THE BELGIANS
FIRST SETTLERS IN NEW YORK AND IN THE MIDDLE STATES

THE BELGIANS
FIRST SETTLERS IN NEW YORK
AND IN THE MIDDLE STATES

With a Review of the Events which led to their
Immigration

BY

HENRY G. BAYER
Lecturer at New York University

*A claim based on Dutch and British official reports,
and on statements by authoritative Dutch and
American historians and geographers*

NEW YORK
THE DEVIN-ADAIR COMPANY
1925

TO

THE BRAVE BELGIAN NATION
WHOSE CHILDREN, WALLOONS AND FLEMINGS,
THROUGH THEIR COURAGE AND PERSEVERANCE
SO USEFULLY CONTRIBUTED TO THE FOUNDING OF THE
UNITED STATES OF AMERICA

THIS BOOK IS DEDICATED.

PREFACE

Search for the truth is the noblest occupation of man; its publication a duty. (*Madame de Staël*)

THE first settlers in New York, New Jersey, Connecticut, Delaware, and Pennsylvania, or the Middle Atlantic States, were Belgian Walloons, according to the Dutch officials and the most prominent Dutch and American historians.

The erroneous teaching that the first settlers in New York and vicinity were Dutch, is to be found only in minor text-books. The authors of those books did not search—so it seems—any of the numerous authoritative works in which this interesting subject is set forth in detail. All the "historians," without exception, agree that those first settlers were "Walloons," that is to say, people from the southern parts of Belgium.

When, in the sixteenth century, appeared in Europe the new religion preached by Luther and Calvin, thousands of Belgians, until then Catholics, became Protestants. Belgium was then governed by the Catholic rulers of Spain, who rigorously persecuted the Protestants; the latter, in great numbers, fled to the northern parts of the Netherlands and elsewhere.

In voluntary exile in Holland, they emigrated again,

vii

and a first group came to Manhattan Island, in 1623, by the boat "New Netherland," under the auspices of the West India Company, a stock company promoted by William Usselinx, a Belgian from Antwerp.

The fact that they sailed from Holland—where they had taken refuge for conscience' sake—has induced many persons to believe that those emigrants were Dutch. But, like their ancestors, those first settlers were natives from the southern parts of Belgium, then called the Comté de Hainaut and the Comté de Flandre, namely from the cities of Avesnes, Valenciennes, Lille, etc.

While the "Walloons" began to pour into Manhattan and other places as early as 1623, it was only after the victorious wars of Louis XIV, in 1658 and 1678, that the cities hereabove mentioned were annexed to France.

Failing to take into consideration or ignoring the dates of transfer of territory just cited, some writers have been under the impression that those refugees in Holland, who emigrated to America, were of French origin, and as a consequence have mistaken the Walloons for "Huguenots." The latter were Calvinists of France, whereas the Walloons were Calvinists of Belgium.

To correct all such errors, to be useful to those interested in the early history of New York, this work has been prepared.

After the discovery made by the Englishman, Henry Hudson, in 1609, discovery in which Van Metteren, Plancius, and Hondius—all natives of the Flemish section of Belgium—played an indirect but im-

portant rôle, rich merchants from Holland sent agents
to Manhattan with the purpose of trading in furs with
the Indians; they erected some trading posts, it is
true, but no permanent habitations.

For business purposes they crossed the Atlantic
back and forth, just as our American business men
are doing to-day. Those Dutch traffickers were the
"first traders" in New Netherland, but not the
"first settlers," for their coming was a visit, and the
length of their stay depended upon their success in
trade, and on the limitation of the license to trade
granted to their employers.

The motives actuating the Belgian Walloons were
very different. With the express purpose of colonizing they came over with their wives and belongings,
they made their home here, children were born to
them and brought up here, and after years of toil and
struggle in their adopted country, those courageous
pioneers were buried in the American soil. They
were the settlers, the first settlers.

They had brought with them a knowledge of the
trades in which they were proficient, and were distinguished for their extraordinary persistence in
overcoming difficulties. They had brought with them
a spirit of freedom and of religious liberty, the basis
of the rights of man, later on so solidly inscribed in
the Constitution of the United States.

In order to help the reader to understand better
what led to the discovery of the Hudson and the coming of the Walloons to New Netherland, several chapters have been devoted to the early navigators, the
Reformation, the history of the Belgians and their

work in the Netherlands, gradually preparing the way for the main object which concerns the first settlements by the Belgian Walloons.

While some chapters may have the appearance of a polemic, the writer has had in view simply the desire to rectify regrettable errors as well as unfortunate popular beliefs, and at no time has it been his intention to be disregardful of the rightful claims of, nor to antagonize, any individual, organization, or nation.

And, since this publication is intended as a souvenir of the tercentenary of the landing of the Walloons on Manhattan Island and their settlement in the Middle States, which glorious anniversary has just been celebrated in New York, Albany, Staten Island, along the Hudson Valley and elsewhere, the second part of this book sketches the "Life and Customs of Old New York."

I extend my sincere thanks to all those who in one capacity or another have been of assistance to me in the preparation of this volume, and especially to my dear friends, Zimri C. Oseland and Richard E. Lambert, Secretary of the Washington Square College, for their stenographic work and reading. I am deeply indebted to Mr. William Harper Bennett, who, so graciously, placed at my disposal his important library on "Americana." Finally, to Monsignor Joseph Stillemans I express my gratitude for having suggested to me the writing of this book.

HENRY G. BAYER.

New York, May 31, 1924.

CONTENTS

xi

CONTENTS

ILLUSTRATIONS

THE SENATE OF THE STATE OF NEW YORK

RESOLUTION INTRODUCED BY SENATOR WILLIAM L. LOVE,
ON MARCH 5, 1924

WHEREAS, the month of May, nineteen hundred and twenty-four, marks the three hundredth anniversary of the arrival of the "New Netherland" with colonists sent out by the West India Company under a charter by the States General of the United Netherlands, and

WHEREAS, the founding of the colony of New Nethland, now the State of New York, was a most important event in the history of the United States of America and of great significance to the people of the Empire State, and

WHEREAS, this colony consisted of thirty-two families, mostly Belgians, and

WHEREAS, Honorable Alfred E. Smith, Governor of the State, in a proclamation, has called upon all schools, churches, civic bodies and municipalities to celebrate this historic event with appropriate exercises and ceremonies,

THEREFORE, RESOLVED (if the Assembly concur), that a joint legislative committee is hereby created to con-

RESOLUTION

sist of three members of the Senate, to be appointed by the Temporary President of the Senate, and five members of the Assembly, to be appointed by the Speaker of the Assembly, to make suitable arrangements for a great State holiday and celebration to be had during the month of May, nineteen hundred and twenty-four.

FURTHER RESOLVED (if the Assembly concur), that the Honorable Alfred E. Smith, Governor of the State, acting upon behalf of the people of the State of New York, extend to His Majesty, King Albert of Belgium, a most cordial invitation to attend such celebration,

FURTHER RESOLVED (if the Assembly concur), that the actual and necessary expenses of the committee in carrying out the provisions of their resolution, not exceeding the sum of fifty thousand dollars, be paid from the legislative contingent fund upon vouchers audited and approved as provided by law.

PART ONE

I have considered the days of old, the years of ancient times.—Psalm ixxil, V5.

The deeds of other times are in my soul. My memory beams on the days that are past.—Ossian's Berrathon.

THE BELGIANS
FIRST SETTLERS IN NEW YORK AND IN THE MIDDLE STATES

CHAPTER I

BEFORE COLUMBUS
TRADE BETWEEN EUROPE AND ASIA

LONG before the time of Columbus, missionaries, travelers and traders visited the Far East—Mongolia, India, China, Japan. They brought back to Europe spices, drugs, dyewoods, ivory, silks, gold and silver, and told wonderful stories of rich lands, curious people and great princes they had seen.

Marco Polo. One of these travelers, a Venetian named Marco Polo, arrived home in 1295 after an absence of many years. He had traveled across Asia, had been for seventeen years in the service of Koublai, Great-Khan (ruler) of the Mongols, and told of Cathay or China and of Cipango or Japan. He made a vivid description of the beautiful cities he had seen, with their gates of bronze and their floors and roofs of gold.

His book, presenting a description of his voyages, one of the most precious geographical documents in existence, turned the mind of Europe to the East and aroused a great desire to reach the rich countries so splendidly described. But the people in Europe knew nothing of any lands on the western side of the Atlantic.

In the latter part of the fifteenth century Venice had gained control of the lucrative trade between Europe and the Indies.

That trade, however, was seriously hampered by the fact that it could not follow a direct and continuous water route. The isthmus of Suez barred the way and the goods brought from the Far East up the Red Sea had to be unloaded, transported across the desert to the Nile and re-shipped to Alexandria (Egypt) for the Mediterranean. In the interest of trade, Europe called for an all-sea route to the Indies.

Prince Henry the Navigator or Prince Henry of Portugal undertook to find the required route, and for nearly seventy years the Portuguese sailors were exploring the Western coast of Africa, endeavoring to discover a way around that mysterious continent into the waters of the Indian Ocean, but in vain!

Diaz. However, in 1487, Bartholomew Diaz (Portuguese) succeeded in reaching the formidable South African cape and, returning home at once, he called it the "Cape of Storms."

Vasco da Gama. The King of Portugal, John II, named it the "Cape of Good Hope," believing that, at last, the way to the Indies was almost as good as opened. And in fact, only ten years later, another brave Portuguese, Vasco da Gama, actually reached India via the Cape of Good Hope, and returned safely to Portugal (1497).

The new route was found, but its length was a serious drawback, since the goods shipped from the East would have to make a voyage of at least twelve thousand miles in order to reach Europe. And, the question arose: might it not be possible to find a shorter way? Such was the great problem of the fifteenth, sixteenth, and seventeenth centuries, and the real motive of the voyages of Columbus, Vespucius, Cabot, Verrazano, Hudson, and others. It was one of such voyages that led to the discovery of the Hudson river.

The impossibility of finding a shorter all-sea route became, later on, sadly evident; a natural water way, such as was dreamed of by the ancient navigators, was not in existence!

Therefore, it required the skill of the modern engineer to create it. Science, stimulated by the spirit of enterprise and the financial power of the nineteenth century, transformed into a splendid reality the wishes of the past generations.

In 1854, Ferdinand de Lesseps, a French diplomat, born at Versailles, conceived the idea of building on the "Isthmus of Suez" a canal which now connects the Mediterranean (Port Said) and the Red Sea (Suez). This canal, inaugurated in 1869, shortens by two-thirds the all-sea route from Europe to India which Vasco da Gama followed. It was the same de Lesseps who started the construction of the Panama Canal.

The Belgians were important subscribers in the Suez Canal enterprise, as well as in the original French stock company of the Panama Canal.

CHAPTER II

DUE to the lack of definite geographical knowledge, an unavoidable and excusable situation for their times, fearless navigators were all blundering in their quest for a shorter route to the Far East. But if not successful in their real purpose, accidentally they made discoveries of the greatest importance to mankind.

Columbus. Christopher Columbus or Christoforo Colombo was born in Genoa, Italy, between 1436 and 1446. An experienced mariner, he was convinced he could discover a far shorter and more direct all-water route to the much-coveted Indies.

Learned men already believed the world to be round, and if this were really true, India, China, and Japan were west of Europe as well as east of Europe.

But Columbus considered the globe to be much smaller than it actually is. He supposed that it embraced but one ocean—the Atlantic—which surrounded the three continents of Europe, Asia, and Africa. He thought also that the Indies faced Europe at a distance of less than four thousand miles. He would make for the "Canaries" and then sail straight

4

west until he reached the eastern coast of Asia. He did not know that a mighty continent—America— barred the way!

He first offered to make the voyage for the City of Genoa, and then applied to John II, King of Portugal; but his offers were not accepted. Finally he succeeded in obtaining the assistance of the King and Queen of Spain, Ferdinand and Isabella, who provided him with all that was required for such a big enterprise.

Columbus fitted out three small vessels: the Nina, the Pinta, and the Santa Maria; of this little fleet he was the Admiral, and when all was ready he and his men went to the little Church of Palos (on the mouth of the river Tinto, Spain), where they attended Mass and prayed for the success of the expedition.

On August 3, 1492, they left Palos while the bells of the Franciscan monastery rang out their good wishes and the people of the small port waved a fond farewell to the daring mariners. His fleet sailed southwesterly toward the Canary Islands—then already known—and reached them on August 12.

On September 6 he set out on his ever memorable voyage across the "Sea of Darkness." In this great undertaking, he was not seeking to find new lands, but a new and shorter way to reach old lands....

Day after day passed but no land was sighted and the sailors were more and more frightened as they found themselves going farther and farther, and they threatened to turn the ship back.

At a certain point of the voyage Columbus met with an experience, and made a decision that perhaps determined the destiny of North America. On October

7, 1492, one of the sailors saw flocks of parrots flying southwest, and argued that the birds were returning to land, which must lie in that direction and he advised the Admiral to change the course of his ship. Columbus recognized the logic of the argument and knew the significance of the flights of birds. He remembered that the "hawk" had shown the "Portuguese" the way to the Azores (Isles of the Hawks). In Portuguese "Acor" means a hawk.

Flemings in the Azores. Concerning those "Portuguese" it is well to say that in 1145, there sailed from Antwerp, Belgium, an expedition of Flemish[1] crusaders who at Lisbon joined with English Knights in order to chase from Portugal the invading Moors. A great number of these Flemish crusaders made Portugal their home, engaged in trade there, and formed a colony of some importance.

According to the usual accounts, the Fleming Van der Berg was driven to the islands in 1432, which is the date of the discovery of the first island of the group, and the news excited considerable interest at the court of Lisbon. Soon, two thousand Flemings settled on the Azores then called the "Flemish Islands," where for generations Flemish was the language spoken.

Colonization had been going on prosperously and in 1466 "Fayal," one of the most important of the Azores group of islands, was presented by Alphonso V, King of Portugal, to his aunt Isabella. She was the wife of Philip the Good, Duke of Burgundy, who

---

[1] The two ethnographical families composing Belgium are: the Flemings and the Walloons.

ruled over Belgium from 1419 till his death which occurred at Bruges, Flanders, in 1467.

The Azores were then the grand rendez-vous for
the fleets on their voyage home from the Indies, and
after 1492, for almost two centuries the Azores were
considered as part of the New World, and from there,
also, the trading boats and colonizing ships sailed
directly to America.

Columbus was now sailing straight for the coast
of North Carolina, and would inevitably have discovered our present continent, had the parrots not
been accepted as guides.

The course of the ship was changed to the southwest, and on October 12, 1492, land was sighted! They
had found a southern section of the western continent:
it was a small island of the Bahama group, which the
natives seemed to call "Guanahani," and here Columbus planted the royal standard of Spain and named
the land "San Salvador" or Holy Redeemer.

The natives came to see the discoverers, and Columbus, believing he had reached India called them "Indians," a name our red men ever kept. But these Indians were not all like those wonderful people of
Cathay and Cipango whom Marco Polo had so richly
described. Instead of wearing clothes of silk and of
gold embroidered satin, they were stark naked, more
or less greased and painted, and were living in the
rudest manner.

Going farther south, Columbus discovered Cuba
and Hispaniola or Haiti. He was sure he had found
the Indies, and as he had reached them by sailing
west, they received the name of "West Indies."

He resolved to carry the news of his success to Spain and set out on his return, January 4, 1493.

In the course of his three other voyages (1493-1502) he discovered Porto Rico, many of the Lesser Antilles, and navigated along the northern coast of South America: Venezuela, Panama, Nicaragua, Honduras, etc. But, he never came within sight of the mainland of the United States.

Columbus died at Valladolid (Spain) May 20, 1506, in the unshaken belief that he had discovered the eastern coast of Asia. He did not dream that he had done something of much greater importance, that he had opened the way to the richest continent on earth.

Cabot. John Cabot or Giovanni Caboto, was born at Genoa, Italy, about 1451, became a citizen of Venice in 1476 and later on moved to Bristol with his family. Bristol was then the principal seaport of England, and the center of trade for the Iceland fisheries. His second son, Sebastian, who accompanied the father on his voyages, was born in Venice about 1474.

The first voyage of Columbus had created a sensation in Europe; the news was received by the Cabots and their English friends with much admiration, and a rival route to the "Indies" was planned by the Cabots, who applied to Henry VII. of England, for permission and aid to go on a voyage of exploration, and the King granted them a license.

They projected to reach the "spice islands of the Indies" by sailing westward, but on a more northern course than the one followed by Columbus.

It is presumed that they sailed together from Bristol in May, 1497, on the vessel "Matthews." They discovered what they supposed to be the Chinese coast "in the territory of the Great Khan," but instead the land they had found happened to be a part of Canada! It was "Cape Breton Island," Nova Scotia, in the gulf of St. Lawrence, and they gave it the name of "Prima Tierra Vista" or First Land Seen. Cabot hoisted the English flag and claimed the country for the British crown.

Returning to Bristol, we find thrifty Henry VII giving "to hym that founde the new isle" the munificent largess of ten pounds with which to celebrate the achievement. The King also granted to John Cabot a yearly pension of twenty pounds to be paid out of the receipts of the Bristol custom-house. But, humorous reader, do not smile: the entire island of Manna-hata was bought by Peter Minuit for twenty-four dollars!

"St. John," now Prince Edward Island, and Labrador were also discovered.

A second expedition took place in 1498, still in the hope of finding a passage to the Indies or to Cipango (now Japan), and again the coasts of Canada were visited. During this voyage, John Cabot disappeared from history and Sebastian assumed command.

The report by Cabot that there were immense quantities of codfish in the vicinity of "Newfoundland," was responsible for the establishment, later, of the largest fisheries in the world. They have since often been the subject of complicated international discussions.

Since the days of the Northmen (Leif Ericson in "Vinland," A.D. 1000) the Cabots were the first Europeans to set foot on the continent of North

America, and their voyages are of the greatest significance in their relations to the subsequent work of English colonization in the Western hemisphere, and in American colonial history.

Americus Vespucius or Amerigo Vespucci, born in Florence, Italy, 1451, emigrated to Spain where he was engaged in fitting out ships for the Atlantic voyages of discovery, and so became acquainted with Columbus.

Vespucius was an able navigator and a learned astronomer, and, after Columbus had made three voyages, he accompanied several Spanish and Portuguese expeditions which explored northern parts of "South America."

During his second expedition with Ojeda and La Cosa—who had been companions of Columbus—which sailed from Cadiz, May 16, 1499, he sighted land on the coast of "Brazil" somewhere near Aracati, while another expedition headed by *Vincente Yanez Pinzon* (also a companion of Columbus) followed in the track of Vespucius and also reached the coast of Brazil but near Pernambuco, January, 1500.[1]

These two expeditions were for account of Spain, and affairs became complicated as *Pedro Alvarez Cabral* accidentally landed in Brazil, May 1500, at a place named by him Porto Seguro (Safe Harbor). Then he called the land he found "Vera Cruz," a name which presently became "Santa Cruz," or land of the Holy Cross, and took possession of it in the name of King Emanuel of Portugal, who immediately

[1] Fiske, Discovery of America, Vol. 2, pp. 93-95

began to prepare an expedition for exploring this new coast.

The King made overtures to Vespucius, and the offer having been accepted by him he passed from the service of Spain into the service of Portugal. Vespucius made several other voyages to South America; that is, to Brazil. He died at Seville, Spain, in 1512.

Columbus all the time was claiming that the lands he had discovered were a part of Asia, whereas Americus Vespucius, in his letters, declared that the lands he had visited—and which we now call South America —were not a part of Asia but a new continent and accordingly he called them a "New World." This divergence of opinions, between the two great navigators, had a decisive influence on the "future name" of the western hemisphere.

Italian discoveries. The discoveries made in the American hemisphere, by Italian navigators, were of the greatest importance. And while we admire the deeds of those illustrious sailors, we do not seem to pay to their memory the tribute that they so justly deserve.

The name "America." In fact, the discovery of America was not a single event, but a very gradual process; it was a case of evolution, and the first voyage of Columbus was the most decisive and epoch-making incident in that evolution.

Vespucius in his letter to Lorenzo de Medici[1] in March or April 1503, calls "Nuvo Mundo" not the supposed "islands of India" discovered by Columbus

[1] Lorenzo II. de Medici, head of the Republic of Florence.

but only the new countries below the equator visited by him (Vespucius) on his third voyage.

The celebrated Dominican friar *Giovanni Giocondo*, of Verona, translated the letter of Vespucius from Italian into Latin and gave it as title "Mundus Novus" or New World.

From a passage in the Latin text of the Nuremberg Chronicle (1493) we learn that this supposed antipodal world in the "southern hemisphere" was sometimes called "Quarta Pars" or fourth part, the other three parts of the earth being Europe, Asia, and Africa.

The name America was first applied only to Brazil, then incidentally to South America, and finally, as will be explained, to the entire western hemisphere by the Belgian geographer Gerard Mercator.

There was not much likelihood, at that time, of naming this hemisphere after Columbus for the sufficient reason that, according to his own repeated declaration, the lands he had discovered were parts of what was already bearing two recognized names, viz. "Asia" and the "Indies." Separate islands and stretches of coast had received their local names as San Salvador, Hispaniola or Veragua, etc.

While it is to be regretted that circumstances prevented the giving of the name of Columbus to this great continent, there remains the satisfaction that "Columbia" is the popular name for the United States.

Saint Dié. In the naming of the new world or the "Mundus Novus" of Vespucius, we will see that the suggestion was made that it might be called "America" and, how it came about is quite interesting.

It happened at Saint Dié, a little French town pleasantly located on the river Meurthe in one of those quiet valleys of the Vosges mountains which Erckmann and Alexandre Chatrian have so charmingly made the locale of their beautiful stories. The town had grown up about a Benedictine monastery founded in the seventh century by St. Deodatus, Bishop of Nevers, and from Deodatus came the name Dié.

René II, who became reigning Duke of Lorraine, in 1473, was a patron of literature and the arts. In his small town of Saint Dié was a college which became curiously associated with the discovery of America, for it was there that toward 1410 the Cardinal Pierre d'Ailly wrote his "Imago Mundi" (Image of the World), the book which greatly influenced the projects of Columbus.

Canon Walter Lud,[1] Secretary and Adviser to Duke René since 1490, had conceived the project (1504) to gather all the geographic data left by the Ancients, and to add to them the new discoveries of the navigators. In this connection, his master, Duke René, had in his possession a description, in French, of the four voyages of Americus Vespucius, and with all such interesting material at hand, he intended to publish a new great work on general geography.

At that time, the cosmography (astronomy and

---

[1] Canon (in French "chanoine") in the Roman Catholic Church, the rank of a dignitary, a member of the Chapter or Council of the Bishop.

geography combined) and the maps of Ptolemy[1] were the basis and the starting point of all studies concerning the universe; but being a very old work, it had become obsolete.

Lud found a precious collaborator in his nephew, Nicholas Lud, who not only became his partner, but gave his house to install a printing shop therein. This Nicholas Lud, in 1508, became himself the adviser and secretary to Duke René, and in 1528, after the death of his uncle Walter, he succeeded him in the high functions of Director of the Mines of Lorraine.

For the execution of his great geographic work Walter Lud took also as assistants two professors of the college of Saint Dié: Mathias Ringmann, born about 1482, either at Orbey, near the monastery of Pairis, or at Villé in Alsace; he was a geographer, a Latinist, a poet, and somewhat of a humorist. The other professor was Martin Waldseemuller, born at Fribourg-in-Breslau, about 1475; he was a geographer and a talented draughtsman.

Lud had just established, at his own expense, a printing shop at Saint Dié, one of the first in Lorraine.

Duke René had communicated to his Chaplain Walter Lud, the French description of the four voyages of Americus Vespucius, and in turn Lud requested Jean Basin, known for the elegancy of his writings, to translate it into Latin. Jean Basin, born at Sandau-

[1] Ptolemy or Claudius Ptolemæus, a well-known Greek geographer, was the most celebrated astronomer of antiquity. His mature life probably extended from 125 to about 160 A. D. His work on general geography was for many ages the chief authority on that subject and did not become obsolete until the beginning of the sixteenth century.

House at Saint-Dié, France, where the new world received the
name "America," 1507.

court, a village of the Vosges, was a vicar of the Church of Notre-Dame.

His translation largely contributed to the success of the book. The narrative of explorations in a new and marvelous world excited great curiosity as shown by the publication of four successive editions within a few months.

As said above, the purpose of this group of learned men of the Vosges (locally designated as "Gymnase Vosgien") was to publish a new treatise on general geography, but as such an important work would take a considerable time, they decided to begin with the publication and distribution of an introduction to the book which they called: "Cosmographiae Introductio."

In this pamphlet the name "America" was given for the first time.

It was a presentation of general facts to facilitate the understanding and study of the great "Cosmography" they were now preparing. Perhaps they intended also to use this "Introduction" as an announcement to the public, and to teach to the people the elements of geography.

Mr. Marcou, in his article entitled "Nouvelles Recherches sur le nom d' Amérique" (New Investigations as to the name America) which appeared in 1888 in the Bulletin of the "Société de Géographie" says that a thorough study of the "Cosmographiae Introductio" shows conclusively that it represents the efforts of several persons. He says that it lacks unity, and that the difference in style is very noticeable if one compares the wording of its chapters.

Mr. Marcou makes the following remarks: "Chapter IX, the longest and the most important indicates by its phraseology that the famous paragraph: 'But now these parts (Europe, Asia and Africa) have been more extensively explored and another fourth part has been discovered by Americus Vespucius—as will appear in what follows—wherefore, *I do not see what is rightly to hinder us from calling it 'America,' i.e., the land of Americus, after its discoverer Americus*, a man of sagacious mind. . . .' must have been written by the one—Jean Basin—who translated into Latin the French version of the four voyages of Americus Vespucius."

"In that pamphlet or elementary treatise of geography, Jean Basin wrote all the passages, four in number, concerning the lands newly discovered, and especially points out Americus Vespucius, which seems very natural, Basin having made a translation of the description of the four voyages of Vespucius, he knew better than any other member of his group all the details relating to the New World."

"Jean Basin is the author of the famous paragraph (reproduced above) which has given celebrity to Waldseemuller. Not only does the elegancy of the style prove it, but other facts confirm such opinion."

Such is the argument of Mr. Marcou as to who gave the name America to the new world.

It was first published at Saint Dié on the 25th of April, 1507. The only copy of the first edition known to exist at present, was picked up for a franc in one of the second-hand book shops on the Paris quays by the geographer, Jean Baptiste Eyries. In 1846 his heirs sold it at auction for 160 francs to Nicolas Yéméniz, of Lyons, and after his death, in 1867, it was sold for 2000 francs, and is now in the possession of the New York Public Library.

Three other editions were published during the same year as the first edition, and a copy of the edition of August 29, 1507, can be seen in the Library of Harvard University.

As already explained, the name "America" at that time applied only to what we now call Brazil, and from then on began to appear on the new maps.

Such is the little story of Saint Dié, and the origin of the name "America."

The house of Lud at Saint Dié, in which the "Cosmographiae Introductio" was printed, still remains. It is located at 7 Place Jules Ferry, and is now occupied by a pharmacist. In July, 1911, a commemorative tablet of white marble was affixed to the building by the "Société Philomathique Vosgienne." This was the occasion of Franco-American festivities under the Presidency of Mr. Robert Bacon, Ambassador of the United States at Paris.

The commemorative tablet reads: "Ici le 25 avril 1507, sous le règne de René II, la Cosmographiae Introductio, dans laquelle le nouveau continent reçut le nom d'Amérique, fut imprimée et publiée par les Membres du Gymnase Vosgien: Gauthier Lud, Nicolas Lud, Jean Basin, Mathias Ringmann et Martin Waldseemuller." Translation: "Here, on April 25, 1507, under the reign of René II, the Cosmographiae Introductio, in which the new continent received the name of America, was printed and published by the Members of the Gymnase Vosgien: Walter Lud, Nicolas Lud, Jean Basin, Mathias Ringmann, and Martin Waldseemuller.''

As to the great geographical treatise, it was published in 1513; a second edition appeared in 1520.

Balboa. On his last voyage, Columbus sailed along the coast of Panama, but in 1513 a Spaniard, Vasco Nunez de Balboa crossed the isthmus of Panama and discovered the ocean called later the ''Pacific.''

As the isthmus of Suez blocked the most important route of commerce in the Old World, so did the Isthmus of Panama in the New World, and Ferdinand de Lesseps, who had built the Suez canal, wishing to duplicate his remarkable work, began the preliminaries to the digging of the Panama canal in 1880. Adverse circumstances placed this gigantic enterprise into the hands of the United States Government who so splendidly finished the work in 1914.

Glorious names, forever connected with the Panama canal, are those of Theodore Roosevelt and William H. Taft, Presidents of the United States; Surgeon General William A. Gorgas, and Chief Engineer Colonel George W. Goethals.

There are, in Belgium, many well known old families by the name of Goethals.

Magellan. Until the time of this great navigator no westward route by water had been found to the Pacific Ocean and the long-sought-for Spice Islands!

Ferdinand Magellan or Fernão da Magalhães, born at Sabrosa (Portugal) about 1480, conceived the vast scheme of circumnavigating the globe. And now in the service of Charles V. of Spain, his little fleet com-

posed of five small ships cleared the mouth of the
river Guadalquivir, on September 20, 1519, and stood
out to sea.

Among the men of Magellan's fleet there were
Belgians: "These five ships were all old and decidedly
the worse for wear. About 280 men were on board, a
motley crew of Spaniards and Portuguese, Genoese
and Sicilians, *Flemings* and French...." [1]

In 1520 he discovered and passed "the straits"
which since then have borne his name, steered his vessels into the great ocean which he called the "Pacific"
just after the heavy storms through which he had
gone, found the "Philippine Islands" (1521), and was
the first to circumnavigate the world.

For some time America was laid down on the maps
as an island, but the later voyages of Vespucius began
to give a new meaning to the work of Columbus who
showed the way across the Sea of Darkness. The true
continental character of the New World became gradually known; although it was not until Magellan made
his memorable voyage round the globe (1519-1521)
that America stood plainly out as an independent
hemisphere.

Yet the greedy merchantmen and unwearied navigators gave little heed to the potential resources
and opportunities of the new land. They stubbornly
scoured the oceans in every latitude, from the Arctic
regions to Cape Horn (extreme S. point of South
America) searching for a passage to the rich countries and jeweled cities of Asia!

Gerard Mercator was a celebrated Belgian geog-

[1] Fiske, Discovery of America, Vol. 2, p. 192.

rapher and mathematician born at Rupelmonde, Flanders, in 1512, the year Vespucius died. He studied at the famous university of Louvain and entered into the service of Charles V. of Spain, to whom he presented two globes superior to anything of the kind that had then appeared.[1]

He is chiefly known from the important method of map projection called by his name, which he published for the first time in 1569, and which was adopted by all map makers. It is that simple method we all use to calculate longitudes and latitudes, in which parallels cut meridians at right angles and are represented by straight lines.[2]

He is known also from certain rules of navigation associated with the above, and called "Mercator's sailing." He wrote several books on astronomy, an atlas, and executed numerous maps and charts.

But, in the history of America, Mercator should be remembered as the first person who indicated on a map the existence of a distinct and integral western hemisphere, and who called the whole by the name "America."[3] In their Cosmographiae Introductio," the Luds and their group gave the name "America" only to Vespucius' New World (below the equator), as shown on the map of 1507 by Waldseemuller, a member of this group, as already explained.

Upon a globe which he made in 1541, Mercator represented the northern continent as distinct from Asia, and arranged the name America in large letters so as

[1] Thomas. Universal Dictionary of Biography.
[2] Bouillet. Dictionnaire d'Histoire et de Géographie.
[3] Fiske. Discovery of America, Vol. 2, p. 152.

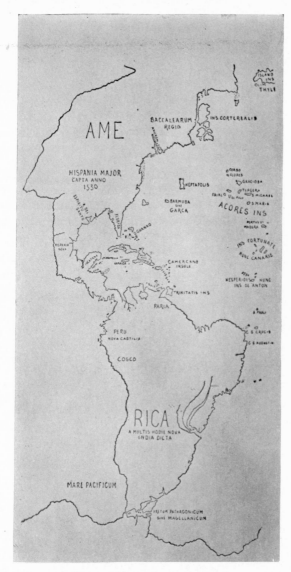

Gerard Mercator's map of 1541.

(First application of the name "America" to the entire continent.)

to cover both northern and southern continents, putting *A-M-E* about on the location of the Great Lakes and *R-I-C-A* just west of the river La Plata, in Argentina. (See map page 20.)

CHAPTER III

IT is the general belief that the first landing made on the "Island of Manhattan" was by Henry Hudson, in 1609.

This, however, is not the case; since the earliest records extant state that as early as 1598, a few Hollanders, in the employ of a Greenland Company, were in the habit of resorting to New Netherland (i.e. New York) not, it is true, with the design of effecting a "settlement," but merely to secure shelter during the winter months. With this in view they built two small forts to protect themselves against the Indians.[1]

Verrazano. And even before 1598, we had the visit to the Bay of New York, of Giovanni da Verrazano, born at Val di Greve near Florence, Italy, in 1485.

The great explorer was in the service of Francis I. of France when he made his voyage along the North American coast. It has been doubted whether he ever made such a voyage, but the discussion which followed simply resulted in the production of additional proof of the authenticity of his explorations.[2]

[1] Stone. History of New York City, p. 9.
[2] Buckingham Smith, who wrote strictures on Verrazano in his "Inquiry" admits that the country could have been so accurately described only "from actual information."

22

There is overwhelming evidence of the reality of his voyage in 1524, which is vouched for by invaluable maps and relations contained in a lengthy "Letter" addressed to his employer, Francis I. This letter is of unique interest, especially for the reason that it contains the first known post-Columbian description of the North Atlantic coast, and the first pen-picture of the Bay and Harbor of New York.[1]

Concerning the bay of New York, here are some extracts from his interesting "Letter": "We found a very pleasant situation among some 'little steep hills' (infra piccoli colli eminenti) through which a 'very large river' (grandissima riviera), deep at its mouth, forced its way to the sea. From the sea to the estuary of the river any ship might pass, with the help of the tide, which rises eight feet." This was about the average rise, and the fact is one that could have been learned only from actual observation. It points to the "bar" as then existing, and gives the narrative every appearance of reality.

Verrazano was cautious, as he possessed only one ship, and he says: "As we were riding at anchor in a good berth, we would not venture up in our ship without a knowledge of the mouth; therefore, we took the boat and, entering the river, we found the country on its banks well peopled, the inhabitants not differing much from the others, being dressed out with the feathers of birds of various colors. They came towards us with evident admiration, and showing us where we could most securely land with our boat. We passed up this river about half a league, when we

[1] J. G. Wilson, Memorial Hist. of the City of New York, Vol. 1, p. 8.

found it formed a most 'beautiful lake' (bellissimo lago), three leagues in circuit, upon which were rowing thirty or more of their small boats from one shore to the other, filled with multitudes who came to see us.'' This beautiful lake was, so far as we can judge, the bay of New York.

Verrazano passed the bar and anchored at the entrance of the Narrows, the position being defined as between ''little steep hills,'' which exactly describes the heights of Staten Island, and the shore of Long Island as far up as Yellow Hook, the present Bay Ridge.[1]   Then far and wide the spacious harbor was surrounded by well-wooded shores, upon which Verrazano and his followers, evidently the first of Europeans to enter the port, gazed with admiration. It never occurred to him that on this ''beautiful lake'' would one day stand a city, which in wealth, population, and importance would eclipse any other city in the world.   The situation was pleasing, but it did not offer what Verrazano sought, namely, an opening to ''India''—that great purpose of all navigators!

It would appear that he did not cross the harbor, as the narrative continues: ''All of a sudden, as is wont to happen to navigators, a violent contrary wind blew in from the sea and forced us to return to our ship, greatly regretting to leave this region, which seemed so commodious and delightful, and which we supposed must contain great riches, as the hills showed many indications of minerals.''

Verrazano would not take his ship through the Narrows into the harbor, on account of his ignorance

[1] J. G. Wilson, Memorial Hist. of the City of New York, Vol. 1, p. 13.

of the situation, and when the wind set upon shore from the sea, he at once decided to get out of danger. Accordingly he says: "Weighing anchor, we sailed fifty leagues towards the east, the coast stretching in that direction, and always in sight of it." Thus he coasted along the shores of Long Island, and discovered an island in triangular form, some ten leagues from the main land, in size about equal to the "Island of Rhodes." [1] This was "Block Island," which is distinctly a triangular island. The circumstance is mentioned here, in order that the reader may appreciate the fact that Verrazano first visited New York, and that he properly describes the coast.[2]

From here Verrazano proceeded to the haven of Newport, after which he coasted northward as far as the fiftieth degree of north latitude (Canada), then returned to France. To the newly discovered country, he gave the name of New France (Nova Gallia), and this discovery formed the basis for a claim by France.

Prior to this, as we have seen, Sebastian Cabot, in the service of Henry VII of England, had explored regions from Labrador to Florida and both nations later made settlements in the country claimed by each.

Gomez. Another visit to the great river was made by a Portuguese. We find him to be Estevan Gomez, the man who had deserted Magellan while he was chief pilot on one of his vessels.

Sailing in the interest of Spain, 1525, he went along the coast of Northern America, and took notice of

[1] The Island of Rhodes in the Mediterranean.
[2] J. G. Wilson, Memorial Hist. of the City of New York, Vol. 1, p. 13.

Cape Cod, Narragansett Bay, the mouths of the rivers Connecticut, Delaware, and Hudson, calling the latter "Rio de San Antonio" (St. Anthony's river). In Diego Ribeiro's map, 1529, the regions from New Jersey to Rhode Island are called "land of Estevan Gomez."

Allefonsce. We must also note the voyage, 1542, of Jean Allefonsce, a native of the old province of Saintonge, France, who came to Canada as pilot for Sieur de Roberval (for some time associated with Cartier, the founder of Montreal).

Allefonsce discovered Massachusetts Bay, and with the aid of Paulin Secalart, wrote a cosmographical description including Canada, the West Indies, and the American coast. This work is in the manuscript department of the Bibliothèque Nationale in Paris, No. 676, and relates to the region of the Hudson river. (See "Northmen in Maine," Albany, 1870.)

The French. Mr. Fiske writes that the river now called Hudson was probably visited also by sporadic French traders who may have ascended it as far as the mouth of the Mohawk, in quest of peltries.

He refers to Weise's "Discoveries of America," Chap. XI, who suggests that the name "Terre de Norumbega" may be a corruption of "Terre d'Enorme Berge," i.e. "Land of the Grand Scarp" from the escarpment of palisaded cliffs which is the most striking feature as one passes by the upper part of Manhattan Island.[1] (See the name Anorumbega on Mercator's map of 1541, page 20.)

Also on the map of "Discourse of Voyages into ye

[1] Fiske. Discovery of America, Vol. 2, p. 547.

Easte and West Indies'' by the Dutch writer, Lin-
schoten, printed in 1598, there is a dotted trail from
the latitude of the Hudson, 40°N. to the St. Lawrence,
showing that the route was one known and traveled at
that time. It is evident, from a variety of considerations that both the Dutch and French used the Hudson, at this period, to engage in trade.[1]

Nevertheless, the fact remains undisputed that to
Henry Hudson belongs the honor of being the first
who attracted public attention to the Island of Manhattan as an advantageous point for a trading post in
the New World.

[1] J. G. Wilson, Mem. Hist. of New York, Vol. I, p. 27.

CHAPTER IV

HUDSON's name was not Hendrick but Henry, for Hudson was not a Dutchman but an Englishman.

Of the personal history of the experienced and skillful navigator not much is known, and the first view we have of him is in the church of St. Ethelburge, Bishopsgate Street, London, in the summer of 1607, whither he had gone with his crew to partake of the Sacrament before sailing under the auspices of the "Muscovy Company" of London in search of a passage to China, across the Polar Sea. Hudson was the grandson of one of the founders of that company. His whole life as known to the world extends over a period of only about four years.

In 1607 and 1608 he made two voyages in the service of the Muscovy Company. During the first he tried to penetrate between Greenland and Spitzbergen and strike boldly across the North Pole; in the second, he tried to pass between Spitzbergen and Nova Zembla, but returned without having achieved any success. At this time (17th century) the Dutch were the richest nation on the globe; their commercial

28

fleet was equal to the those of England, France, and Germany together. A thousand vessels were built annually in Holland and an extensive trade was carried on with all the nations of Europe.

But their main source of supply was the Indies (East Indies), and to secure themselves against competition, the merchants engaged in this traffic had, in 1602, obtained a charter of incorporation from the States General under the name of "Dutch East India Company."

And now, to render the commerce more lucrative, it became desirable to shorten the passage to the Indies. The voyage to China by the only known route—that via the Cape of Good Hope, first made by Vasco da Gama—consumed about two years! Some time before the two voyages of Hudson, three Dutch expeditions had already tried to find a way through the Polar seas, but they encountered nothing but ice and snow, and returned after having endured unheard-of hardships. These expeditions were those of 1594, 1595, and 1596-97 in which the learned Fleming Petrus Plancius was the chief promoter.[1]

The news that voyages by Hudson, for account of England, were in progress made the Dutch East India Company uneasy. Indeed, the finding by their rivals of a shorter route to India would prove of serious competition.

The reputed historian Emanuel Van Meteren, Minister of the Netherlands at the Court of St. James, acquainted Hudson with some correspondence he had received from friends in Holland, and induced the

[1] J. G. Wilson. Mem. Hist. N. Y., Vol. I, p. 141.

navigator to go and see them, as they desired to secure his services.

Van Meteren is often called the "Dutch historian." In reality he was a Belgian, born at Antwerp in 1535.[1] He was taken, at 15 years of age, to London by his father to be brought up in mercantile pursuits. He was a relative of the celebrated geographer Ortelius,[2] with whom he traveled all over England and Ireland, and at whose suggestion he wrote his famous history of the Netherlands. He continued to reside in London until his death, 1612. He was Minister of the Netherlands at London for the last 30 years of his life.

The first account which appeared in print of Hudson's voyage for the East India Company was in 1611, in a supplementary volume of Emanuel Van Meteren's History of the Netherlands from 1595 to 1611.[3]

Hudson accepted the invitation transmitted to him by Van Meteren, and in 1609 he arrived at The Hague, where he was received with great honors. Plans for another expedition through the Polar seas were discussed. Petrus Plancius, who had a thorough knowledge of maritime affairs, warmly seconded the efforts to search for a northeastern passage to India and placed his cosmographical studies and the maps he had prepared, at the service of Hudson and gave him

[1] Thomas. Dict. of Biography, under "Meteren."

[2] Abraham Ortelius born at Antwerp in 1527, became the geographer of Philip II, King of Spain. Was an intimate friend of Gerard Mercator and Justus Lipsius. His "Theatrum Orbis Terrarum" Antwerp, 1570, is the first atlas known; he wrote also the first geographical dictionary called "Synonymia Geographica," 1578.

[3] Henry C. Murphy's Brochure: "Henry Hudson in Holland." See also Mary Booth's "History of New York." App. "q," p. 838.

advice as well as all his published works. Beyond
question, those two men had enjoyed many a personal
conference during those weeks that Hudson was in
Amsterdam preparing for his great voyage.

This Plancius was also a Belgian, born at Dran-
outre, near Ypres, Flanders, in 1552. "He became
celebrated in more than one respect. Having been
ordained in 1577, he preached in divers parts of Brabant, especially at Brussels, where he preached six
years, but this city falling into the enemy's hands,
he passed into Holland disguised as a soldier. He
came in 1585 to Amsterdam, where he immediately
resumed the ministry. Here he opposed Arminius
and the Lutherans, and later on the Remonstrants."

"In 1618 he assisted at the Synod (ecclesiastical
council) of Dordrecht where he was chosen, with
others, to superintend the translation of the Old
Testament."

"He contributed, in the meanwhile, to the elucida-
tion of geography, astronomy, navigation, and other
mathematical sciences, and was one of the principal
projectors of the Dutch expeditions to the East Indies.
The first Dutch ship sailed thither by the aid of charts
which Plancius had constructed. He likewise, advised the expeditions to Nova Zembla, in the hope of
discovering a nearer way to China, in which project he
was very much engaged in 1608."

"He may be truly said to have been in this manner
accessory, in an especial degree, to the discovery of
the Hudson River and New Netherland, to which we
now find him sending a vessel in company with

others (1621)." He died at Amsterdam, May 25, 1622.

This biography is from O'Callaghan's History of New Netherland, Vol. 1., p. 94. The historian says that there is a sketch of the life of Plancius in "Wagenaar's Beschryving der Stad Amsterdam," vol. 3, from which he took most of the above particulars. The French dictionaries by Dezobry et Bachelet, and by Gregoire, say that through his astronomical and nautical science he rendered great service to the commerce of Holland, and James Grant Wilson in his "Memorial History of the City of New York," vol. 1, p. 141, calls him the Hakluyt and Purchas[1] of Holland.

And now that the "Amsterdam Chamber" had promised to defray the expenses of the new enterprise, it was finally decided to make that new attempt to reach India by the Northeast, with Hudson in command.

The contract made by the Amsterdam Chamber alone and signed by two directors in its behalf, was concurred in by the whole East India Company before the sailing of the expedition. In consequence of Hudson's ignorance of the Dutch language, the instrument was executed on his part with the aid of Jodocus Hondius, as interpreter.[2]

Here are some extracts from the contract: "On January 8, 1609, the directors of the East India Com-

---

[1] Richard Hakluyt, born in 1553. A celebrated English geographer; professor of geography and navigation at Oxford.
  Samuel Purchas, born in 1577. A famous English geographer and compiler of travels.
[2] Henry C. Murphy's Brochure: "Henry Hudson in Holland." Also Mary Booth's "History of New York." app. P. Page 837.

pany of the Chamber of Amsterdam, on the one part, and Henry Hudson, Englishman, assisted by Jodocus Hondius, of the other part.''

Another extract: ''......for which said voyage the directors shall pay to the said Hudson, as well as for his outfit for the said voyage, as for the support of his wife and children the sum of 800 guilders ($320.).

It was signed: Dirk van Oos, J. Poppe, Henry Hudson, and lower down Jodocus Hondius, witness[1].

Once more, we find in this Hondius a Belgian. Jodocus (that is, Joost or Justus) Hondius, who acted as the interpreter, adviser, and friend of Hudson, was an eminent engraver—a Fleming by birth, who had fled from his country during the revolutionary troubles. He first went to London but afterwards removed to Amsterdam, where he died two years after the document was signed.[1]

Dr. Thomas in his ''Universal Dictionary of Biography'' describes him as follows: ''Hondius or De Hondt (Jodocus or Josse), a skillful Fleming engraver and geographer, born at Wacken, Flanders, about 1550. He had a high reputation as an engraver on copper. He worked in London, and afterwards settled in Amsterdam, where he engraved maps of superior quality, and published new editions of the ''Grand Atlas'' of Mercator. He died in 1611.

Having thus reviewed the useful rôles played by Van Meteren, Plancius, and Hondius, in the preliminaries of the memorable voyage of Hudson, which opened the way to the permanent settlement of Europeans in

---

[1] Henry C. Murphy's Brochure: ''Henry Hudson in Holland. See also Mary Booth's ''History of New York.'' app. P. p. 837.

what is now the City of New York, the State of New York, and other places, we must remember the interesting fact that those three gentlemen were Flemings, that is to say Belgians of the northern part of Belgium.

It is evident that their fame as learned men, their high standing and powerful influence in the Netherlands, were, to the greatest extent, responsible for this third voyage of Henry Hudson—which revealed Manhattan—with its subsequent beginning of colonization by the Walloons in 1623—that is to say by Belgians of the southern part of Belgium.

The valuable contributions of those three Belgians to the discovery of the Hudson River, after the attempt to reach India by the north, will come as a revelation to many. Of this great and important event, little is commonly known other than the citation that Hudson was in the service of the Dutch East India Company when he visited Manhattan and the Great River.

But now that attention has been attracted towards those who rendered the discovery possible, those who were responsible for it, we will give them full credit, as O'Callaghan has done, for Plancius, in his History of New Netherland. The names of the Flemings: Van Meteren, Plancius, and Hondius cannot be dissociated from the glorious name "Henry Hudson."

On the 4th of April, 1609, Hudson departed from the Port of Amsterdam on his boat the "Halve Maen" (Half Moon). It was a yacht or Dutch galliot, a clumsy kind of brig, with square sails upon two masts. It was a relatively safe craft, but a slow sailer

EMANUEL VAN METEREN.

PETRUS PLANCIUS.

of 60 tons burden, and manned with a crew of 20 men, partly English and partly Dutch.

As at that time there were so many Belgian exiles in Holland, and as the three influential Flemings just mentioned had so prominently participated in the preliminaries of this expedition, the question arises: is it not likely that there were Belgians among those sailors as there were in Magellan's crew? If there were any Flemings among them they could easily have been mistaken for Dutch, as Dutch and Fleming are often confused.

Hudson had been instructed to pass by the north and northeast of Nova Zembla in his search for a route to India, and he faithfully followed those instructions until the cold became so intense that his sailors could not continue to perform their duties. Now and then surrounded by mountains of ice, or thrown in unknown currents, the crew had become mutinous and Hudson was forced to turn back.

Obliged to abandon his project to go to Asia by the north seas, he was now endeavoring to reach it by searching for a passage through the American continent. He had studied Verrazano's charts and reports, and had good reasons to believe that some communication with the sea existed at about the 40th degree of latitude. He sailed as far down as Virginia, then taking a northerly direction he anchored at Navesink, N. J.[1] on September 2nd, and reached Sandy Hook on the 3rd.

On the 6th, John Coleman, an Englishman, with 4 seamen, went to sound the Narrows. Coleman was

[1] Not to be spelled "Neversink." (U. S. Geographic Board.)

killed by the Indians and buried upon a point of land called "Coleman's Point."

On the 11th of September, the Half Moon carefully steered through the Narrows, came in full view of Manhattan Island. Hudson never dreamed that one day it would become the melting pot of innumerable nationalities, the home or business place of millions of people, a formidable financial power, the seat of great institutions of learning, and the talk of the world.

Hudson had a mission to fulfil. He was satisfied that he had, at last, found a passage to China for the river stretched far off to the north. He began to ascend the river, reached the Highlands on the 14th, and anchored above the present city of Hudson on September 17th.

From the 18th to the 22nd of September, he proceeded on his way up the river, but navigation having become difficult, a boat was sent several leagues in advance to measure the depth of the river. Only 7 feet of water, and variable soundings halted any further advance. According to some opinions he reached a point above the present city of Albany, others place it below that city.

While he had accomplished a feat of the greatest importance for all times, he was far from China—the objective of his voyage. At this time, the famous French navigator, Samuel de Champlain, the founder of Quebec, was at the lake which bears his name, and within only 100 miles of Hudson.

From September 23rd to October 3rd the return voyage was continued and on the 4th of October, 1609, he set sail for Holland to report on his discoveries. Hudson wrote that the land was of the finest kind for tillage, and as beautiful as the foot of man ever trod upon.

He stopped at Dartmouth, in Devonshire, on the 7th of November, 1609, where he was detained by the British authorities, who questioned his right to be in the service of a foreign power.

His employers—the Dutch East India Company—were not aware of his return, and his report reached them several months after his arrival at Dartmouth. He was kept in England, but later on his vessel, the Half Moon, with its cargo, was sent to Holland.

Immediately, the English Muscovy Company made preparations for another attempt to reach Asia through the northern regions, and appointed Hudson as commander. He sailed northeast again until the ice forced him to steer westward, and after many hardships discovered, in 1610, the strait and the vast bay, both of which bear his name. On the return voyage of 1611, his crew mutinied and forced the heroic commander with eight men into a small boat, which was turned adrift and never more heard of! Such was the tragic end of the great and gallant navigator ....to whom our gratitude has forgotten to erect a single monument.

The dates given above, concerning his trip on the river, are from the log book of the Half Moon, by Robert Juet, mate.

The Great River. What we call now the Hudson, went through many names: Groote River (Great River); Manhattans or Manhattes or Manhattos

Rivier; Noort Rivier (North River); Montagne or Montaigne Rivier; Mauritius or Maurits River, in honor of Prince Maurice of Nassau.

Grande Rio de Montagnes, by Verrazano; Rio de San Antonio, by Gomez.

Cohohatated, and Shatemuc and Mohicannittuck, by the Indians.

Manhattan. Juet, Hudson's mate, wrote in the log book of the Half Moon that on the return voyage from the headwaters of the stream, they anchored, on October 2nd, 1609, in the bay now known as Hoboken, and notes specifically that it was on "that side of the river that is called Manna-hata," where "there was a cliff that looked of the color of a white green.[1]

This cliff, known as Castle Point, for many years the residence of the Stevens family, a most honored name so closely connected with that great institution of learning called "Stevens Institute of Technology," now under the able and learned leadership of Dr. Alexander Crombie Humphreys, is near the "Elysian Fields" at Hoboken.

The significance of the reference to this cliff is not that it more clearly defines the place of anchorage, but the more important fact that it fixes beyond all question the district of country to which the original inhabitants gave the name, which after passing through many changes in orthography, is now written "Manhattan" and is applied specifically, to the island which throbs with the activities of the metropolis of the nation.[1]

DeVries confirms Hudson's or Juet's application of

[1] J. G. Wilson, Mem. Hist. of N. Y., vol. 1. pp. 33-34.

the name to the above location. Relating his return voyage from a visit to Hartford, in 1639, De Vries wrote: "Arrived about evening at the Manattes, opposite Fort Amsterdam." [1]

As we are now nearing the end of the presentation of voyages having direct or remote connections with settlements in America, a few lines concerning Hennepin will be in order.

Louis Hennepin. This Recollet friar, a Walloon, born at Ath (Belgium) in 1614, a missionary in Canada, explored the Illinois river and Minnesota, and discovered the Falls of St. Anthony.

After his return to Montreal he went to France, where he published a narrative of his experiences, under the title: "Description de la Louisiane nouvellement découverte" (Description of Louisiana newly Discovered). Paris 1683.

First Mention of Niagara Falls. His other book: "Nouvelle découverte d'un très grand pays situé dans l'Amérique, entre le Nouveau Mexique et la Mer Glaciale" (New Discovery in America of a very large country between New Mexico and the Glacial Sea), Utrecht 1697, has the earliest known engraved plate showing "Niagara Falls," and a fine map containing results of explorations north of Lake Superior.

Some of the descriptions it contains are of great interest; and from that time forth the French became familiar with the Lake Superior country, and began to extend their alliances among the northwestern Indians.[2]

---

[1] N. Y. Hist. Coll. Sec. Ser., 1: 261.
[2] Fiske. Discovery of America, vol. 2, pp. 538-40.

CHAPTER V

THE first settlers in New York were Belgians (Walloons) as will be proved in the following chapters. They came to New York in 1623, but some writers say 1624.

With the purpose, perhaps, of disproving the true nationality of those first settlers, it has been said in certain quarters that the Belgians came into existence only in 1831, (after the revolution which gave them their independence), whereas it is well-known that they were already at war with Julius Cæsar in the years 57 to 51 B.C. See "Commentaries" of Cæsar on his wars, which contain the initial description of Belgium.

The Belgians, as history shows, were often "annexed" by some great power, and passed constantly from one foreign domination to another. As a consequence, their present territory is by far smaller than that occupied by them in earlier times.

In order to give to the reader a correct idea of the antecedents of the Belgians, a brief account of their long and complicated history follows.

Walloons and Flemings. The Belgian people belong to two different races, the Walloons and the Flemings.

Belgium is divided into nine provinces, the Walloons occupying one-half of this territory (south): Hainault, Namur, Liege, Luxembourg, and southern Brabant, and the Flemings the other half (north): West Flanders, East Flanders, Antwerp, Limbourg, and northern Brabant.

The Walloons are the lineal descendents of the old "Gallic Belgae" (or Celtic people); that is to say, of the inhabitants of the ancient Belgian Gaul, and the people of the southern provinces of Belgium were designated by the name of Walloons very likely on account of their Gallic origin.

In transition from the Latin and Romance languages to the tongues of the North, the "g" is often changed into "w," and so Guillaume becomes William, and guerre, war; the Prince de "Galles," in French, is the Prince of "Wales," and so the name Gaulois would become Waalsch or Walloon. The Flemings and the Dutch call the Walloon a "Waal" and give to the Walloon country the name of "Waalsch."

The Gauls and Romans were called by the modern English and Germans the "Wealas" meaning "stranger" and the expression "oon" stood for "one" or "a"; thus, for them, a Walloon was one stranger, a foreigner.

They have a literature of their own, and their language called "Walloon" is still spoken in Belgium; it contains a greater number of Latin words than French. In its early form it was born directly from

Latin; the Celtic and German elements to be found in it are of secondary importance.

It is not, therefore, a "French dialect" nor "corrupt French," as many believe. It is a dialect or branch of the primitive Gallic or langue d'oil,[1] the Romance tongue which was to serve as the transition between the dying Latin and the French about to be born. This explains the extensive use that the Walloons have made of the French language. Walloon, like the other dialects of the Romance language, is older than French, the latter being a composite of those dialects.

Here is a Walloon proverb, with French and English translations:

Inn omm sainz argein esst u leu sain dain.

Un homme sans argent est un loup sans dents.

A man without money is (like) a wolf without teeth.

The difference between the two languages—Walloon and French—will be recognized by the trouble and labor some Belgian and French linguists went to, in writing comparative dictionaries on the subject. They are:

Cambresier.   Dictionnaire wallon-français....Liége, 1787.
Remacle.   Dictionnaire wallon-français....Liége, 1823.
Grandgagnage. Dictionnaire étymologique de la
                 langue wallonne.............Liége, 1845.
Hubert.   Dictionnaire wallon-français.......... 1856.
Chavée.   Dictionnaire français et wallon..Paris, 1857.

[1] "Langue d'oil," name given in the middle ages to the Romance language spoken north, from the river Loire to the Rhine, and comprising many dialects, the fusion of which gave birth to the French language.

The Flemings. The Flemings are of Teutonic stock. In primitive times, invaders from the East, beyond the river Maas, brought into Belgic Land new populations.

The territory occupied by the Flemings was covered with marshes and little strips of land called Vladen, Vladeren or Vlandren, and the inhabitants were then known as Vlamen. Today, at home, they call themselves Vlamings (Flemings), and their territory, in their own language, is Vlaanderen (Flanders).

Their language is called "Flemish"; it is a Teutonic tongue. Taking into consideration the changes in pronunciation and spelling necessarily brought in after many centuries, it is believed that Flemish and Celtic were the languages of Belgium before the arrival of the Romans; it is certain that Latin but very slightly entered into it.

In their general physiognomy Flemish and Dutch of to-day offer a close resemblance, but differ in many points. Flemish was polished by literary culture before Dutch, and under the name of "Vlaemisch" or "Brabantisch" it was, in the fifteenth century, the general and written language of the "Seventeen Provinces," called "Pays-Bas" or "Netherlands," that is to say, Belgium and the Dutch country together. Flemish had then succeeded to Latin in the charters and literature; the ordinances of the 14th, 15th, and 16th centuries were in Flemish. In the 10th century, this language was in use in the entire territory of Picardy.

Early in the 15th century, the Flemish cities had poetical societies called "Chambers of Rhetoric."

The great fame of the Flemings in the fine arts does not need to be recalled.

Walloon is not so extensively spoken by the Belgians as Flemish, the Walloons making considerable use of the French language which is also used by a large number of Flemings.

Celts and Gauls. About the 12th Century, B. C., appeared the Celts[1] and towards the 6th Century, B. C., they seem to have become the dominant people in Europe. The Belgae or Belgians belong to this race.

The Celts invaded Northern Italy (Gallia Cisalpina), and all the territories between the Rhine, the Alps, the Mediterranean, the Pyrenees, the Atlantic Ocean, and the North Sea, (Gallia Transalpina). In this part of Gaul were Belgium and France of today. Other Celts, with "Belgius" as their chief, overran Macedonia in 279 B. C.

The Prefecture of Gaul, comprised the Transalpine Gaul, Great Britain, and Spain.

The continent of Gaul is described by Julius Cæsar in Chapter I of his "Commentaries," as follows:

"Gallia is all divided into three parts: whereof the 'Belges' do inhabit one, the 'Aquitanes' another, and those which they call 'Celtes' and we 'Galles' a third; all these differ each from other, in manner, language, and in laws. The 'Belges' are most war-like."[2]

Gallia Belgica. The Belgae or Belgians inhabited the vast territory limited to the north and east by the Rhine; to the south by the Vosges Mountains, the

---

[1] Branch of the Aryan family or primitive peoples of Central Asia.
[2] Celts and Gauls are often presented as synonymous names, the Gauls being Celtic people.

rivers Marne and Seine; to the west by the Ocean, the English Channel, and the North Sea. Such was the size of the country occupied by the primitive Belgians when the Roman legions attacked them and fought them for several years.

There were more than twenty independent tribes, with over a million and one-half people. Among those who inhabited sections corresponding to the present limits of Belgium were the Morini, the Menapii, the Aduatici, the Eburones, the Nervii, and the Treviri. Finally Cæsar conquered them in the year 53 B.C., and referring to the peoples of Gaul, he wrote: "Horum omnium fortissimi sunt Belgae," or "Of all these the Belgians are the bravest."

The Romans gave to the Belgic soil, here above described, the name of "Gallia Belgica," or "Belgian Gaul."

Nova Belgica. Later on, we shall see that the territories of New York and vicinity, occupied by the Belgians and the Dutch during the early days of settlement, are designated on the maps, by the name of "Nova Belgica," or "New Belgium."

The same name, implying the recognition of the true nationality of the first settlers in New York, is also to be found in the official Dutch seals of 1623 and 1654, as well as in the seal of Peter Stuyvesant, Dutch governor of New York. (See chapter XV.)

Belgae of Britain at the time of Julius Cæsar. It appears that the southeastern part of the island, now the county of Kent, was occupied by the Cantii, an influential tribe which in Cæsar's time was divided among four chiefs. To the west, the Regni held the

modern counties of Sussex and Surrey. Still further
west, the "Belgae" occupied the country from the
southern coast to the Bristol Channel, including nearly the whole of Hampshire, Wiltshire, and Somerset-
shire Counties.[1]

Roman Period. The Belgians remained under
Roman rule for more than 400 years, and became well
acquainted with the customs of civilization, while Lat-
in had become the language of their government.
During the Roman Empire, Belgian Gaul had been
extended as far as Basel (Switzerland) and under
Constantine was divided into four provinces: First
Belgica, capital Treves, Second Belgica, capital
Rheims, First Germania, capital Mayence, and Second
Germania, capital Cologne.

In the Roman itineraries we find many names of
Belgian cities of today, such as Tournai (Tornacum),
Menin (Minariacum), Gembloux (Geminiacum), Nas-
sogne (Nassonacum), Arlon (Orolaunum), etc. The
Romans left also the Latin names of several rivers
of Belgium: Scaldis (Scheldt), Mosa (Maas), Legia
(Lys), Urta (Ourthe), Sesmarus (Semois), Sabis
(Sambre), Loetia (Lesse), etc.

In many places are to be found Roman antiquities,
the tracks of roads, the marks of camps, cemeteries,
and villas, attesting the prosperity of the Gallo-
Roman period. Indeed, under the Emperor August-
us, successor to Cæsar, the Empire had reached a high
degree of material and intellectual prosperity. But
at the religious point of view what a sad spectacle!

[1] T. Wright. The Celt, the Roman and the Saxon, ch. 2; J. N. Larned.
Hist. for Ready Ref. vol. 1, p. 318.

They worshipped an infinity of gods, some symbolizing vices, and recognized thousands of divinities!

The first seeds of Christianity probably took root in the Belgic lands very early through Roman soldiers who had become Christians. During the third century A. D. appeared the first Christian missionaries among the Morini and the Nervii. Those fervent apostles were persecuted by the ferocious Rictovare, Prefect of Gallia Belgica, under the emperors Diocletian and Maximian. Saint Victoric and Saint Tuscien were martyrized near Amiens, and Saint Piat and Saint Chryseuil near Tournai, and other Christians perished by the thousands.

The great Roman Emperor Constantine from a pagan had become a Christian and the persecutions were stopped; from then on Christianity made rapid progress on Belgian soil. In the fourth century appeared Saints Materne, Servais, Martin, and Victrice, whose names are also those of many churches in Belgium.

Batavians. The Romans called the inhabitants of Holland the Batavians (Batavi) from a tribe that inhabited the "island of the Batavians," now Bommeler-Waard. In the 6th and 7th centuries the name Batavians disappears, to be replaced by the name of "Friesians."

When Cæsar undertook to conquer the Gaul, he made a treaty of alliance with the Batavians, who by this act kept their independence. But under the Emperor Tiberius, his son Drusus took possession of their country and they were placed under Roman rule.

Civilis, chief of the Batavians, raised his countrymen against the Romans, A.D. 69-71, but in vain. They made their submission and were again allowed in the Roman alliance. Three different tribes now inhabited Holland: the Batavians, the Friesians, and the Bructerians.

Carausius. Towards the end of the 3rd century, a Belgian (Menapi) named "Carausius," who had become a Roman general, was in charge of a flotilla to defend the coast of the Atlantic against the pirates, when suddenly he debarked in Great Britain, where he forced the Roman legions, A. D. 287, to recognize him as emperor, and where he reigned for six years.

He conquered the Island of the Batavians, which afterwards he gave to the "Franks," thus facilitating for the latter their entry into Gaul.

Germania and the Goths. The Germans occupied, then, all the countries between the Rhine and the Vistula, and between the Baltic Sea and the Danube. These tribes dashing from the east took possession of the Roman soil. Then came the Franks, of more interest to Belgium because they established there a social order.

Frank Period. The Franks were not a particular tribe but a federation of Germanic peoples. The Roman Empire had fallen into full decadence and the Franks (5th century) starting from the Island of the Batavians, in the north, began the invasion of Gaul, which later on they conquered entirely.

The first Franco-Belgian kings were: Pharamond, Clodion, Mérovée, Childéric, and Clovis. Mérovée was the founder of the Merovingian dynasty; Childéric, like Mérovée, made Tournai (Belgium) their capital.

Of the Merovingian dynasty of Frankish kings, Clovis, born in A. D. 465, was the most illustrious. Considering the Kingdom of Tournai as too small, he decided to conquer the entire Gaul. Converted to Christianity, he was baptised at Rheims, the old metropolis of Second Belgica.

The Franks having become the dominant people of Gaul, they founded there several little kingdoms and the country took the name of "France," whose history really begins with the reign of Clovis.[1] The latter died at Paris in A.D., 511, and his kingdom was divided among his four sons, who later on overcame the "Burgundians" with whom the fortunes of Belgium became afterwards associated.

The Frankish, or French emblem of royalty was the fleur de lys (lance-head) or lily flower, which some say was named from the Belgian river Lys, crossed by Clovis and his army.

In 561, the vast Frankish empire was again divided into: the kingdoms of Paris, Burgundy, Austrasia, and Neustria with Belgium lying partly in both of the two latter countries. Grave dissensions between the rulers of Austrasia and Neustria created terrible civil wars, which weakened the Merovingian dynasty.

In those two kingdoms, the high dignitary of the royal households had the title of "Mayor of the Palace," and in the course of events this dignitary became the real power holder. In the 7th century those high positions were held by the Walloons Pepin

[1] Bouillet. Dict. d'Histoire, pp. 693 and 700.

of Landen,[1] Pepin of Heristal[2] and Charles Martel, all from "Hesbaye," a geographic zone of Belgium or part of the old principality of Liege.

Pepin of Heristal was chosen as chief by the Austrasians, and forced the Neustrians to accept him as Mayor of the Palace, and for 27 years he governed these Frankish States.

His son Charles surnamed Martel, meaning the "hammer," born in A.D. 691, at Jupille (near Liege, Belgium), ruled for a long time over France.

The Friesians (Hollanders formerly called Batavians) had separated themselves from the Franks, but Charles Martel vanquished them in A.D. 736 and they were reinstalled in the Frankish union. He introduced among the Friesians the Christian civilization in protecting Saint Willebrord, their apostle who came from Ireland, then called the "Isle of Saints."

The Merovingian kings who had become rulers only in name, as their States were governed by the Mayors of the Palace, were called the "Sluggard Kings" or "do-nothings." This peculiar situation brought on a change of dynasty.

Pepin the Short, having been proclaimed king of the Frankish States, founded a new dynasty called "Carlovingian," after the name of his father, Charles Martel, and so ended the dynasty of the Merovingians.

His son and successor was Charles, called Charlemagne, or Charles the Great. This Frankish monarch crowned emperor in A.D. 800, by the Pope Leo III, ruled from 768 to 814, over Belgium, France, Ger-

[1] From Landen, a locality N. W. of the City of Liege.
[2] From Heristal, a locality N. E. of the City of Liege.

many, Switzerland, and a portion of northern Spain and Italy. He imposed the Frankish institutions on the Friesians, who were isolated in the midst of dunes and marshes.

The place of his birth is not certainly known, but Belgium claims him as her son, asserting that he was born in Liege "from which Province all of his ancestors came," and the city of Liege, on one of its public squares, has erected an equestrian statue of him.

Charlemagne, more than a thousand years before the Belgians finally obtained their complete independence, made of his Belgic domain an independent circuit in his vast empire, virtually mapping out the provinces. During his reign many great cities of Belgium saw their start and most of these old towns grew up about a monastery, where grammar, rhetoric, dialectic, arithmetic, geometry, music, and astronomy were taught.

In the 7th century, Belgium was justly called the "Land of the Saints." Here is a list of names of founders of monasteries or churches around which the following Belgian cities originated during that century:

Saint Amand }
Saint Bavon } Ghent.......Province of East Flander.

Saint Remacle { Stavelot
              { Malmedy   Province of Liége.

Saint Vincent, Soignies..........Province of Hainault.

Saint Lievin, Alost........Province of East Flander.

Saint Trond, Saint-Trond.......Province of Limbourg.

Saint Waudru, Mons...........Province of Hainault.

Saint Itte
Saint Gertrude } Nivelles........ Province of Brabant.

Saint Monulphe
Saint Lambert } Liége............Province of Liége.
Saint Hubert

Saint Gery, Brussels............Province of Brabant.

The memories of other saints are very dear to the Belgains. Saint Gudule, for instance, the Patron Saint of Brussels, was the niece of Pepin of Landen, and the god-child of St. Gertrude.

The little city of Hal, near Brussels, known all over the world for pilgrimage meetings around its celebrated miraculous statue of Our Lady, saw its primitive church consecrated by Saint Hubert, in 727. A large sanctuary, one of the most beautiful churches in Belgium, a masterpiece of pure Gothic architecture, replacing the old church, was blessed in 1409 by the Archbishop of Cambrai: Pierre d'Ailly, the author of "Imago Mundi," mentioned before in the "Naming of America."

The city of Treves, once in Belgium (now in Germany) also became a center of monastic life.

Charlemagne died in 814, and quarrels between his son, grandsons, and other relatives ended in the compact of Verdun, 843, which divided the great empire into several kingdoms, whose history is very intricate. Lothaire II, formed the kingdom of Lothairingia, which itself was later on divided into Upper Lothairingia (Lorraine) and Lower Lothairingia (Eastern Belgium and the Rhenish Province).

Period of Feudalism in the 9th, 10th, and 11th centuries. Formal feudalism began after the death of Charlemagne.

The "feudal system" or "division and distribution of tracts of lands" among conquerors or lords, and later on "momentary and conditional grants of lands" by the lords to some of their subjects or followers, dismembered Belgium into big areas called "feuds" or "fiefs," which constituted the origin of the Belgian provinces. They were: the County (earldom) of Flanders; the Duchies of Brabant, Limbourg, and Luxembourg; the Counties (earldoms) of Hainault and Namur; the Principality (princedom) of Liege and the Marquisate of Antwerp. Each of them were ruled by a personage with a title such as Count, Duke, etc., generally corresponding to the denomination of his domain.

The above names of the old territorial divisions of ten centuries ago, with Flanders now divided into East Flander and West Flander, are still the names of the nine provinces forming the Kingdom of Belgium today.

In the chronicles the first important families of the feudal period are called Belgian "princes." The country now called Netherlands had her Counts of Holland and Zealand, Dukes of Gelderland, Lords of Friesland, etc.

Feudalism was a social system of privileges and rights for the few, and submission or servitude for the masses; a society divided into two distinct groups, the landed and the landless. It was adopted and maintained for centuries in many countries of Europe.

The nearest approach to the feudal system in the United States started with the Dutch in 1629. Their purpose was to promote the settlement around New Amsterdam and along the Hudson by adopting a system of large landed estates. It was provided that any member of the community who in four years should carry to the Colony 50 families at his own expense, should have a large tract of land, over which he should have extensive civil and criminal authority under the title of "Patroon." He should also have on his estate the monopoly of weaving and some exclusive trading privileges.

It was thus definitely proposed to establish a feudal system, known here as the "Patroon System" of land holding.[1]

The Crusades. During the period from the 11th to the 13th century, the world witnessed the "Crusades," or military expeditions against the Turks, who had taken the Holy Land and Jerusalem, and persecuted the Christians.

The Pope Urban II, assembled, in 1095, at Clermont —Ferrand, in Auvergne (France), a Council, at which he himself presided, and there the first Crusade was decided upon by bishops, knights, and the people, amidst the cry of "God wills it!"

Peter the Hermit, born at Amiens, had become the preacher of the First Crusade; he rode through many states of Europe and excited the Christian world against the Moslems. After having accompanied the Crusaders to the Orient, he came back to Belgium and

[1] Bassett. A Short History of the United States, p. 73.

founded, near Huy (Province of Liege), the monastery of Neu-Moutier where he died in 1115.

In the Crusades the Belgians played the dominant rôle. The hero of the first Crusade was "Godfrey de Bouillon," [1] Duke of Lothier, a Walloon, born at Baisy, Belgium, who became Lord or Advocate of Jerusalem, refusing the title of "King" offered him by his followers. To Holy Land he gave feudal laws, known as the "Assizes of Jerusalem;" they represent the most complete code of feudal institutions. Another chief of the first crusade was the Fleming, Robert II, Count of Flanders, commanding a division of Flemings, French, and Italians.

The fourth Crusade was undertaken by another Belgian, Baldwin IX, Count of Flanders and Hainault. He was chosen Emperor of Constantinople in 1204, and solemnly crowned in the Basilica of Saint Sophia (magnificent church erected in Constantinople, in 537, by Justinian I, Emperor of the East; it is now a famous Turkish mosque).

Communes. Feudalism led to liberty! The feudal system had given to the nobles exclusive civil and political rights but the "communes" did not remain inactive: they had raised themselves through their industry and commerce; they had formed a splendid labor organization, known as the "Corporation of Trades"; they had become a power, and they asked for their rights and liberty.

Thus, the 12th, 13th, and 14th centuries saw the

[1] Bouillon, a small city in the Province of Luxembourg (Belgium). Its old feudal castle belonged to Godfrey, the Hunchback, who legated it to his nephew, Godfrey de Bouillon.

creation, organization, and development of "communes" or "cities" with rights and privileges for the people such as the commoners or burghers had never before enjoyed. Under this system of freedom in administration and public affairs, commerce, industry, as well as literature and fine arts, developed immensely. The functions of the men then representing an administration were as follows:

1. The Aldermen who had the administration of the finances and exercised the judiciary power, formed the Board of Aldermen.
2. The Councillors who took part in the administration of the city, formed the Board of Councillors.
3. The Mayor was the head of the administration, over which he presided. Sometimes there were two mayors, then one presided over the Board of Aldermen and the other over the Board of Councillors, but the latter was the subordinate of the former.
4. A Treasurer, and 5. A Secretary.

The composition of the administration of a commune, or city, of that time, is still the same in Belgium now-a-days, except that the Board of Aldermen is no longer a court of justice, and that each alderman is now the head of a department, such as finance, public works, etc., except the police, of which the head is a Commissioner, under the Mayor.

Under the auspices of freedom in local matters, new cities came into existence and rapidly developed. Industry became extraordinarily prosperous; Flanders was the richest country on earth. Bruges, called the Venice of the North, had the most important market in Europe, not only for linen (flax) and cloth (woolens) but for all other products, as she was the warehouse of the producing countries of the globe. She was also a financial power: the first "commerce exchange" was established there in 1360.

Bruges had 200,000 inhabitants and Ghent 150,000, with 50,000 weavers; Ypres had also 200,000 inhabitants, with 4,000 cloth factories; Louvain had no less than 150,000 inhabitants with 40,000 weavers; Tournai counted 2,500 weaving looms.

Liege with 120,000 inhabitants had a fine reputation for cloth and arms making; Huy was known for her manufactured metals, and Dinant was exporting her artistic copper works called "dinanderies."

Important and prosperous also, were the cities of Brussels, Courtrai, Mons, Namur, Audenarde, Alost, Tirlemont, Furnes, Grammont, etc.

The Flemish "Hanse"[1] or association of some Belgian and foreign cities, contributed largely to the expansion of commerce. First Bruges, and later Antwerp became the warehouses of the Hanse, whose vessels were on all the seas of Europe to exchange the Belgian products (linen, cloth, metals, etc.) for those of far distant countries (silks, furs, spices, etc.).

The power of the Belgian cities was so great that each of them could supply an army of from 10,000 to 20,000 men.

From an intellectual viewpoint, progress was as great as the prosperity of the communes. It was at this time that the Romance language received the

[1] Hanse. Name given in the Middle Ages to a commercial association or league of European cities; "hanse-town," a city belonging to the Hanse.

greatest attention through the zeal of the "trou-
veres,"[1] charming poets, the fathers of the French
language. The same period registers Van Maerlandt,
the father of Flemish poetry, author of "Sentences
from Aristotle," "The War of Troy," etc.

And in the fine arts, the part of the communes was
perhaps still greater. The wealth of the people of
Belgium helped architecture—of Gothic style—to
reach its height, and their country was embellished
by such splendid monuments as the Cloth-Hall of
Ypres (destroyed by the Germans during the great
war); the Cloth-Hall of Bruges, with its incomparable
belfry; the remarkable City Halls of Brussels, Louvain, Bruges, Audenarde, etc; the beautiful cathedrals
of Notre-Dame at Tournai and at Hal; St. James and
St. Paul at Liege; St. Bavon at Ghent; Ste. Gudule at
Brussels; Notre-Dame at Antwerp; St. Rombaut at
Malines; etc. (Some were not finished until the 15th
century.)

> "Then most musical and solemn, bringing back
>   the olden times,
> With their strange, unearthly changes rang the
>   melancholy chimes."
> "I beheld the pageants splendid, that adorned
>   those days of old;
> Stately dames, like queens attended, knights who
>   bore the Fleece of Gold."
>
> *(Longfellow. From the "Belfry of Bruges.")*

However, the extensive privileges granted to the
people, their quarrels and their revolts, brought about,

[1] Trouvere, or poet of the langue d'oil; "troubadour," or poet of the langue d'oc, divisions of the Romance language.

during the 15th century, a most severe decline in the prosperity and happiness of the communes.

Burgundian Period. Burgundy conquered by Cæsar passed through many vicissitudes and had become a Duchy. Located at the East of France, it had Dijon as capital, and is now part of France.

Philip the Bold, son of King John II of France, was placed in possession of the Duchy, in 1363, and so the "House of Burgundy" sprung from the royal house of France.

The cause of the accession of the House of Burgundy in Belgium was the marriage, in 1384, of Philip the Bold to Margaret, sole heir of the Count of Flanders.

To Philip the Bold, first Duke of Burgundy, succeeded in direct lineage: John the Fearless, Philip the Good, Charles the Bold, and Mary of Burgundy.

At first the dukes of Burgundy had only Flanders, but Philip the Good added finally to his domain the rest of Belgium (1443), except the Principality of Liege. He took also the counties of Holland and Zeeland and the Duchy of Gelderland. The Belgian communes were opposed to the political schemes of the Burgundian princes and violent outbreaks occurred.

Philip the Good instituted at Bruges, in 1430, the famous order of the "Golden Fleece," [1] composed of thirty-one Knights chosen from among the most powerful Lords, and forming under the presidency of the Grand Master, the Duke of Burgundy, a Council to aid the sovereign in the difficult matters of the

[1] The insignia was a long necklace of solid gold, with a golden sheep as a charm.

State. He protected letters and the fine arts, encouraged public construction, and presented the Library of Burgundy (Bibliothèque de Bourgogne) with rare manuscripts. Philip the Good contributed to that great artistic and literary movement of the 15th and 16th centuries, called the "Renaissance." His time saw the Van Eycks, famous Flemish painters, to whom is attributed the invention of oil painting; Memling, one of the greatest painters of the Flemish school; the Walloon painter, Roger de la Pasture; the historian Philip de Commines who became minister of Louis XI; etc.

Some of the cathedrals and public monuments, mentioned in the previous paragraphs on the Communes, were finished during the Burgundian period.

Under the reign of Charles the Bold, the art of printing was introduced in Belgium. In the Flemish city of Alost, where he was born, Thierry Maertens installed a press in 1473.

Mary of Burgundy, only child of Charles the Bold, succeeded her father, and married, in 1477, Maximilian, Archduke of Austria. This marriage transferred the states of the House of Burgundy, comprising Belgium and Holland, to the "Habsbourgs" or "House of Austria."

Mary died accidentally, in 1482, at the age of 25, leaving to her husband two infants: Philip the Fair and Margaret of Austria. Her death terminated the powerful house of Burgundy, which had ruled over Belgium for a century.

Austro-Spanish Period. In 1482, Maximilian began his regency of the Lowlands—Belgium and part of Holland — and in 1493 succeeded his father, Frederic III, as Emperor of Germany, or head of the Holy Roman Empire, and transferred to his young son Philip the Fair, the Lordship of the Lowlands and Burgundy. This prince married, in 1496, Joanna of Spain, daughter of Ferdinand and Isabella, holders of the crowns of Aragon and Castile. One year later Margaret, sister of the young Prince Philip, married Don John, brother of Joanna and heir to the throne of Spain. But the latter died prematurely, and so the Belgian Prince, Philip the Fair, already heir to the Austrian domains, became also heir apparent of the Crown of Spain. Indeed, after the death of Isabella, 1504, he fell heir to her possessions and became ruler of Castile.

Two consequences resulted from these events. The first was that Philip the Fair, who was already Archduke of Austria by his father, became head of the "House of Austria," that ruled over Spain, and which was now called the "Austro-Spanish House." The second consequence was, that later on, Belgium was turned over to Spain. Under Philip the Fair, Brussels was the the capital of the Lowlands.

Then came Charles V, born at Ghent, in 1500, son of Philip the Fair and of Joanna. He was brought up by his aunt, Margaret of Austria, now regent of Belgium, and educated by William of Croy, Lord of Chievres (Hainault) and by Adrian Boyens of Utrecht, famous professor at the University of Louvain, who became Pope under the name of Adrian VI.

The great emperor ruled over the Lowlands (Belgium and Holland) and the other states of the House of Burgundy; the Italian states of Naples, Sicily, Sardinia, Genoa; the Duchy of Milan; Spain and her immense colonies in America. He was also proclaimed Emperor of Germany. He took pride in saying that "the sun never set on his domain."

Francis I, King of France, was the great rival of Charles V and during their wars the advantages were on the side of Charles. As a result, the French lost Tournai which passed definitely to Belgium in 1521. They lost also the Battle of Pavia, Italy, in 1525, where Francis I was made prisoner and tendered his sword to the Belgian General Count Charles de Lannoy, commander of the troops of Charles V.

Les Pays-Bas. At the time of Charles V, the seventeen provinces of the Belgians and the Dutch represented by counties, duchies, etc., were grouped together under the name of "Pays-Bas" or "Netherlands"; they were: Limbourg, Luxembourg, Brabant, Flanders, Namur, Hainault, Antwerp, Malines, Franche-Comté, and Artois, in the south; Zeeland, Holland, Utrecht, Gelderland, Over-Yssel, Friesland, and Groningen, in the north.

This grouping of territories was called "Pays-Bas" (a French word meaning low-lands) owing to the orographic aspect of the country.

The name Pays-Bas (plural) when translated "Netherlands" (plural) in English must mean, in this period of history, the seventeen Belgian and Dutch provinces of that time, mentioned hereabove.

The country we now call in English "Netherlands" (plural) is not the same as the one of old. Netherlands of to-day is what is often loosely termed "Holland," and what the Dutch call, officially, Nederland (singular) and not Nederlanden (plural), which should make it in English Netherland, and not Netherlands.

This remark is important as many persons are under the impression that the word "Netherlands" means, at all times, the Dutch territory only. This error has placed on the Dutch side many Belgians of renown in literature, arts, and sciences, and is misleading in many other ways.

In 1548, the Pays-Bas were incorporated into the empire of Charles V, and formed the "Circle of Burgundy." At this time, the Low-Countries had a population of 3,000,000 people, and no other country, north of the Alps, was more populated in comparison of size.

In 1555, at Brussels, Charles V abdicated the Pays-Bas or Netherlands to his son, Philip II, and soon thereafter transferred the rest of the empire to his brother Ferdinand I. Then he retired to the monastery of St. Just, in Spain, where he died in 1558.

Spanish Period. This was for Belgium, what the 16th century was for Europe: a revolutionary period which brought suffering, destruction, and ruin.

Philip II began to rule over the Pays-Bas in 1555. His education had made him essentially a Spanish king, and he met with unpopularity in many ways. In 1559, he confided the government of the seventeen provinces of the Netherlands to his sister, Margaret of Parma, and to help her in her task, he formed a Council of State, in which there were: William of

Orange (William the Silent); the Count Egmont, and the Count Hornes. These three men played an important rôle during the religious troubles.

After making these dispositions, Philip sailed for Spain, where he resided most of the time.

During the reigns of Charles V and his son, Philip II, appeared Martin Luther and John Calvin, with their new religion: the "Reformation," or· "Protestantism," which will be the subject of Chapter VI, as this religion played its rôle in the emigration of Belgians to Holland, and from there to New York.

The contests of the Catholic ruler, Charles, with the Protestants were continued with greater vigor by his successor, Philip. But Protestantism in the Netherlands was gaining more and more followers, and Philip, his representative the Duke of Alva, and others, having made many mistakes and gone to excesses, the northern provinces, whose population had largely increased by the flight of the frightened Walloon and Flemish Protestants of the southern provinces, succeeded, after terrible struggles, in breaking away from the Spanish domination and detached themselves from the Pays-Bas.

United Provinces. Indeed, in 1579, the north formed the Dutch Republic of the "United Provinces." At first, they numbered only five, but increased to seven: Zeeland, Holland, Utrecht, Gelderland, Over-Yssel, Friesland, and Groningen. In this way the "seventeen provinces" were broken up.

Belgian Protestants, Walloons and Flemings, by the thousands, had fled to foreign countries, mainly to Holland and England. The southern provinces

(Belgium) remained under the rule of Philip and were known as "Pays-Bas Espagnols" or "Spanish Netherlands."

Shortly before his death, which occurred in 1598, Philip II conceived the project of detaching Belgium (the Spanish Netherlands) from Spain, and to make it some kind of separate state, on feudal principles, in favor of his daughter, the Infanta Isabella, who married Albert, Archduke of Austria. In 1599, they were received by the Belgians as the new rulers of the Spanish Netherlands.

War started again! Spain wanted to reconquer the lost provinces of the north, now a Dutch Republic. The armies of the latter were commanded by Prince Maurice of Nassau, son of William of Orange, and those of Spain by Albert. The Dutch were successful at Nieuport, on the Belgian seacoast, but lost at Ostend after a memorable struggle which lasted three years.

Finally, and after long discussions, was signed at Antwerp, in 1609, at the time of the voyage of Hudson to America, a twelve year truce by which Spain recognized the independence of the Dutch Republic of the United Provinces, each contracting party keeping the territories then in their possession.

Albert and Isabella took advantage of this truce, to remedy and to improve the sad conditions in which Belgium found herself after a revolution of forty years, and continuous wars.

When they began to rule, the country offered a pitiable spectacle: the artisans and laborers had fled from the cities; the harbors were blocked; Belgian industry and commerce had taken refuge in England, Germany, Rotterdam, Middlebourg, but especially in Amsterdam; the countryside, laid waste by the war, was depopulated and agriculture ruined; churches and monasteries were destroyed.

Under these new rulers everything seemed to gain life again and to take a turn for the better. But it was mainly in literature, art, and science that the change was the greatest. Justus-Lipsius, a Fleming, celebrated philologist and professor at Iena, Leyden, and Louvain, was the main figure of a group of famous literary men, among whom Henri Dupuy, philologist; Aubert Lemire, historian; the Jesuit, Andrew Schott, professor of Greek and rhetoric at Louvain, Toledo, Saragosse, and Rome; Philip Cospeau, or Cospean, a Walloon, famous preacher who became Bishop of Nantes and pronounced the funeral oration of Henry IV, King of France.

In mathematics, Simon Stevin, to whom is due the theory of inclined planes; the Jesuit Gregoire de Saint-Vincent, one of the greatest surveyors of the 17th century, called by the famous Leibnitz as equal to Galileo.

It is during this period that Father Bolandus, of the Jesuits, following the project of Heribert Rosweide, began the publication of the "Acta Sanctorum" or "Deeds of the Saints."

It was also the time of the celebrated Flemish painter Peter-Paul Rubens, born at Antwerp, 1577,[1] and of his numerous famous pupils: Van Dyck, Ten-

---

[1] Max Rooses. "Rubens" English translation by Harold Child, vol. 1, p. 15,

iers, Snayers, Jordaens, etc., who made the renown of the Flemish school, while sculpture had a distinguished representative in Francis Duquesnoy, of Brussels.

Not long before the inauguration of Albert and Isabella, Belgium counted among her scholars the geographers Ortelius and Mercator, already mentioned in a previous chapter, and Andrew Vesale, of Brussels, the most eminent anatomist of the sixteenth century.

In 1543, he published his great work on anatomy, "Seven Books on the Structure of the Human Body," which brought immense improvements in the science. Senac, the celebrated French physician, compared it to the discovery of a new world. Vesale was the physician of the Emperor Charles V.

After the death of Albert (1621) and Isabella (1633) many governors for Belgium were successively appointed by Spain, and the twelve year truce having expired, war with the Republic of the United Provinces was renewed, and France started to attack the possessions of Spain.

The weariness of eighty years' war between Spain and the northern Protestant provinces, the advantageous offer made by Spain, and the fear of the Dutch Republic to see Belgium pass to France, were inducements to make peace, and this was signed at Munster, in January, 1648, between Spain and the Dutch United Provinces.

But the struggle with Louis XIV, King of France, continued and in 1658 the French Marshal Turenne won over the Spaniards the Battle of the Dunes, near Dunkerque. This victory permitted the Minister

Mazarin to dictate to Spain the Treaty of the Pyrenees (1659), the first that gave Belgian territory to France. Indeed, Philip IV, then King of Spain, had to give to France as dowry to the Infanta Maria Theresa, whom Louis XIV married, the province of Artois, part of the Province of Luxembourg, and the southern parts of Flanders and Hainault. Later on the Franche-Comté and part of Namur went also to the French crown.

Louis XIV wanted the dismemberment of the Spanish monarchy and coveted the annexation of all Belgium, (Spanish Netherlands). But the Dutch Republic had no desire to have France as a neighbor, and formed an alliance with England and Sweden, which stopped for a while the progress of Louis XIV, and forced him to sign the treaty of Aix-la-Chapelle (1668) by which France kept her conquests in Belgium, namely: Charleroi, Binche, Ath, Douai, Tournai, Audenarde, Lille, Armentieres, Courtrai, Bergues, and Furnes, and their dependencies. These formed a line of fortified places along the French border. Some of them, such as Lille, Armentieres, Bergues, and Douai, never returned to Belgium.

But war (1672-1678) continued against the Dutch Republic, which was fighting to maintain her industrial, commercial, and maritime supremacy. After many struggles and successes, now on one side, then on the other, was signed the treaty of Nimegue, in 1678, first between France and the Dutch, then between France and Spain, compelling the latter to give to Louis XIV fifteen more cities of Hainault and Flanders, and so Belgium had, again, to pay for the cost of the war!

Those two treaties, the one of the Pyrenees, in 1659, and the one of Nimegue, in 1678, each made at the expense of Belgium, permitted France to widen her territory.

The lands taken from the Belgian Flanders formed the "French Flanders" with Lille as capital. To-day, those lands compose the greatest part of the Departement du Nord, one of the richest of France. The lands taken from Hainault, became the "French Hainault."

The old territory of Hainault, and the sections thereof transferred to France, deserve special mention, for this Belgian Walloon soil has a close connection with the early history of New York. From Hainault came most of the first settlers in New York and vicinity.

Hainault. It was, primitively, inhabited by those brave Nervii, whom Cæsar vanquished with their Chief Boduognat, and was called "Hannonia", by the Romans. Later on, it received the name of Hainault (Hainaut in French) from the River Haine, which flows through the country. As early as the 5th century it had its own Rulers and Counts, and through marriages it was several times united to Flanders. In 1427, it was occupied by Philip the Good, Duke of Burgundy, and under Charles V it was, as we have seen, a part of the Seventeen Provinces or Pays-Bas, and after the secession of the northern provinces it was in the group (which remained to Philip II of Spain) called then the Spanish Netherlands, or Pays-Bas Espagnols.

Valenciennes and Avesnes. The treaties hereabove

mentioned, made by Louis XIV in 1659 and 1678, enabled him to form the "French Hainault" with Valenciennes as capital, and such cities as: Avesnes, Condé, Maubeuge, Le Quesnoy, Landrecies, Jivet, Charlemont, Philippeville, etc.

The dates of 1659 and 1678 are of importance, as any previous date having a connection with the territory of Hainault belongs to the history of the Walloons of Belgium and not to the history of France. Thus, Jean Vigné—and not Jan Vigne—of a family of Valenciennes, said to be the first white male child born in New York, was the offspring of a Walloon family of Belgium, and Jesse de Forest, known for his activities in bringing his Walloon countrymen to New York, in 1623, was of the same nationality.

During the summer of 1922, several French newspapers printed long patriotic articles, reproduced here in America, about Jesse de Forest, born at Avesnes, "France." While the eulogy of de Forest was well deserved, their enthusiasm made them forget the above page of history, and the chronology attached thereto!

Yes, Avesnes and Valenciennes are now, and have been for many years, in France, but were not at the time of Vigné and de Forest.

Notwithstanding the Treaty of Nimegue, the wars of Louis XIV soon were renewed. William III of Orange, the implacable enemy of Louis, formed the League of Augsbourg (1686) with Austria, Spain, Holland, Sweden, Saxony, Bavaria, and added England, after he had dethroned James II and had become himself King of England. Once more, Belgian soil became the battleground of the formidable wars of the French monarch, which brought to Belgium and France extreme misery. For the time being, the Treaty of Ryswyk (1697) terminated the disastrous struggle.

But on top of this came the wars of the Succession of Spain (1701-1713) which brought into Belgium a strong French occupation. Affairs were now complicated through the death of Charles II, King of Spain, 1700, who had named as his heir the Duke Philip of Anjou (Philip V), grandson of Louis XIV.

England and Holland, guided by the anti-French policy of William III, signed at The Hague, in 1701, the Treaty of the "Great Alliance," by which they agreed to take from Philip V all his territories except Spain herself, and after the terrible battles of Audenarde, Malplaquet, and Denain, the Treaty of Utrecht (1713) brought an end to the wars of the great Louis, who had to make concessions to the Dutch Republic.

By this treaty, Spain and her possessions in America remained with Philip V, while Belgium (the Spanish Netherlands), the states of Milan, Naples, and Sardinia went back to "Austria." However, the latter, by the special treaty of the "Barrier" (1715) must allow the Dutch Republic (the United Provinces) to garrison troops in certain fortified Belgian cities, on the western frontier, as a barrier against French aggression. The cost of this military Dutch occupation was to be paid by the Belgians; it stipulated, furthermore, the closing of the River Scheldt to Belgian commerce, thus increasing the ruin and humiliation endured by the unfortunate country, for a century.

The Spanish period had lasted from 1555 to 1713 and Belgium from Spanish Netherlands became now the "Austrian Netherlands."

Austrian Period. Charles VI, then Emperor, appointed, 1717, as Governor-General of Belgium (Austrian Netherlands) the Prince Eugene, who let the Marquis de Prié take charge.

The dissatisfaction of the Belgians with the shameful Treaty of the "Barrier" in 1715, the antipathy for the Governor, who thought that the people had too much political liberty, the complications of the imposition of taxes, etc., brought in violent riots, arrests, and severe punishments: Francis Agneessens, of Brussels, 70 years old, chief of a labor corporation, was beheaded, 1719.

The same treaty which, to the profit of the Dutch, had closed the Scheldt, precipitated the ruin of Antwerp and took away from Belgian commerce its main outlet towards the sea, thus preventing participation in international transactions.

And when in 1723 the "Ostend Company" was formed to do business with the Indies and the East, complaints and threats of war were sent by the Dutch and English—who feared competition—to the Emperor, Charles VI, and the latter ordered the suspension of the new company for seven years, and even its dissolution.

Charles VI left all his Austrian possessions to his daughter Maria Theresa, who soon after the death of her father found herself attacked by the rulers of many countries (1740-1748), who coveted parts of her empire. She had married the Prince Francis of Lorraine, and succeeded in gaining to her cause Hungary, England, and the Dutch Republic.

The War of the Austrian Succession brought the invasion of Belgium by the the armies of Louis XV, King of France, who took a great part of Flanders, while his Marshal de Saxe defeated the Anglo-Dutch troops at Fontenoy (1745). All the Belgian provinces (Austrian Netherlands), except Luxembourg and Limbourg, fell into the possession of the French monarch, and were crushed by taxes of all kinds.

But, Louis XV himself changed the entire situation. Now desiring a reconcilement with Austria, he restored the Belgian provinces to Maria Theresa and signed the peace of Aix-la-Chapelle (1748), which also stipulated the suppression of the annual subsidy which the Treaty of the Barrier had caused the Belgians to pay to the Dutch, for the army of occupation of the latter. Furthermore, Francis of Lorraine, husband of Maria Theresa, became Emperor of Austria.

The death of the great Empress Maria Theresa, which occurred in 1780, was much regretted by the Belgians, whom she had treated with kindness.

Her son, Joseph II, now the ruler of Austria and Belgium, was a dangerous despot, who went headlong into innovations and reforms in religious and civil matters which exasperated the people, and made them ripe for the revolution which exploded in 1789.

Belgian United States. This revolt of the people for their liberties, known as the "Brabant Revolution," was successful, and as it led to the formation of the "Belgian United States" deserves special mention.

There were now two parties in Belgium: first, the "Statistes," who desired the maintenance of the old Brabant Constitution, and had for chief Van der Noot; he wanted to free Belgium from the domination of the Austrians, with the help of other foreign powers; and, second, the "Vonckistes," who had for chief Vonck, a lawyer of Brussels, who desired to modify the institutions of the country in applying modern ideas.

Van der Noot formed a committee to go and negotiate with the cabinets of London, Berlin, and The Hague, where they received fine promises, as the statesmen of those countries wanted to intimidate Joseph II.

Vonck had formed an army composed of young patriots. Circumstances made the two chiefs meet: one wanted to negotiate, and the other to act; but Van der Noot accepted the plan of Vonck, who had secured for his army the services of Col. Van der Meersch, of Menin, in Flanders.

This little army had four thousand patriots, poorly equipped and slightly drilled, but full of enthusiasm, whereas the Imperial Austrian Army, whom they had to face, was composed of from fifteen to twenty thousand well-drilled soldiers.

Van der Meersch and his men entered the Province of Brabant and there he read to his troops the "Manifesto of the Brabant People," which proclaimed the loss of the sovereignty of Joseph II over Brabant.

Then they advanced towards the cities of Turnhout and Diest.

An Austrian army corps commanded by General Schroeder was sent against them, and Van der Meersch, who had neither cavalry nor cannon, thought it unwise to engage battle in open field. Using strategy, he fell back towards Turnhout and succeeded in drawing the Austrians into the city, where after a furious five hour battle in the streets, he forced the Austrians to retire, leaving cannons and ammunition in the hands of the patriots. (Oct. 26, 1789.)

This victory encouraged the patriots and quickly propagated insurrection in all the Belgian provinces, which made themselves free.

The propositions of Joseph II, who now renounced his innovations, were rejected and the States General, composed of fifty-three representatives of the liberated provinces, assembled at Brussels, voted—January 10, 1790—a federation under the name of "Etats-Belgiques-Unis" (Belgian United States) which, unfortunately, lasted less than a year.

In this struggle for liberty and religion, General Pierre Malou, of Ypres, played a very important rôle. Later on, he came to America and became a priest and an educator; he is buried under St. Patrick's church, New York. (See chapter XVI.)

The coalition of Statistes and Vonckistes had brought success to the revolution; their subsequent division prevented them from getting the benefits of it. Discussions as to political programs became bitter, and differences so irreconcilable that the Vonckistes entered into negotiations with their former foes, the Austrians, making them propositions which the latter refused, and during the first days of December, 1790, General Bender at the head of his Austrian troops, entered Brussels. Thus Belgium was, again, under the domination of Austria.

It would appear that the adventure of the Statistes and Vonckistes was well remembered after the Belgian revolution of 1830-1831, which gave, finally, to the Belgians their independence, for they hastened to adopt as their national motto: "L'Union fait la Force." (Unity makes Might, or In Union there is Strength.)

May the Flemings and the Walloons in their present and future struggles never forget those two episodes of their national history...the one where disunion brought only regrets and humiliation, the other where union gave happiness and prosperity.

The plea for this remembrance comes from the shores of the Hudson River, where the spirit of understanding and good-will of the old Belgians of 1623 is still alive; a plea from the United States of America, whose motto "E Pluribus Unum" is a counterpart of the one of the Belgian United Provinces of today.

Joseph II died in 1790, and a few years later the "Austrian Netherlands" or Belgium passed to France.

French Period. The "French Revolution," which had commenced in 1789, and witnessed the taking of the Bastille, the suppression of feudal privileges, the "Declaration of the Rights of Man," the voting of the Constitution of 1791 which made each citizen equal before the law, the proclamation of the French Republic

of 1792, the creation of the metric system, the behead-
ing of King Louis XVI, and his wife Marie Antoinette
(sister of Joseph II, mentioned in the previous paragraph) etc., also saw the wars between France and
Austria, again taking place on Belgian soil!

The French General Dumouriez sent into Belgium
an army of 80,000 men, won the battle of Jemmapes
(1792), took Mons, entered Brussels, and made himself master of all Belgium.

The port of Antwerp, blocked by the closing of the
Schedt, was reopened, 1792; this port through Dutch
agitation, had been closed to European commerce for
a century.

An offensive launched by the Austrians won from
the French the battle of Neerwinden (1793). Then
came the battle of Fleurus (1794) won by the French
General Jourdan, and the consequence of this victory
was the definite annexation of Belgium to France. It
was proclaimed in October, 1795, by the "Convention
Nationale" (French Revolutionary Assembly, which
succeeded to the "Assemblée Législative"), and two
years later Napoleon Bonaparte, through his treaty
of "Campo-Formio" with Francis II of Austria, had
the annexation confirmed. This marked the end of the
"Austrian Netherlands," composed of the Belgian
Provinces.

But the same year (1795) the Dutch were also conquered by the French and this was the end of the
Dutch Republic of the Seven United Provinces as
well. The latter was now known as the "République
Batave," (Batavian Republic, 1795-1806).

Belgium was divided by the French revolutionists

into nine departments, corresponding, almost, to the nine Belgian provinces of today, and the enduring little country now followed the destinies of France.

Then came into light Napoleon Bonaparte (later Napoleon I), son of Charles Bonaparte, a noble Corsican, and of Letizia Ramolino; born at Ajaccio, Corsica[1], in 1769, he studied at the military school of Paris, fought for the new French Republic,[2] and forced Austria to sign the Treaty of Campio-Formio, mentioned above.

Back from his successful campaign in Egypt, he suppressed the "Directoire," a name given to the short-lived French Government formed during the Revolution, became Consul and finally Emperor in 1804, as Napoleon I. Then took place his memorable expeditions against Austria, Prussia, Poland, and Russia.

He distributed the thrones of Europe among his relatives, and his brother, Louis Bonaparte, received the one of Holland, which from the Batavian Republic became the Kingdom of Holland, 1806, annexed to France in 1810, and free, again, in 1814.

The armies of Europe allied against the great Napoleon, victoriously entered Paris in 1814, and the Treaty of Paris (May, 1814) detached Belgium and Holland from the French Empire, while the Treaty of London (June, 1814) written by the governments of Europe, ordered the union of Holland and Belgium as a "balance of power" or "European equilibrium," and invited Prince William of Orange-Nassau to

[1] The State of Genoa sold the Island of Corsica to France in 1767.
[2] First French Republic 1792-1804.

operate the fusion of the two countries by means of conciliation and liberty. William took possession of the Government of Belgium, August, 1814.

Napoleon had abdicated and was sent to the little Island of Elba (in the Mediterranean). The treaty of Paris stipulated also that France would retain her limits only as they were in 1792, and Louis XVIII became King of France.

Dutch Period, or Holland and Belgium as one Kingdom, 1815-1830.

Napoleon escaped from the Island of Elba, March 1, 1815, returned to France and began his "Reign of One Hundred Days." The powers refused to recognize Napoleon, who had already organized an army of 220,000 men, and the Allies again directed their troops against France. There were the Austrians, commanded by Schwarzenberg; the Russians, who came to support the Prussians commanded by Blucher; the British, the Hanovrians, the Dutch, and the Belgians, commanded by Arthur Wellington (an Irishman, called the Iron Duke), who had his headquarters at Brussels.

Napoleon won over the Prussians the Battle of Ligny (near Gembloux, Belguim), and his Aide, Marshal Ney, won over the British the Battle of Quatre-Bras (near Nivelles, Belgium).

The next day, June 17, 1815, took place the famous battle of Waterloo, near Brussels, in which Napoleon was definitively defeated by Wellington and Blucher. The great French warrior was interned on the Island of St. Helena (Africa), where he died May 5, 1821.

The reunion of Belgium and Holland, through the

"Congress of Vienna" (1814-1815), ratifying the treaties of Paris and London, became the Kingdom of the Netherlands or Royaume des Pays-Bas. Prince William of Orange-Nassau became the ruler of the new kingdom, being known as William I.

The union of Belgium and Holland brought immense prosperity to both countries; Holland had colonies and an important maritime commerce, while Belgium possessed great agricultural and mineral resources. But there existed, since the sixteenth century, between the Belgians, who had remained Catholics, and the Dutch, who had become Calvinists, an antagonism which the subscribing powers to the Treaties of Reunion of the two nations seemed to have overlooked.

The antagonism was accentuated by the unwise and crafty policy of the new King William I. His sympathies were exclusively Dutch, and partial. He wanted to subordinate Belgium to Holland, though the latter numbered only one-half of the Belgian population.

The Belgians complained against the reactionary new constitution, which declared that the reformed faith was that of the sovereign; the press complained against the lack of liberty; the people were against the monopoly of civil education as directed against Catholic teaching. There was dissatisfaction about the law that imposed a knowledge of the "Dutch" language on candidates for official positions, and soon the Belgians found themselves excluded from important offices in all branches of the government. Among other grievances were the numerous taxes applied on all kinds of Belgian products of the farm and industry, in order to pay the old debts of Holland. The High Court of Justice was at The Hague, and so were all the great institutions of the Government of the Netherlands (now Holland and Belgium together), including the Bureau of Mines, although the mines were in Belgium, Holland having none of her own.

The policy of William I had made the union of the two countries a failure, and the Belgians revolted openly.

The Revolution. On August 26, 1830, the Opera "La Muette de portici"[1] was performed at the theatre of Brussels. A revolutionary scene occurs in that opera, with a song urging to combat. Over this song, the audience, rising in a body, took up the refrain ending with:

> Amour sacré de la patrie,
> Rends-nous l'audace et la fierté!
> (O supreme love for our fatherland,
> Give us, again, courage and pride!)

Repeating this song, the excited audience rushed to the street where noisy crowds joined them, and the Belgian revolution for independence was on its way. The house of Van Maanen, Minister of Justice of William I, and the offices of his subsidized newspaper the "National" were ransacked; the Dutch colors were torn down, and replaced by those of the old flag of Brabant (the red, yellow, and black), which continues to represent the standard of Belgium today. Then took place some negotiations between the Belgians

[1] French opera in five acts, poem by Scribe and Delavigne, music by Auber, 1828.

and the Dutch, with the revolution spreading to Liege, Antwerp, Louvain, Bruges, etc.

Belgian delegations went to the States General at The Hague and while there, Dutch troops entered Brussels, on September 23rd, and terrible fighting between the Belgian patriots and the Dutch army took place, ending September 26th, when the latter decided to retreat.

As in the American revolution for independence, valiant soldiers of France generously helped the Belgians in their struggle for freedom. It is often forgotten that brave men from Belgium—Flemings and Walloons—also fought in the war of the American revolution on the side of the patriots. (See chapter XVI.)

A provincial government was formed and the Dutch were expelled from all the Belgian cities. However, they still kept Maestricht, and the fort of Antwerp, where they bombarded the city. The Provincial Government, organized on September 26, 1830, proclaimed the independence of Belgium, issued a decree assuring the freedom of the press, teaching, association, and worshipping, and convoked the first National Congress.

Independence. This Assembly composed of two hundred representatives, elected by the people, met at Brussels on November 10, 1830, and had for its main purpose to give to Belgium a definite government. It confirmed the proclamation of the independence, pronounced the loss of any right of the House of Orange-Nassau over the sovereignty of Belgium; endowed the country with a Constitution; established a constitutional, representative, and monarchial government, and elected as King of the Belgians the Duke of Nemours, one of the sons of Louis-Philip I, then King of France.

For political reasons the French monarch could not allow his son to accept the Belgian crown, and Baron Surlet de Chokier, President of the National Congress of Belgium, was appointed Regent, February 21, 1831. The Constitution, carefully studied, had been adopted on February 7, 1831.

The independence of Greece had been proclaimed (February 3, 1830) at about the same time as that of Belgium, and the throne of Greece was offered by the great powers of Europe to Leopold, Duke of Saxe-Cobourg-Gotha, who declined the offer. He consented to become the ruler of the Belgians, and as Leopold I was, at Brussels, on July 21, 1831, inaugurated King of Belgium.

On August 9, 1832, he married Louise-Marie d'Orléans, daughter of Louis Philip I, King of France. The beloved Queen died at Ostend in 1850.

For centuries, Belgium had shown her great ability in industry and the fine arts, and now at the very beginning of her freedom she gave to the world another proof of her wonderful initiative and skill; Belgium built the first railroad on the European continent: the line from Brussels to Antwerp was inaugurated on May 5, 1835.[1]

William I of the Netherlands tried, by all means, to overthrow the new Belgian monarchy, but in 1838

[1] Railroads originated in Great Britain, but were quickly introduced and perfected in the United States.

public opinion in Holland clamored for peace with Belgium. The treaty which definitively separated Belgium from Holland was signed at London April 19, 1839, and William I continued to rule over his own people.

The sovereignty and perpetual neutrality of Belgium was recognized and guaranteed, in appropriate form, by Great Britain, France, Austria, Russia, and Prussia. It was this document that the latter (Germany) scorned, in 1914, as a "scrap of paper," which flagrant violation of agreement revolted the civilized world.

Soon William of the Netherlands displeased the Dutch themselves by the presentation of a huge budget which was rejected (1839), and by his marriage to a Belgian Catholic Lady, the Countess d'Oultremont. He abdicated in 1840 and went to Berlin where he died in 1843. His son William II had succeeded him at the time of abdication; this King was the grandfather of the present Queen Wilhelmina, who succeeded to her father, William III, in 1890.

The reign of Leopold I had been a period of organization and consolidation of the national institutions and independence of Belgium, an era of peace and of material and intellectual progress. He died on December 10, 1865, deeply regretted by the entire nation and, like George Washington, he justly deserved the sublime title of "Father of his Country." Leopold I was the uncle of Queen Victoria of England.

He had three sons and one daughter: Prince Louis Philip, who died very soon after his birth, Prince

Leopold, who succeeded to his father as Leopold II, Prince Philip, Count of Flanders, the father of present King Albert I, and Princess Carlotta, who married the Archduke Maximilian of Austria. The latter became Emperor of Mexico at the request of Napoleon III, and was shot by Mexican revolutionists on June 19, 1867. The unfortunate Empress Carlotta, grief-stricken, went insane.

King Leopold II worked on the same lines as his father; both made Belgium great. His initiative and perseverance gave to Belgium that rich and immense African territory of over 900,000 square miles called the "Congo," in which Americans, associated with Belgians, have big interests. He died on December 17, 1909, after a peaceful reign of more than forty-four years, during which Belgium prospered immensely.

Prince Albert, born in 1875, succeeded his uncle, Leopold II, as King Albert I. Belgium had now become the most densely populated country of Europe, with great agricultural, industrial, and commercial activity to be seen throughout the realm, with literature and fine arts flourishing, and with friendly relations with all nations well established, when suddenly —on August 4, 1914—the peaceful country of King Albert was invaded by the Germans, at the very beginning of the Great War.

His patriotism and splendid heroism during this long period of great suffering, strengthened the courage and endurance of his valiant soldiers, with whom he shared hardship and privation. Their wonderful resistance, as illustrated by the troops of General

Leman, and patient perseverance, won for both King and men the admiration and sympathy of the world. The devotion of the beloved Queen Elizabeth was a true demonstration of her high qualities of womanhood in time of uncertainty, danger, and adversity. Her exemplary deeds were a consolation to the mothers of many lands, whose sacred contributions and sacrifices had been accompanied by so much grief.

The firm attitude of Cardinal Mercier was a constant moral comfort for the Belgian population, once more under a foreign domination,—the most oppressive and abominable of them all.

In the few preceding pages we have reviewed the history of Belgium, a history, alas! so full of suffering, devastation, and sad memories! What the generous people of the United States have done for the Belgians, during the Great War, in their hour of distress and great need, will remain, forever, one of the best pages in the long history of the admirable little country.

And the Belgians say that to express to America their thanks and gratitude there are no words of appreciation high enough, and they add: We cannot reciprocate adequately, God alone can and...will reward the country of Washington, Lincoln, Roosevelt, Wilson, and Hoover....

On top of that unlimited help which Belgium received, comes—and again from America—the greatest act of "intellectual solidarity" of all times.

The people of this liberal country have decided to rebuild, at the cost of one million dollars, the University of Louvain[1] wantonly destroyed by the Germans in 1914. The destruction of this university, together with its library, was a deliberate act: the torch was put to it. The books, more than 250,000, and priceless manuscripts were reduced to ashes, and the buildings burned to the ground!

What a contrast in the sentiments of nations! On one side wilful destruction, and on the other voluntary contributions for reconstruction, by scholars, teachers, and pupils of that multitude of American schools and universities! All responded, and each individual gladly contributed, according to his means; even children—good little souls—sold their old clothes, as we read in the papers, in order to be able to participate more liberally in this noble work of international fraternity.

May the American example of supreme good-will among men prevent, in the future, the odious destruction of shrines of education and temples of God!

Conclusion. We have seen in the antecedents of the Belgians, their forced submission to foreign powers, beginning with the conquest of the Gauls and continuing for almost 1900 years! The Belgic territory was the football of diplomacy, the victim and plaything of unscrupulous potentates, the favorite battleground of foreigners.

We have seen their constant longing for freedom and their subsequent revolts in order to gain liberty.

[1] Founded by John IV, Duke of Brabant, in 1425. The new building, erected through the generosity of the people of the United States, will be dedicated in 1925; the plans of this important work have been drawn by the well known American architect Mr. Whitney Warren, of New York.

But always under the domination of a stronger nation possessing great and well-drilled armies, the little country—while keeping her traditions and her own languages—never saw the possibility of breaking away from foreign rule, till the revolution of 1830.

It is incredible that some people should say that the Belgians did not come into existence until 1830! The truth is that they were already in existence at the time of Julius Cæsar, and that they got their independence in 1830. Between these two dates, they did not disappear from earth!

In the present chapter, we have seen that they remained where Cæsar had found them and that for long periods they fell, against their will, under the rules of the Romans, Franks, Burgundians, Austrians, Spaniards, Austrians again, French, and Dutch, and that now and then some of these masters in their "transfer of property" were clipping off parts of Belgian soil, leaving...what is left to-day: an area of 11,380 square miles, in which more than seven million people are crowded.

The fact that the great powers of Europe did, finally, grant "independence" to the Belgians, is sufficient proof of the European official recognition of their antecedents as a nation.

CHAPTER VI

THE REFORMATION

DISORDERS IN FRANCE. TROUBLES IN THE BELGIC AND DUTCH PROVINCES OF THE NETHERLANDS

THE RENAISSANCE or revival of letters, arts, and science in Europe, which marked the transition from medieval to modern history, began in Italy and gradually spread and developed in other countries from the 15th to the 17th century.

It took humanity back to the original writings of antiquity, to Greek, Latin, and Hebrew manuscripts. During the Middle Ages[1] the important Greek and Latin works were mainly kept in the monasteries, where monks made duplicate copies of them. The progress in the art of printing[2] favored the diffusion of a greater literary culture. "Humanism" was the name given to the doctrine of the "humanists" or scholars of the Renaissance period, who were mastering the Latin language with Vergilian elegancy.

In this great intellectual movement Desiderius Erasmus, the Dutch theologian, was a conspicuous

---

[1] Historical period of Europe from the downfall of Rome, 476, to the conquest of Constantinople, 1453.

[2] Johann Gutenberg, 1397-1468, a German printer, is the reputed inventor of movable type; also the Dutch Laurens Janszoon Coster 1370 (?)-1440.

humanist in the lowlands of Holland and Belgium, then called Pays-Bas or Netherlands. The classic letters and science made great progress in the Belgian provinces; painting, sculpture, and architecture decidedly underwent the Italian influence; the music of the school of the Lowlands imposed itself and dominated that of all other countries. It reached its apogee with the Walloon Roland de Lattre (Orlandus Lassus), born at Mons in 1520; he was called the "Prince of the Musicians."

The Reformation. The Renaissance partly introduced, and greatly fostered, changes in religious matters, and brought in the "Reformation" or Protestantism, which, during the 16th century, separated from the Roman Catholic Church great portions of the people of Europe.

Several times before this, the Albigenses[1] in France, Arnauld de Brescia in Italy, Wyclif in England, and John Huss in Bohemia, rebelled against the Catholic Church and refused to submit to its authority, but unsuccessful they soon disappeared with their partisans, or at least left no important traces.

Luther. Luther followed their path; he began to dogmatize in 1517 and converted part of Germany. Zwingle introduced the new doctrine in Switzerland, Calvin in Geneva and in a great part of France, Knox in Scotland, and Henry VIII in England.

While the name "Reformation" was given to the religious phase of the Renaissance and embraced all the sects which since the 16th century had adopted the

[1] A sect of religious reformers named from Albi, in southern France.

new ideas, it was more particularly applied to the Calvinists than to the Lutherans.

Martin Luther, born in 1483 at Eisleben, Saxony, was the son of a mine-digger.

In the Lowlands, Erasmus, without wishing to depart from the Catholic Church, injured her by his criticism of the monks, the relics, and the single life of the priests. People lost confidence in the clergy and in the Church itself.

The first symptoms of the Reformation in the Lowlands appeared in Antwerp, in 1518, a few months after the posting of the Thesis of Luther at Wittenberg, Saxony, and Augustinian Fathers publicly preached his doctrines at Dordrecht, Holland, and Antwerp, Belgium.

The Catholic Emperor, Charles V, born at Ghent, Belgium, in 1500, who ruled over Germany, the Lowlands, Spain, etc., was opposed to the heretic doctrines of Luther. At first he had recourse to measures of conciliation. He summoned the German princes to assemblies called "Diets," where these new doctrines were condemned; the Lutherans protested against the decisions of the Diets, hence their name "Protestants." The one held at Worms, Germany, in 1521, prescribed measures for the suppression of Lutheran writings, and magistrates should sue the followers of Luther and pronounce the penalty of death and the confiscation of property against the printers who, without the sanction of the proper authorities, printed books concerning religion.

But the new doctrine continued to propagate, and Charles V organized an inquisition of State or repressive system, 1522, and intolerance went to terrible excesses. The new faith was practiced only in secret. The Emperor increased his severity, dreadful penalties were prescribed for those who would discuss religion without being theologians, and for those who knowing heretics did not denounce them, etc. It spread terror and stopped the expansion of Lutheranism, but the dispersion of its communities brought into the Lowlands new sects more radical, such as the "Anabaptists," in 1523.

Anabaptists.   The Anabaptists had for chief Storck, a German, who from a disciple of Luther became his enemy as he went farther than Luther in the religious reforms. He gained to his cause Thomas Munzer, another Anabaptist reformer and radical, who preached that God did not want, any longer, kings or magistrates on earth. He incited the people to insurrection and pretended to reestablish the Kingdom of Christ by the sword.

He had under his orders 40,000 fanatic followers who began their bloody attacks on the partisans of Luther, and took the town of Muhlhausen, when the troops of the Confederated Princes met them and defeated them at Frankenhausen. Munzer was executed in 1525.

The Anabaptists succeeded in taking the town of Munster, June, 1535, but soon thereafter they were violently attacked and almost exterminated.

Anabaptism had made rapid progress in the South of the Lowlands, but after the defeat at Munster it lost its revolutionary character and became less dangerous. In some countries, later on, the Anabaptists were identified with the Presbyterians.

Placards. By new "Placards" or proclamations, the government of Charles V was now trying to reach the clandestine press, which issued anonymous books with disguised titles concealing their true character, and sometimes bearing false approbations of ecclesiastical authorities. The old severe penalties were confirmed, and new ones were added.

A veritable reign of disorder broke loose not only in the Lowlands but throughout the Empire of Charles, where some princes who had become Protestants hanged their Catholic subjects, while others who had remained Catholic killed their Protestant subjects. In less than thirty years, the progressing and studious world of the Renaissance had transformed itself into a quarreling, restless, fighting society of the Reformation.

Peace of Augsbourg. Such was the sad and painful situation brought by the introduction of Lutheranism at the time of Charles V, who marched his armies against the reformers, and defeated them at Muhlberg, April, 1547. Less successful in a second encounter, Charles was forced, in 1555, to sign the "Peace of Augsbourg" or Peace of Religion, between Catholics and Lutherans, granting to the latter the free exercise of their faith.

The Bavarian city of Augsbourg is also famous in history for the Diet of 1530, at which the "Augsbourg Confession" or formula of Lutheran faith, written by Philip Melanchthon, was introduced; for the "Augsbourg Alliance" of 1534, between Francis I of

France and the Lutheran princes against Charles V;
for the "Augsbourg Interim," a sort of compromise
between these two parties, offered by Charles V at
the Diet of 1548; for the "Peace of Augsbourg" of
1555, mentioned above; for the "League of Augsbourg" of 1686, between Austria, Bavaria, Sweden,
Saxony, etc., against the encroachments of Louis XIV
of France.

Martin Luther died at Eisleben, Saxony, on February 18, 1546, after having devoted the last years of
his life to polemics with the numerous sects who had
sprung from the Reformation. Charles V, who had
devoted a great part of his life in opposing the Protestants, died in 1558, at the Monastery of St. Just, in
the old Province of Estremadura, Spain.

Calvin. Philip II, son of Charles, was now the master of Spain and of the Lowlands or Netherlands
(Belgium and Holland). The new Catholic ruler had
to face the doctrine of Calvin, the second great leader
of the Reformation. Jean Calvin, born in 1509 at
Noyon, in Picardy, France, was the son of a cooper
named Cauvin, and like Luther had been brought up
in the Catholic faith.

Having adopted the principles of the Reformation
he began to propagate them in Paris in 1532. Threatened with prison he took refuge in several cities, and
in Basle (Switzerland), he published, in 1535, his
"Institutes of Christianity" or outline of the doctrine
of the innovators, which became a kind of a catechism of the Reformed French.

In 1536, he was appointed professor of theology at
Geneva, Switzerland, where the Reformation had just

been adopted. Two years later he was banished from the country for his extreme rigorism, went to Strasbourg, where he propagated the new doctrine, and was recalled to Geneva in 1541. From this time on he became a formidable power in that city and was called the "Pope of Geneva."

He made the Council adopt his articles of faith and his ordinances on ecclesiastical discipline; he wanted to reform the morals as well as religious beliefs, and letting his ardor run riot, he allowed to be burned at the stake the famous Spanish physician and theologian Michael Servetus, who was a reformer himself.

Calvin, who died at Geneva in 1564, differed from Luther by reforms much more radical, proscribing all exterior exercises of worshipping, and all ecclesiastical hierarchy, rejecting mass, the dogma of the Transubstantiation, the invocation of saints, etc.

From Geneva, Calvinism spread to several cantons of Switzerland, and then to France, Belgium, Holland, England, etc., and later on to America, with the arrival of the Walloons in New Amsterdam, in 1623.

Huguenots. In France, the Calvinists received the nickname of "Huguenots," which name at that time was considered as opprobrious. The origin of this word is not very plain; some make it derive from the name of a certain "Hugues" who was the head of a religious and political party of Geneva, and which name is pronounced, in French, as the first two syllables of the word "Huguenots." Others ascribe its origin to the German "eidgenossen" or "bound by oath," name first applied to the inhabitants of Geneva who had rebelled and leagued against the Duke of Savoy. But, there are other suggestions for the origin of the name.

The name Huguenots was given, in France, to the partisans of the Reformation, but especially to the disciples of Calvin. From the point of view of nationality there was, and is, a plain distinction to be made between the Walloons or Belgians, and the French, and therefore to call "Huguenots" the Walloon Calvinists who first settled in New York, in 1623, is not correct, since the word applied to the "French" Calvinists only.

Struggles of Calvinists. In France, the Calvinists fought for a long time to obtain the free exercise of their religion, but were repressed by Francis I, Henry II, and Francis II. The Conference of Poissy, near Paris, in 1561, between Catholics and Protestants, gave the latter some hope, until the massacre of Huguenots at Vassy (Department of Haute-Marne) in 1562 became the signal of civil wars.

Though greatly weakened by defeats at Dreux, 1562; St. Denis, 1567; Jarnac and Moncontour, 1569, the Calvinists had obtained important concessions by the Treaties of Amboise, 1563; Lonjumeau, 1568, and St. Germain, 1570.

Catherine de Medici. The crafty Catherine de Medici, mother of the weak Charles IX, King of France, and Regent during his minority, was clever in politics but without scruple, and during the religious wars, tried to reign by holding the balance of power between the religious factions. She was artful, perfidious, and a strong believer in astrology!

Fearing the influence which the chiefs of the Huguenots had gained at Court, she conceived the infernal project of exterminating all the Protestants living in Paris or elsewhere in France, and having succeeded in obtaining the consent of her son, the King, the slaughter took place on that fatal night of August 24th, 1572. It was called the "Massacre of St. Bartholomew's Day," because it was customary to call an unusual event by the name of the saint honored in the Catholic Church on the day of the event. And, according to such custom, we find, in history, the name of "Massacre of St. Brice's Day," given to the killing of Danes in England for political reasons, on November 13, 1002. St. Bartholomew, one of the twelve Apostles, himself a victim of intolerance, was martyrized in Armenia, about A.D. 71.

The most contradictory opinions have been set forth as to the number of people who were killed, no figure being lower than 1,000. Among them was the Admiral Gaspard de Coligny, (born in 1519; died in 1572) who had fought with the Reformers in several wars. In many provinces, however, the Governors refused to execute the sanguinary orders of Charles IX. A great number of Catholics fell also, assassinated by personal enemies who took advantage of the turmoil.

This terrible act cannot be imputed to the Catholic Church, for it was the work of a cunning woman who would favor or rebuke Catholics and Protestants alike, according to her own political interests.[1] During the odious performance, which she had instigated,

1 Larousse. French Dict.; Bouillet. Dict. d'Histoire; Dr. Thomas. Dict. of Biogr.

the Catholic Bishops protected the Protestants so far as they were able.

What a pity, that men in the name of religion should, on that very same ground, forget themselves to the point of becoming fratricides, thus violating the rules of religion and the law of God!

Edict of Nantes. This massacre gave rise to a new civil war which lasted till the accession of Henry IV, who was a Protestant but became Catholic, to the throne of France, 1589. He assured to his Protestant subjects, in 1598, the freedom of their religion by a decree known as the "Edict of Nantes."[1] It authorized the exercise of the Calvinist faith except at Court and in Paris; it granted to the Protestants four universities or academies, and other privileges. But later on, Louis XIV suppressed those privileges one by one, and in 1685 he repealed that Edict all together.

Exodus of Calvinists. After this revocation, began the great exodus of French Calvinists or Huguenots, carrying with them their wealth and industry, to the great disadvantage of France. They emigrated to England, Holland, the Protestant states of Germany, Denmark, Sweden, and America. Many came to Massachusetts and Virginia, but much greater numbers went to South Carolina and New York.

In Boston, the marks of their residence are plentiful. In the State of New York they founded New Rochelle, in 1688, after the name of the French city "La Rochelle" in the Dept. of Charante-Inférieure,

[1] French City of the Dept. of Loire-Inférieure.

where Calvinism had appeared as early as 1534, and became a great Calvinist center from 1557 on.

Louis XVI, in 1787, granted them a new Edict of tolerance, and soon thereafter the French Revolution of 1789 assured them complete liberty.

Calvinism in Belgium. We shall now go back to Belgium, to note the effects of Calvanism under Philip II, having already reviewed those of Lutheranism under Charles V.

Philip II, son and successor of Charles V, confided, in 1559, the regency of the "Seventeen Provinces" of the Pays-Bas, or Netherlands, to his sister Margaret of Parma, and by doing so he eliminated the danger of rivalry between William of Orange and Count Egmont, as both were hoping to be appointed to this high position of Regent.

In order to help her in her delicate functions, Philip formed a Council of State, composed of William of Orange, stathouder or governor of Holland, Zeeland, and Utrecht; Count Egmont, governor of Flanders and Artois; Count Hornes, director of the navy; Count Berlaymont, member of the Council of Finance; Viglius, president of the Privy Council, and Granvelle, Bishop of Arras, (later a Cardinal) who was in great favor with the King. The last three, who had been in the service of Charles V, formed the "Consulta" or Secret Council, and Margaret, the Regent, had to be guided more particularly by their advice.

Heresy, propagated in the "Seventeen Provinces" by German soldiers of the armies of Charles V, had made progress. The ignorance of religion was great among the people and their morals were corrupted;

a spirit of independence was everywhere, while the clergy and their ceremonies were laughed at. Such a situation was embarrassing the government and rendered its task difficult.

Philip had left for Spain, his favorite place of residence, and the government headed by the Catholic Regent Margaret was functioning at Brussels. Philip, with all his Spanish tendencies, was unpopular and the insurrection against him had, as will be seen, two different phases: the first was essentially national; it united the mass of the nation against the Spanish policy of the King, while the second was rather of a religious character favorable to Calvinism, and this drew the Catholics and the King nearer together.

Supported, at the start, by practically the entire nobility, William of Orange and Count Egmont gained an enormous influence in the Council of State, and posed as the defenders of the country. They drew up a political program, anti-Spanish and anti-absolutist, and gradually reduced the authority of Granvelle. They wanted, first of all, the departure of the Spanish troops, and on this subject they created a sharp agitation. Those troops left in 1561.

Count Egmont was of a pleasing personality, and his brilliant victories over Henry II of France, at Saint-Quentin where he commanded the Flemish cavalry, and at Gravelines, had puffed him up with pride. A splendid soldier, but unacquainted with the difficulties of politics and administration, he often hesitated between the advantage of a vain popularity and his duties towards his sovereign. This weakness brought him under the influence of William of Orange, and to his doom.

William of Nassau, Prince of Orange, called later "The Silent," born in Germany, 1533, was a shrewd politician, ambitious and stubborn, who, under the pretext of defending the national liberties, made a clever use of the Reformation and of the high position conferred upon him by Philip II, to assure for himself a great following in the Netherlands.

His religious principles were of great elasticity. Under Charles V he gave up Lutheranism for Catholicism, showing attachment to the latter, under Philip II, while secretly he was the confidant of all the leaders of the Protestant Party.

Philip had obtained from the Pope, Paul V, the erection of fourteen new Bishoprics and Granvelle was appointed Cardinal. These measures dissatisfied the Protestants and the nobility, and William of Orange, Egmont, and Hornes protested to the King. Intrigues having induced the Regent Margaret to ask the recall of Granvelle, this was done.

With the departure of Granvelle coincides the appearance of revolutionary symptoms, transforming the character of the insurrection against Philip II. From national, it became essentially religious as a result of the progress of Calvinism.

Calvinist Organization. Protestant ministers entered the cities under disguise, and in the evening, behind closed doors, evangelized their converts in some hostelry or in secluded spots. They had, already, made proselites at Lille, Arras, Douai, Mons, Audenarde, Ghent, Mechlin, Tournai, and Valenciennes, and in the Northern Provinces, especially in the ports of Holland and Zeeland, owing to their steady relations with England. In 1563, the Synod of the Walloon Churches in the provinces of Artois, Flanders, Brabant, and Hainault, was formed, and Antwerp soon became a strong Calvinist place, a rallying center for the Flemish and Walloon communities. Calvinism penetrated into the ranks of the nobility and the merchant class, but recruited its adepts mainly among the poorer classes and the working people, who converted themselves in the hope of ameliorating their situation.

Notwithstanding the recommendations of Philip, the magistrates did not dare to act against thousands of Calvinists, and governmental troops came to prevent preaching, and to disperse the Protestants who were obliged to hide themselves or to emigrate.

Since the departure of Granvelle, the Regent Margaret was at the mercy of the Lords, and the government had, in fact, passed into the hands of the Council of State, where the triumvirate composed of William of Orange and the Counts Egmont and Hornes, was now dominant, and where the partisans of Granvelle lost all influence.

The Council of State, 1565, entrusted Egmont with a mission to Philip in order to obtain a modification of the "Placards," or edicts against the Protestants, and to change the political regime by giving a more important rôle to the Council of State and to the States-General. But Egmont did not obtain the slightest concession.

Soon, the country was flooded with pamphlets

against the King, in which the free exercise of the new religion was advocated. Besides, the industrial crisis and the high cost of living that characterized the year 1566, raised popular discontent to the highest pitch.

The Calvinists of the Netherlands (Belgium and Holland) followed the program of the French Calvinists or Huguenots. Their constant propaganda among noblemen of small means increased the strength of the opposition. Conventions held at Spa, in the Walloon country, led, in 1565, to the famous "Compromis des Nobles" (League among nobles) in which the first signers were Louis of Nassau, brother of William of Orange, Henry Brederode, and Philip Marnix. Within a few weeks, hundreds of signatures were obtained.

The official functions of William, Egmont and Hornes prevented them from signing also, but the adherence of knights of their house indicates that they approved of the "league."

The avowed purpose of this league of noblemen, was to maintain the liberties of the country, especially that of religion, and to oppose the inquisition, while the real and secret purpose seems to have been to weaken the authority of the King.

The leaguers promised, under oath, to support one another, and for form's sake, declared to Philip their loyalty and attachment to the Catholic religion.... How much better it would have been to speak openly, instead of having recourse to plots and intrigues!

The next year, 1566, four hundred of these noble leaguers went to Brussels and presented to Margaret a petition in which they expressed their devotion to the King, and requested the Regent to suspend all pursuits against the heretics, till the King had read their request. Margaret seeing this large delegation became frightened, and the Count Berlaymont, while trying to reassure her, told her that they were only "gueux." [1] In the Netherlands (Belgium and Holland) the Protestants or revolters against Philip II kept this name, during their war for independence.

The effects of the revolutionary agitation of the nobility commenced to show: resistance against heresy became weaker and hesitating, and the number of Calvinists was growing all the time. Reformers from Germany, France, England, and Switzerland appeared, preaching in the woods or some secluded places to thousands of people who had come to hear them. Later on, they held meetings near the cities of Antwerp, Tounai, Ypres, Bruges, etc. At Ghent they wanted to make use of a church.

Bewildered, the Regent Margaret did not dare to depend upon the Catholic party alone, and was afraid to break with William of Orange, Egmont, and Hornes.

The nobles gathered at Saint Trond, Belgium, took advantage of the effervescence to ask from Margaret a complete amnesty, and as William, Egmont, and Hornes had, already, allowed the league of nobles to accept the offer, made by the Calvinist merchants, to hire mercenaries in order to oppose might by might, they expressed to the Regent the threat of calling

[1] Meaning "beggars"; probably an allusion to the fact that many of those noblemen were without means, or had contracted debts.

friendly help from other lands. Louis of Nassau was commissioned by his brother, William of Orange, and the nobility to raise troops in Germany in case Philip II should send a Spanish army.

Philip authorized his sister, Margaret, to grant a limited amnesty provided leagues and intrigues ceased.

Iconoclasts. While the nobles were plotting and the Calvinists were preaching, suddenly bands of "iconoclasts" [1] appeared in the industrial region of Flanders, August, 1566, and reached, rapidly, Antwerp, Ghent, Ypres, etc., extending their wanton destruction to the north, in Zeeland, Holland, and Friesland.

Churches and convents in the vicinity of Saint-Omer, Menin, Courtrai, Ypres, Ghent, etc., were ransacked. Egmont was sent to those unfortunate cities, but his presence seemed to encourage the iconoclasts rather than to intimidate them, and as he was the Governor of Flanders, Margaret expressed her discontent over the disorders and asked him to bring them to an end. She sent two regiments to Lille to repress the riots, and Egmont reproached her for using force....

Pillage continued for several days. Four hundred churches and monasteries were ransacked. William of Orange, who had been sent to Antwerp to maintain order, left the menaced city without prescribing sufficient measures of safety, and went to Brussels to assist at a meeting of the Knights of the Golden Fleece....During his absence the rich church of Notre-Dame was devastated and pillaged; the dam-

---

[1] Image-breakers, or certain religious parties devoted to the destruction of images that were venerated.

age was estimated at several million francs, and priceless objects of art were taken away or destroyed.

Terrible devastations took place in Flanders, Holland, Zeeland, Gelderland, Friesland, Brabant, and in sections of Hainault, mainly at Tournai, where the Church of Notre-Dame suffered greatly. The provinces of Namur, Luxembourg, and Artois escaped devastation. In many cities, the Catholic services were interrupted.

"One fact usually forgotten," says the Protestant minister, William Elliot Griffis, "is that at Ghent itself, the Protestant mob, led by three fanatics, followed the bad example of the inquisition, persecuted violently their Catholic fellow citizens, and pillaged the churches and convents. In the same place where Spaniards had burned people alive for differences of opinion, these rowdy Ghenters, in the Friday Market-Place, burned alive four minor friars and two Augustinian fathers. At Bruges, a few weeks later, two minor friars were given to the flames kindled by brutal hatred in the name of religion." [1]

It was the age of intolerance, not the age of religion! Religion, no matter its particular denomination, forbids violence and murder, commends brotherly love and self-restraint.

During those times of calamity, Margaret learned to know her nobles who instead of comforting her were scaring her, and in this way extorted from her, for the dissidents, permission to assist at the sermons, and pardon for the leaguers. The Regent protested that those concessions were given against her will, and

[1] W. E. Griffis. Belgium: The Land of Art, pp. 209-210.

in the report she sent to Philip relating the devastations that had just occurred in the Netherlands, she accused William of Orange and the Counts Egmont and Hornes of having declared themselves, in words and in deeds, against God and the King.

After the bloody riots and destruction of places of worship, came general indignation and reaction in favor of the Catholics, and the noble leaders became opposed to the Iconoclasts.

To maintain order, Margaret dispatched William of Orange to Antwerp, Egmont to Flanders, and Hornes to Tournai. William authorized preaching in Antwerp, became more and more embroiled with Margaret, refused to the latter the new oath of loyalty she had requested from all those in office, and finally went to place himself in surety in Germany. Egmont allowed preachings where they had taken place before, and where the troubles had started, while Hornes, at Tournai, did practically the opposite of what he had been ordered to do.

The Regent ordered several Catholic nobles, among them Noircarmes and Mansfeld, to reestablish order at Valenciennes, Maestrich, Utrecht, Antwerp; the rebellious cities submitted, and for the time being calm existed.

Repressions. Duke of Alva. When news of the terrible destruction made by the Iconoclasts reached Philip II, he decided to punish the culprits and the noble Governors who had not used their power to prevent or suppress the troubles. And, in his anger, instead of going himself to the Netherlands he committed the political mistake of sending the Spaniard

Ferdinand Alvarez of Toledo, Duke of Alva, 1567. In this very same year, in Antwerp, was born Usselinx, the founder of the West India Company, under whose auspices the Walloons came to New York in 1623.

When it became known that the Duke of Alva was expected in the Netherlands, with an army of 10,000 men, more than 100,000 Protestants implicated in the last disorders fled from the southern part of the Netherlands (the Belgian Provinces) to the north of the Netherlands (the Dutch Provinces), where Protestantism spread steadily and strongly.

The Regent Margaret of Parma, informed of the great authority given to Alva, resigned and left for Italy, where she died in 1586.

One of the first acts of Alva was to establish, under the name of "Council of Troubles," a court called by the people "Blood Council," to judge those who had participated in the rebellion. It was this Court that found Egmont and Hornes guilty of high treason; they were beheaded in the Public Square at Brussels, on June 5, 1568. This double execution was another political error which was greatly resented.

The severity of Alva was heavy; he ordered the arrest and summary condemnation of several hundred persons, and to impress still more the people who were already living in a state of fear, he built a great citadel at Antwerp.

William of Orange, who had fled to Germany, recruited there an army of Protestants, but he failed before the better strategy of Alva. Louis of Nassau, who had won a victory in Friesland, was defeated by the Spaniard at Jemminghen (Nassau, Germany).

Having pacified the Provinces, Alva decided, 1569, to replenish the treasury of Spain by introducing in these Provinces of the Netherlands the oppressive system of taxes in use in his own country; this aggravated the economic crisis already created by his regime of terror. It was at this time that Philip II ordered the Duke of Alva to proclaim a general pardon, 1570. Soon thereafter, he obtained his recall. and as he was preparing to return to Spain, suddenly a formidable insurrection occurred, 1572.

Insurrection in the North. In the north of the Netherlands, in the waters of Holland, William of Orange had organized a fleet manned by the "gueux" and commanded by William de la Marck. The Spaniards could not prevent these men from taking the important port of Brielle (in the Island of Voorne) which became the cradle of the Dutch Republic of the Seven Provinces, to be formed later. Indeed, this success was the signal of a general uprising in Holland and Zeeland.

As a reward, William of Orange appointed de la Marck Governor of Holland, and the latter persecuted the Catholics with ferocity, as is shown by the martyrdom of Gorkum (S. E. of Rotterdam) in which nineteen priests and friars were tortured and hanged, July 6, 1572, (a few weeks before St. Bartholomew's Day), while churches and monasteries were pillaged.

In the South of the Netherlands, Mons was taken by Louis of Nassau, and several cities of Flanders and Brabant were occupied in the name of William of Orange.

Alva turned against the Protestant cities of the

North, but the extreme rigor he used in the ransacking of Zutphen (Gelderland) and Naarden and Harlem induced many cities to continue their resistance.

The second campaign of William of Orange, like his first, failed, and the repression was terrible. Malines and other cities became the prey of the disorderly Spanish troops. Philip II, realizing that he had made a great mistake in the appointment of the Duke of Alva, finally recalled the stern general, 1573.

He was replaced by don Louis Requesens, who favored peace; Requesens suppressed the Council of Troubles, reduced the taxes and, in the name of the King, proclaimed an amnesty for those who had participated in the uprising, and who would become reconciled with the Catholic Church. These concessions not having brought the expected results, hostilities against the revolters started again.

Siege of Leyden. The city of Leyden (Holland) was besieged and William of Orange saved the place by breaking up the dikes and flooding the land, 1574. The next year, the city, as a reward for its vigorous resistance to the Spaniards, was endowed with a Protestant university which has acquired a brilliant reputation.

At this time, 1575, there functioned against the Catholics of the North of the Netherlands a "Blood Council" presided over by Snoy, Lieutenant of William of Orange, in Friesland. This court ordered the most terrible penalties. Governor don Requesens died suddenly in 1576.

The Council of State took charge of the affairs of the country, but without being able to put an end to

the disorders. The States-General entered into negotiations with the revolted provinces of the North, and
in October, 1576, delegations from the latter arrived
in Ghent to discuss, with the delegates of the Southern
provinces, the means of an understanding.

Spanish Fury. While they were deliberating, news
came that the Spanish troops of the Citadel of Antwerp, who had not been paid for some time, had
mutinied, ransacked, and burned the city, besides killing more than 6,000 of its inhabitants. The pillage
was estimated at sixty million francs. This terrible
outbreak was called the "Spanish Fury."

Pacification of Ghent. Under the sad influence of
this "fury" the delegates reached an agreement, 1576,
known as the "Pacification of Ghent," which included
the recall of the Spanish army, the suppression of the
terrible ordinances of the Duke of Alva, the restitu-
tion of ecclesiastical property, etc.

Don Juan, son of Charles V, succeeded don Requesens as Governor. He adhered to the "Pacification of
Ghent" through his "Perpetual Edict," dated from
Marche, in the Walloon country, but stipulated that
the Catholic religion should be reestablished everywhere, February, 1577.

However, the agreement between North and South
was soon forgotten, and troubles and fights between Catholics and Protestants were renewed. Don
Juan won the battle of Gembloux, 1578, in which
thousands were killed, but soon thereafter he was
defeated at Rymenan, near Malines. He died at
Namur the same year, (1578).

He was succeeded by Alexander Farnese, son of Margaret of Parma, who was, as we have seen, the Regent of the seventeen Belgian and Dutch Provinces of the Netherlands, at the beginning of the reign of her brother Philip II.

CHAPTER VII

FORMATION OF THE DUTCH REPUBLIC

SECESSION OF CATHOLICS AND PROTESTANTS

UNDER the new Governor, Alexander Farnese, grave dissensions arose between Catholics and Protestants, and especially when the Calvinists of Ghent, directed by Ryhove and Hembyse, forbade the exercise of the Catholic faith, threw in prison the Bishops of Bruges and Ypres with other noble Catholics, and ransacked churches and monasteries.

Flemish and Walloon Catholics were utterly dissatisfied, and the latter formed a new party known as the "Malcontents," who sought an understanding with Governor Farnese. To cope with this reaction, William of Orange endeavored to combat the Calvinist regime of terrorism going on at Ghent and in other cities, but without avail.

These new excesses against Catholics induced the Southern Provinces, Artois and Hainault, and the cities of Lille, Douai, and Orchies to form the "Confederation of Arras," January, 1579, which had for purpose the maintenance of the Catholic religion and obedience to the King of Spain.

Dutch Republic. In that same month of January, 1579, the Protestants of the North formed the "Union of Utrecht," through which the party of William of Orange profited. This "Union" resulted, later on, in the formation of the Dutch Republic.

At first, only five provinces: Holland, Zeeland, Utrecht, Gelderland with Zutphen, and Friesland, entered the Union. Over-Yssel entered it at the end of 1579, and Groningen with Drenthe much later. These provinces, which were part of the group of the Seventeen Provinces called Netherlands or Pays-Bas already at the time of Charles V, continued the struggle against the Catholic South, and finally declared themselves "independent," 1581. They separated from Spain, and formed the Dutch Republic of the Seven United Provinces.

Spanish Netherlands. The ten other provinces located in the South: Flanders, Antwerp, Malines, Brabant, Limbourg, Namur, Hainault, Luxembourg, Artois, and Franche-Comté, remaining loyal to Philip II of Spain, took the name of "Spanish Netherlands" and were sometimes called the "Catholic Netherlands."

William of Orange, now stathouder or head of the government of the revolted United Provinces, having proposed to the States-General the deposition of Philip II, the latter retaliated by issuing against William an edict of proscription, and by promising a sum of money and privileges to the one who would bring before him William of Orange dead or alive, 1580. To this, William answered by a manifesto, in which he made bitter accusations against the King of Spain.

In 1584, William of Orange was assassinated in his home at Delft (S. Holland) by the young fanatic

Balthasar Gerard, who was arrested and torn to pieces.

Prince Maurice of Orange-Nassau was studying at Leyden when his father was murdered. He was immediately elected President of the Council of State and appointed, later on, Captain-General and Admiral. He won several important battles over the armies of Spain, and greatly contributed to Dutch independence.

Philip II died in 1598, and was succeeded by his son, Philip III.

After long discussions at The Hague between Belgian representatives of the "Spanish Netherlands" and those of the "United Provinces," a "Twelve Years' Truce" was signed at Antwerp, 1609, each side keeping the territories then in their possession. But it maintained the closing of the important River Scheldt (Belgium).

While this agreement was taking place, Henry Hudson was exploring the "Great River" and paved the way for the arrival of the Protestant Walloons now, for conscience's sake, in exile in the Dutch Republic.

After the expiration of the Twelve Years' Truce with the Dutch, war was resumed and continued until the reign of Philip IV. But the Republic of the United Provinces obtained, 1648, the "recognition of their independence" by Spain, at the Peace of Munster, Westphalia. This Treaty, again, maintained the closing of the River Scheldt (Antwerp) and Spain abandoned to the new State considerable territory of the Belgian Provinces; in Brabant: Breda, Bois-Le-

Duc, Bergen-op-Zoom; in Flanders: l'Ecluse, Hulst, Axel; and in Limbourg: Maestricht, etc.

Unlike the Truce of 1609, a final and formal peace had now been made and the United Provinces were acknowledged as a free and sovereign state. At the time of the Truce, the Spaniards had only treated with them "in quality of" and as holding them for independent provinces.

Results of the Revolution. It depopulated Belgium, then called Spanish Netherlands. As all her ports were closed, it reduced her commerce to almost nothing and thus all commercial transactions favored Rotterdam, Middlebourg, and Amsterdam; it ruined Belgian industry through the expatriation of her skilled craftsmen; it crushed agriculture with enormous taxes to be faced by the farmers; it created hatred among the people; it marked a bitter religious and political division within the former Netherlands, now separated and forming a Calvinist North detached from Spain, and a Catholic South adhering to Spanish rule.

A striking contrast, was the picture presented by the Dutch United Provinces. The crops had, indeed, failed there also, but the entire command of the sea, which they preserved, and the free importation of corn secured plentiful supplies; the ports were crowded with vessels, and by the thousands, Walloon and Fleming Protestants from the South, flocked to the North and made the new Dutch Republic prosperous and great.

"The men who prepared the greatness of the Netherlands were not Hollanders, but Walloons, Flemings,

Brabanters, Calvinists of the South." [1] And, Mr. Corwin says: "The Walloons inhabited the southern provinces of Belgium; the Protestants of these provinces, being persecuted, fled to Holland, and these are the Walloons of history. They carried with them many useful arts and enriched their adopted country." [2]

Lesson to the World. We have seen, briefly, the sad history of the Reformation in several parts of Europe; the long suffering of the people, people belonging to the same country; quarrels and fights bringing exhaustion and ruin; brothers becoming enemies on a question of religion; bitterness going so far and so deep, as to reach destruction of places of worship, and murder!

All this, in the name of religion, religion: the way to honor God! What a grave error on the part of men who wanted to honor the One who, in his infinite comprehension of human welfare, had said: "Love thy neighbor as thyself." What a horrible sight it must have been to the Creator who had so expressly forbidden excesses, by his words: "Thou shalt not kill."

May Catholics and Protestants alike, in every part of the world, remember that above all they are Christians, that malice is contrary to their own religion, that hatred for each other undermines the strength of the State, and fortifies the enemies of the Nation.

One of the best performances of good citizenship is

[1] Douglas-Campbell. The Puritans in Holland, England and America.
[2] Edward Tanjore Corwin. Manual of the Ref. Church in America, pp. 16-17.

the strict observance of reciprocal respect between Catholics and Protestants. Tolerance and understanding between countrymen or citizens, is for the State a solid bulwark against its foes within and without, as well as a valuable asset to the nation. Tolerance is true Christianity, understanding is true patriotism, both are equally agreeable to God!

In a beautiful address to the graduates of New York University, 1923, Dr. William H. Nichols, while not referring to religion but to the safeguard of the nation, said in part: "By a faction, I understand a number of citizens, whether amounting to a majority or a minority of the whole, who are united by some common impulse of passion or of interest adverse to the rights of other citizens, or the permanent and aggregate interests of the community.

"I have no quarrel with men associating themselves together for the benefit of their section or calling, whatever it may be, as long as they advocate nothing contrary to the public good.

"Our country is like our body. You cannot injure one part of it without damaging the rest. I feel assured that there is no one within the sound of my voice who would consciously do anything to injure our country. This land is 99% patriotic, however much noise the other fraction of one per cent may make. Let us not forget this when we are stirred by the strange ways so many have of showing their patriotism, when not brought to their senses by some real danger to the nation."

This, indeed, was a plain and splendid presentation of the duty of every loyal American, of every good

Christian.   Catholics and Protestants alike do possess these qualities.   As good Christians they will forgive and forget the past; as loyal citizens they will, together, work for the expansion of the prosperity and fame of the United States, while other religious denominations, not less patriotic, will fraternally contribute to the greatness of the beloved country.

CHAPTER VIII

THE BELGIANS IN THE DUTCH REPUBLIC
USSELINX AND THE DUTCH WEST INDIA COMPANY

UNDER Philip II, at the time of the Duke of Alva, 1567, the northern provinces of the Netherlands had a population of not over eight hundred thousand.

The security those provinces, now a republic, offered, combined with the freedom of religion and the activity of commerce, drew to their shores vast multitudes of Belgian Protestants (Walloons and Flemings), and also some Catholics. This emigration of artisans and rich merchants, transferred thither the advantages of their enterprise and skill.

The population of the towns became so overflowing, that it was found impossible to build houses fast enough to shelter all the newcomers. Within two generations, the new Dutch Republic of the Seven United Provinces had two million inhabitants, and had become one of the first class powers of Europe.

Emigration to other Lands. Belgian Protestants emigrated not only to the Dutch Republic, but to other countries, such as the Palatinate, Sweden and England; to the last had gone more than one hundred thousand Walloons and Flemings, represented by skilled artisans, laborers, and traders.

Made England Prosperous. The English people were then mainly devoting themselves to agriculture and wool-raising. But soon afterwards, this influx of Belgian craftsmen so familiar with weaving, lace-making, the manufacture of woollen, linen, and silk fabrics, and other industries, transformed the island into a nation of manufacturers and merchants, whose prosperity and influence became enormous, and are still felt to-day.

In London, Canterbury, Norwich, Southampton, and other cities of England, Walloon churches were founded more than a century before the revocation of the Edict of Nantes, and in Canterbury, as early as 1561, the Walloons were granted the use of the crypt of the cathedral as a place of worship.

However, it was to the Dutch United Provinces, more easy to reach, that the bulk of the Belgian emigrants went. There, they were to be found in every city, but more particularly in Amsterdam and in Leyden; the latter is of real interest to the American people, to the descendants of the Walloons, Huguenots, and Pilgrims alike.

Pilgrims and Walloons at Leyden. England had, also, her church troubles with the "Independents" or "Separatists" or "Congregationalists." These Puritans manifested a disposition to break away from the "Anglican Church" altogether, and to form communities of their own.

At first, they were often called "Brownist Churches," after Robert Brown, a divine of the time, who was for a while a zealous maintainer of the duty of separation.

After King James' Hampton Court Conference with the Puritan divines in 1604, and his threatening words to them, nonconformity began to assume among the churches more decidedly the form of secession.

The leader in the Puritan exodus to New England was William Brewster, son of a country gentleman who had, for many years, been postmaster at Scrooby in Nottinghamshire. Staunch Puritan that he was, Brewster had not hitherto favored the extreme measures of the Separatists. Now he withdrew from the church and gathered together a company of men and women who met on Sunday, for divine service, in his own drawing room at Scrooby Manor, where the Pilgrims originated.

In organizing his independent Congregationalist Society, Brewster was powerfully aided by Richard Clifton and John Robinson. Another important member of the Scrooby congregation was William Bradford, of the neighboring village of Austerfield, afterwards Governor of Plymouth for nearly thirty years. He became the historian of his colony, and to his picturesque chronicle we are indebted for most that we know of the emigration that started from Scrooby and ended in Plymouth.

It was in 1606, two years after King James' truculent threat, that this independent church of Scrooby was organized. Another year had not elapsed before its members had suffered so much at the hands of officers of the law, that they began to think of following the example of the Walloon and Flemish Calvinists in escaping to the Dutch Republic.

After an unsuccessful attempt in the autumn of

1607, they succeeded, a few months later, in accomplishing their flight to Amsterdam, where the Belgian Protestants had already secured a home.

But there, they found the exiles who had preceded them so firmly involved in doctrinal controversies, that they decided to go further in search of peace and quiet. They reached Leyden, in Southern Holland, in 1609, just when the Spanish Government had granted to the Dutch the "Twelve Years' Truce." During eleven of these twelve years the "Pilgrims" remained in Leyden; their numbers increased from three hundred to more than one thousand.

In spite of the relief from persecution, the Pilgrims were not fully satisfied with their new home. They wished to preserve their English speech and English traditions, and to find some favored spot where they might lay the corner-stone of a great Christian state. It was too late in the world's history, to carry out such a scheme upon European soil; the only favorable outlook was upon the Atlantic Coast of America.

And so, in July, 1620, the English at Leyden, after negotiations with the authorities of their native country and the Virginia Company, trusting in God and in themselves, made ready for their departure.[1]

A small ship, the "Speedwell," of some 60 tons burden, was bought and fitted out in Holland, and early in July those who were ready for the formidable voyage left Leyden for embarkation at Delft Haven. Soon thereafter the vessel sailed for Southampton, England.

[1] J. Fiske. The Beginnings of New England, ch. 2. Also in: G. Punchard. Hist. of Congregationalism, vol. 1; G. Sumner. Memoirs of the Pilgrims at Leyden (Mass. Hist. Soc. Coll.)

The Mayflower. On their arrival there, they found the Mayflower, a ship of about 180 tons burden, which had been hired in London, awaiting them with their fellow passengers, partly laborers employed by the merchants, partly Englishmen like-minded with themselves who were disposed to join the colony.

The ships, with perhaps 120 passengers, put to sea about August 5th; but the Speedwell was soon pronounced too leaky to proceed without being overhauled, and so both ships put in at Dartmouth after two days' sail. Repairs were made, and they started again; but when about one hundred leagues beyond Land's End, Reynolds, the master of the Speedwell, declared her in great danger of sinking, so that both ships again put about. On reaching Plymouth Harbor it was decided to abandon the smaller vessel, and thus to send back those of the company whom such a succession of mishaps had disheartened.

Cape Cod. At last, on September 6th, the Mayflower left Plymouth and set sail for the English possession of Virginia, as the passengers thought. Nine weeks from the following day, on November 9th, they sighted the eastern coast of Cape Cod. She took from Plymouth 102 passengers, besides the master and crew; on the voyage one man-servant died and one child was born, making 102 (seventy-three males and twenty-nine females) who reached their destination. Of these, the colony proper consisted of thirty-four adult males, eighteen of them accompanied by their wives and minor children (twenty boys and eight girls); besides these there were three maid servants and nineteen man-servants, sailors and craftsmen.

Some well informed English people claim that the Pilgrim Fathers, in their second attempt to leave England, did not sail from Plymouth, but from Immingham Creek in North Lincolnshire, where a memorial, presented by the Sulgrave Institution of the United States, has just been erected (1924) by the Anglo-American Society of Hull.

Of the thirty-four men who were the nucleus of the colony, more than half are known to have come from Leyden.

On November 11th, the Mayflower had rounded the Cape, and found shelter in the quiet harbor on which now lies the village of Provincetown, Massachusetts. On the same day, an armed delegation visited the nearby shore, finding no inhabitants. Some days were spent in exploring Cape Cod Bay, and the harbor since known as Plymouth Bay was chosen for the settlement of the colony.

Landing. The exploring party landed, as is believed, at the famous Plymouth Rock, in Massachusetts, on December 11th, 1620.

Tradition divides the honor of being the first to step on the Rock, between John Alden and Mary Chilton. It was not till December 16th that the Mayflower was anchored at the chosen haven.[1]

A hard winter and much suffering fell on the new settlers, and within four months nearly half their number had perished. At one time, during the winter, only six or seven had strength enough left to nurse the dying and bury the dead; of the eighteen wives mentioned above, only four survived. But

[1] F. B. Dexter. The Pilgrim Church and Plymouth Colony.

more colonists arrived a few months later, by the boat "Fortune."

On the 5th day of April, the Mayflower set sail on her homeward voyage with scarcely more than half the crew which had navigated her to America, the rest having fallen victims to the epidemic of the winter. She carried back not one of the immigrants, dispiriting as were the hardships which they had endured.

Soon after the departure of the Mayflower, John Carver, the first Governor, died (1621); and William Bradford was chosen to fill the vacant office, with Isaac Allerton as his Assistant.[1]

Plymouth, outside the bounds of the London company, could not profit by the original patent. But in 1621 it received a grant from the Council for New England. The terms were not satisfactory; the colonists desired a charter like that of Massachusetts Bay, but the gift was denied them.

Without a frame of government from the Crown, they were therefore thrown on their own initiative. The result was the "Mayflower Compact," signed November 21, 1620, by each male adult except the servants and two hired seamen. It created "a civil body politic" on democratic lines, but fully subservient to the royal authority. In the absence of a charter, it was the basis of civil government in Plymouth until the colony was united with Massachusetts in 1691.[2]

As to the name "Plymouth," Morton (Memorial

[1] J. G. Palfrey. Hist. of New Eng. vol. 1. Also in: J. A. Goodwin. The Pilgrim Republic.
[2] John Spencer Bassett. A Short Hist. of the U. S.

56) assigns as a reason for adopting it that "Plymouth in Old England, was the last town they left in their native country, and they received many kindnesses from some Christians there."

Mrs. Robert W. de Forest, in her work: "A Walloon Family in America," vol. 1, page 18, says "that with the Pilgrim Fathers had gone to America some of Jesse de Forest's compatriots." (Walloons.)

Jamestown. The "Pilgrim Fathers," it must be remembered, were not the first settlers on the American soil, now called the United States. Before their time, other English gentlemen adventurers had tried colonization in the southern section of the country, and the "Jamestown Settlement" begun in Virginia in 1607, by Englishmen, is properly considered the birthplace of the American nation.

Near Norfolk, Virginia, from April 26 to December 1, 1907, was held an important international exposition—called the Jamestown Exposition—to commemorate the tercentenary of the settlement of white people in the United States. On this occasion President Roosevelt invited all the nations of the world to participate, and to send to Jamestown representative battleships or military delegations.

Fulton. This celebration coincided with the international maritime exposition of Bordeaux, through which the French wanted to honor the centenary of the invention of Robert Fulton: the application of steam to navigation.[1] Fulton had made his initial trials in France, on the River Loire.

[1] Publisher's Note: The author of this book was the Commissioner to the United States for this French Exposition.

This application of steam, one of the most useful, pacific and beneficent of all inventions, which so extensively contributed to immigration and development of trade, easily and rapidly bringing together the people of very dissimilar countries, facilitating the study of languages, science and fine arts, has generously disseminated education and wealth.

Robert Fulton was born at Little Britain, Pennsylvania, in 1765. In 1807, his "Clermont," the first steamboat that navigated the Hudson River, made a successful voyage from New York to Albany and back. She travelled at the rate of five miles an hour. Fulton died in New York in 1815.

Belgians in Holland. We will now return to the Dutch Republic, where we found that the Walloon and Flemish Calvinists had preceded the Pilgrims and the Huguenots. In that very same city of Leyden, where the Belgian refugees were in great number, many people in the United States could learn of their Belgian ancestry through the archives of the "Walloon Library."

The great exodus of Belgians towards the United Dutch Provinces, had, within two generations of these Provinces, seen the population rise from 800,000 to over 2,000,000! This enormous increase made their naval and military forces formidable. The Walloons and Flemings, from whom the Dutch gained a knowledge of many branches of manufacture, had not only made the Dutch Republic possible, but powerful and wealthy.

The important city of Amsterdam, on the Zuider Zee, had naturally attracted great numbers of them, and the "Eglises Wallonnes" or Walloon Churches, were numerous in this city as well as in other sections of the Dutch Republic, where Walloon colonies had been formed. Leyden had its Walloon church as early as 1584. These communities, while they acquired to a certain degree the language of their adopted country, retained their own; and the Walloon families, though not infrequently allied by inter-marriages with those of their hosts, preserved for many generations a character distinctly that of their original country. The Walloon churches while retaining their own ritual and mode of government, became incorporated with the ecclesiastical establishment of the nation.

The contribution they made to the industrial, the intellectual and the religious strength of the people was of incalculable worth.[1]

In Amsterdam we find the Fleming Petrus Plancius preaching the gospel, as he had done in Brussels, drawing maps for the first Dutch navigators who planned to reach India by the sea, and advising Henry Hudson as to his arctic explorations which, incidentally, led to the discovery of the great river and subsequently to the present enviable situation of New York.

And in Amsterdam, we find that other Fleming, Josse Hondt (Jodocus Hondius), a famous geographer who was the counsellor, interpreter, and friend of Hudson. While in the same rich Dutch city, most prominent was William Usselinx, the real founder of the West India Company under whose

[1] Baird. Hist. Huguenot Emigration to America, vol. 1. p. 151.

auspices the Belgians came to New Amsterdam, now New York. He was an important merchant, from Antwerp, who had followed his countrymen to Amsterdam.

The exiled Belgians did not intend to remain permanently in the Dutch Provinces. They breathed a new element of commercial strength into the atmosphere, and at the same time were putting their shrewd heads together, to devise some method by which Belgium might be delivered from the Spanish yoke. They well knew that the wide possessions of Spain were open to the resolute attacks of a vigorous foe.

Finally, they originated the gigantic scheme of a warlike company of private adventurers, who should conquer or rule the Spanish settlements, seize the Spanish transports, and cut off all communication with her Transaltantic dependencies. And they proposed to name it, very appropriately, the West India Company.

The obstacles in the way of putting so vast a project into execution were very great. John of Barneveld was at the head of affairs in the Dutch Republic, and advocated peace. He was too practical a philosopher not to appreciate the enormous advantages his country had just gained. The victorious return of the Belgians to their native provinces would only remove commerce and political leadership to the south, and was in no case to be desired. He was fully determined to prevent the existence of any such warlike corporation as the one under consideration. But the Belgians found energetic allies. The lower classes in the Holland towns favored them because Barneveld was hated

for his aristocratic proclivities. Influential men from
the other Dutch provinces lent their aid because the
Advocate aimed at an overweening influence for Holland. The House of Orange gave them the hand of
fellowship, because this great family aspired to wider
dominion and to a less limited authority than they had
hitherto possessed.[1]

Usselinx. The leader of the Belgian party was
William Usselinx, an exiled Antwerp merchant of
noble descent, whose force of will was simply marvelous, and whose magnetic influence over his countrymen was so great that they seemed to think with his
brain and act with his hand. His ready pen kept the
political life of Holland in one continual ferment. He
was opposed to peace with Spain under any circumstances. His arguments were convincing, and his wit
was as flashing and as quickly unsheathed as a sword.

Thus two parties were formed; they were divided
on almost every question of public interest. The Belgian party were strict Calvinists and democrats, and
their policy was to carry on the war with Spain until
Belgium should be freed. The Barneveld party were
Arminians (arminianism, the doctrines of Arminius
and his followers, opposed to Calvinism, chiefly as
holding a less rigorous view of the divine sovereignty), aristocrats, republicans, and quite content to
give Belgium over to the Spaniards.

The question of the West India Company was
agitated for nearly thirty years. Its actual existence
dates from the year 1606. That is, commissioners
were named from the Assembly at that period, and

[1] Martha J. Lamb, Hist. City of New York, Vol. 1, p. 23.

discussions were frequent in regard to it. But Barne-veld, who was at the head of the Assembly, never seri-ously thought of confirming the corporation. He only wished to use it as a threat for the intimidation of Spain, and it was chiefly by this menace that the twelve years' truce was accomplished, which played so important a part in the history of the Netherlands.

The wrangling between the two political parties grew more fierce as the details of the peace negotia-tions became known. The river Scheldt was to be closed, Antwerp thus ruined; Belgium given up, and all attacks upon the Spanish forbidden. The peace party maintained the principle of excluding strangers from every employment, and of concentrating all pub-lic offices in a few patrician houses of the old stock. The impoverished, but proud and fiery Belgian exiles looked with dismay at their gloomy prospects in the event of the truce being agreed upon, and put forth all their energies towards the completion of the West India Company. Usselinx wrote a series of pamphlets, in style simple and effective, and which belong to the most remarkable productions of that class of literature. They created such a sensation, and attracted the attention of contemporary historians to such a degree, that the most distinguished of them all, Emanuel Van Meteren, reprinted one of them entire.

But the pamphlets, like the plan for the West India Company, served only to accelerate the conclusion of the truce. A cessation of hostilities for twelve years was signed by the representatives of the two nations in 1609. It was a signal victory for the aristocratic party.

But ten years later the great statesman Barneveld paid for it with his life. No sooner had the Calvinistic faction gained the ascendency than the West India Company became a fixed fact. And it was due almost entirely to the herculean exertions of Usselinx.[1]

Mrs. Martha J. Lamb and Mrs. Burton Harrison in their "History of the City of New York," vol. 1, page 25, conclude: "It is singular that a man who has earned so honorable a place in history should be so little known to the world.

"It is true that he never held an official position, yet he founded two great commercial companies, which were so prolific in results that, had justice been properly meted out, his name would have been immortalized. He contributed more than any power to annihilate Spain. He brought to New York the nation in which the principle of free communities—the vital principle of American liberty—was carried out to its full extent. He made Sweden a maritime power. And by the success of his enterprises he was, in 1629, instrumental in saving Holland from the Spanish yoke, —an act so vast in its consequences that for it alone he deserves the eternal gratitude of all Germanic Europe."

In the above paragraph, the reference made by Martha Lamb to Usselinx and Sweden will be explained in Chapter X, under "Swedish West India Company."

[1] Martha J. Lamb. Hist. City of New York. Vol. 1, pp. 23-25.

The Belgians, in great numbers, had emigrated to Sweden, and as early as 1624 William Usselinx, the promoter of the Dutch West India Company, had drawn up a plan for the promotion of a similar company in Sweden.[1] These are the two great commercial companies Martha Lamb is referring to.

But for his great West India Company, Usselinx had not confined his efforts to Amsterdam alone; Zeeland, the "Sea-Beggar" Province, was a fair and promising field for his purposes, and while he left Plancius (already mentioned) and another Belgian, François Francken, a member of the High Council of State, to carry on the work in the commercial capital of Holland, he himself succeeded in interesting influential men of Middelburg.[2]

As a consequence, the States of Zeeland appointed a Committee of Three (of whom Usselinx himself was one), to meet a number of gentlemen from various cities of Holland, who had evidently been appointed a committee on the subject by the States of Holland, after their discussion concerning it. There were eight representatives from Amsterdam; Dordrecht, Delft, and Rotterdam were each represented by three; Harlem and Leyden, each by two; and seven other cities, each by one. All these with the three from Zeeland constituted, therefore, the rather large committee of thirty-one members. They were charged with the duty of drafting a patent, or "license"—"vergunning," the historian Van Meteren calls it, which is the Dutch for license—or charter, for a West India Com-

[1] Fred R. Jones, in Hist. of N. America, edited by Lee, Vol. 4, p. 44.
[2] James J. Wilson, Mem. Hist. of N. Y., vol. 1, p. 85.

William Usselinx.

pany, and they assembled and addressed themselves to this task in October, 1606.

Delays, postponements, and then the twelve years' truce interrupted the progress of the scheme. The charter was granted only on June 3, 1621, stipulating that a sum of not less than seven millions of florins ($2,800,000) be subscribed as capital. All were invited to subscribe to the stocks of the venture, and the Belgians responded generously to the call of their leaders.

> "West India can bring Netherland great gain,
> Lessen the might, divert the wealth of Spain."

The company was divided into five branches or "chambers," with headquarters in the principal cities of the Republic; the Amsterdam chamber was the most important and to it were assigned all affairs relating to New Netherland. The management of the whole company was entrusted to a general executive board of nineteen members, called the "College of the XIX." They adopted the democratic principles of the Belgians, and accorded to the shareholders a voice in all important proceedings,[1] which unusual advantage greatly contributed to securing the capital for the great enterprise.

The Dutch West India Company was modeled after the Dutch East India Company, whose charter dated from March 20, 1602, and whose stockholders received big dividends: the lowest was 15% in 1605, and the highest 75% in 1606.

The West India Company having been thus or-

[1] Martha Lamb. Hist. of N. Y., vol. 1, p. 47.

ganized for effective operation, what was it empowered to do? For the space of twenty-four years after July 1, 1621,[1] it was to have the privilege, to the exclusion of all other inhabitants or associations of merchants within the bounds of the United Provinces, of sending ships for purposes of traffic to the countries of America and Africa that bordered on the Atlantic Ocean, and those on the West Coast of America on the shores of the Pacific. The remainder of the globe was assigned to the East India Company.

It was authorized to form, in those waters, alliances, offensive and defensive, and to erect forts; to declare war and to make peace, with the consent of the States General, under certain conditions; to appoint governors and other officers in friendly or conquered territories where they had established themselves; to make laws and to administer them.

It was obliged to advance, in every way possible, the material welfare of the lands taken up for commercial and colonization purposes. The company had other privileges, but those just cited were the principal ones.

Manhattan Island had, at that time, been known for several years and visited by Dutch trading boats. The "United New Netherland Company," a name assumed, in 1614, by an association of merchants who had sought to develop the resources of the region, together with all the others trading with the countries on the Atlantic Coast, was absorbed by the great West India Company.

There followed now a period of several years when

[1] James G. Wilson. Mem. Hist. of N. Y., vol. 1, p. 93.

the West India Company reached the height of its financial success; the climax of prosperity was attained in 1628, when Admiral Piet Heyn, of the Company, took the Spanish Silver Fleet, worth eleven and one-half millions of florins ($4,600,000.), while the value of the prizes brought home, about the same time, by other fleets of the company, aggregated more than four million of florins ($1,600,000). Hence the West India Company felt justified in declaring a dividend of 50% in 1629.

And now will begin the interesting story of the Walloons who were anxious to emigrate to America.

CHAPTER IX

THE WALLOONS PREPARE FOR EMIGRATION TO THE NEW WORLD

On the eastern coast of America, in the very heart of the country not only claimed but partly occupied by England, into the very portion that divided her northern colony (New England) from her southern colony (Virginia), the Hollanders were diligently penetrating and establishing a nucleus for profitable trade. This led James I of England, to direct his Ambassador at The Hague, Sir Dudley Carleton, to address a remonstrance to the States General, 1621.[1]

"By degrees, the fame of the New World reached the ears of the artisans of Amsterdam; and some of the Belgian refugees applied to Sir Carleton for formal encouragement to emigrate to 'Virginia.' The Ambassador, having no power to make arrangements with them, communicated their application to the King, by whom it was ordered to be referred to the Virginia Company. But the conditions which the Company offered did not appear to have been satisfactory to the Walloons; and the abortive negotiations ended."

"Thus Virginia lost the advantage of having an

[1] James G. Wilson. Mem. Hist. of N. Y., vol. 1. p. 142.

ingenious, brave, and industrious race added to her perhaps too homogeneous population. What Virginia lost New Netherland gained. Cosmopolitan Amsterdam was to impress its character upon cosmopolitan Manhattan." [1]

Jesse de Forest. Now, who were those Walloons? The head of this group of applicants to Sir Dudley Carleton was Jesse de Forest, who with his wife and children went to Holland, 1615, where his father and brothers had already gone.

Born in Avesnes, Belgic soil of Hainault,[2] about 1576, he was a splendid type of Walloon, gifted with energy, initiative, and perseverence, and he used these qualities for the benefit and welfare of his countrymen. One of his descendents, Mr. Robert W. de Forest, of New York, by his splendid acts of philanthropy and his protection of intellectual organizations, shows that he has inherited the qualities of his illustrious ancestors who were most important among the early pioneers in New York and Connecticut, and during the War of the American Revolution.

The petition to the English Ambassador, written and signed by Jesse de Forest, then living in Leyden, was in French—the language of the Walloons—and was dated February 5, 1621.[3] It applied for permission to settle in Virginia, fifty or sixty families, Wal-

---

[1] Brohead. Hist. St. of N. Y., vol. 1. p. 147; London Doc. vol. 1. p. 29; N. Y Col. Mss. vol. 3. p. 10.

[2] Avesnes became French only after the victorious wars waged by Louis XIV on Spain, thus after 1658-1678.

[3] It is by mistake that the Documents relative to the Colonial History of New York, vol. 3, and Mr. Brohead in his History of the State of N. Y. vol. 1, present the date of the petition as 1622, since this document was inclosed in Sir Dudley Carleton's letter of July 21, 1621.

loons and French, all of the reformed religion. A translation of this petition into English will be found at the end of this chapter.

Accompanying this document was a Round-Robin, signed by fifty-six men, most of them heads of families, the whole number comprising two hundred and twenty-seven men, women, and children. Jesse de Forest was, of course, one of these fifty-six signers and he proposed to take with him his wife and their five children.

Within the circle of the Round Robin were a few words promising that the signers would settle in Virginia "under the conditions set forth in the Articles which we have communicated" (the petition), and ending rather significantly "and not otherwise." This inscription is also in the handwriting of Jesse de Forest.[1] A photographic reproduction of this interesting document is to be found within this chapter. The greater number of those petitioners were members of the Walloon Church of Leyden.

The names on the "Round Robin" of the Petitioners to the British Ambassador, Sir Dudley Carleton, for permission to settle in Virginia, 1621, will be found below.

(Their signatures are preserved in the British Public Record Office, London. State Papers, Colonial, vol. 1, No. 54.)

With
Wife and 4 children... Barbe, Adrien, dyer.
Wife and 4 children... Billet, Jan, tiller.

[1] Mrs. Robert W. de Forest's "A Walloon Family in America" vol. 1, p. 20.

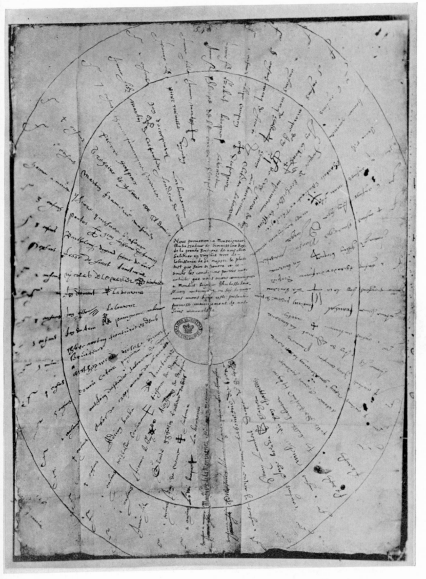

Round-robin annexed to the application of Jesse de Forest.
(The original measures 18x13½ inches.)

Young son............Broque, Gillam, tiller.
Wife and 2 children...Broque, Louis, tiller.
Young son............Broque, Robert, tiller.
Wife and 1 child......Campion, Flipe, textile worker.
Wife and 4 children...Campion, Jean, textile worker.
Wife and 1 child......Censier, Michelle, textile worker.
Wife and 5 children...Catoir, Ernou, textile worker.
Wife and 2 children...Channy, Challe, (mark of) tiller.
Wife and 2 children...Conne (Coinne) Jacque, tiller.
Young son............Cornille, Piere, vine-grower.
Wife and 5 children...Clitden, Francor, tiller.
Wife ....Damont, Jan, tiller.
Wife and 1 child......Desendre, Antoin, tiller.
Wife and 8 children...Digand (Digaud) Barthelemy, sawyer.
Young son............De Carpentier, Martin, copper found-
                       er.
Wife and 2 children...Du Carpentry, Jan, tiller.
Wife and 1 child......De Crenne (Cranne) Jean, postman.
Wife and 4 children...De Crepy, Abel, textile worker.
Wife and 5 children...De Croy, Jan (mark of), sawyer.
Wife and 2 children...Du Four, Theodor, textile worker.
Wife and 5 children...De Forest, Jesse, dyer.
Young son............De Le, Philippe, carpenter.
Wife and 2 children...De La Marlier, Nicolas, dyer.
Young son............De la Mot, Jan, tiller.
Wife and 2 children...De Pasar, Polle, textile worker.
Wife and 2 children...Du Pon, Michel, hatter.
Wife and 5 children...De Trou, Jan, textile worker.
Wife and 4 children...De Violate, Anthoyne, vine-grower.
(Bachelor)...........Fourdrin, Franchois, textile worker.
Wife and 7 children...Farnarcque (Farvarque) Thomas,
                       locksmith.
Wife and 1 child......Framerie, Martin, musician.
Two children.........Flip, Marie (in the name of her hus-
                       band, a miller).
Young son............Gantois, P., student of theology.
                     Gaspar, Pierre.
Young son............Ghiselin, Claude, tailor.

Wife and 3 children... Gille, Jan, tiller.

Wife and 5 children... Gourdeman, Jan, tiller.

Wife................. Gremier, Antoine, gardiner.

Wife .... Lambert, Henri, textile worker.

(Bachelor)........... Lechielles (Lespielle) Jacques, brewer.

Wife and 3 children... Le Geay, Pontus, textile worker.

Wife and 4 children... Le Jeune, Gregoire, shoemaker.

Wife and 6 children... Le Rou, Jan, printer.

Wife and 1 child...... Le Roy, Jerome, textile worker.

Wife and 5 children... Le Ca, Jan, tiller.

Wife and 4 children... Le Ca, George.

Wife and 5 children... Maton, Philippe, dyer, and two servants.

(Bachelor)........... Mousnier de la Montagne, student of
medicine.

Mousnier de la Montagne, pharmacist and surgeon.

Wife and 4 children... Martin, Antoine.

Young daughter....... Martin, Jenne.

(Bachelor)........... Quiesnier (Quesnee), Pierre, brewer.

Wife and 6 children... Sage, Jan, textile worker.

Wife and 4 children... Woutre, Gouerge.

(The presentation of spelling of those names is as near as a careful and patient examination could set forth.)

Their petition had been turned over to the "Virginia Company," and the answer was not at all what Jesse had hoped for. His great object was to have his colonists dwell together and apart from others, so that they might maintain their religion as well as their language. But the Virginia Company thought otherwise.

The directors said that they saw no "inconvenience" in having 300 Walloons and French settle in

Virginia. On the other hand, they "esteeme it so
Royall a favour in His Ma'tie and so singular a benefit to the said Walloons and ffrenchmen, to bee
admitted to live in that fruitful land" that, in fact,
they could do nothing for them but—give them good
advice. They did, moreover, "conceive it not expedi-
ent that the sayd ffamilies should sett downe in one
grosse bodie," but they offered to place them "by
convenient nombers in the principall Citties, Bor-
oughs and Corporacions in Virginia." [1]

The disappointment of Jesse de Forest and the
other petitioners was great, though their demands
seemed to have been somewhat excessive, and coming
from people established in the Dutch Republic must
have appeared rather suspicious to the English authorities, though those Walloons had no political
designs.

Aware of the uneasiness of the English Government, the "West India Company" did not delay arrangements to secure their title to New Netherland
by more extended actual occupation. "By virtue of
their charter," and before their final organization,
they "took possession of the country" in the year
1622, and "trading vessels" were promptly sent
out.[2]

The voyages of the Dutch ships, at this time, generally occupied about seven or eight weeks. On clear-
ing the channel, they laid their course for the Canary
Islands; whence they stretched across the Atlantic
toward Guiana (or Wild Coast) and the Caribbees,

[1] Mrs. Robert W. de Forest's "A Walloon Family in America" vol. 1,
p. 21.
[2] Brodhead, Hist. St. of N. Y., vol. 1, p. 149.

and then ran obliquely toward the northwest, between the Bahamas and the Bermudas, until they made the coast of Virginia. By steering this circuitous southern course, they avoided the severe gales of the North Atlantic, and had the opportunity of refitting, when it was necessary.

At first, the name "Virginia" was applied to the whole region from about 34° to 45° north latitude, or approximately from North Carolina to Maine, while the name "West Indies" was a vague expression to designate any point in the Western hemisphere or North and South America.

Jesse de Forest was persevering with his plan to bring his countrymen to the new world, and now made several applications to the Dutch authorities.

Brodhead, in his "History of the State of New York," tells us that the Provincial States of Holland, ascertaining that several families of Walloons had applied to Sir Carleton for permission to emigrate to Virginia, thought that "they should rather be secured for the West India Company;" and the subject was referred to the directors of that corporation, to consider "what could be therein done for their service."

The directors promptly reported that the emigration of these Walloons would be "very advantageous" to the Company; and that immediate measures should be taken to secure them, and to give them employment, until the company should be formally organized, and be able to send them out as "colonists." The views of the directors were approved by the Provincial States, and the attention of the magistracy of Amsterdam was officially directed to the subject, April, 1622.[1]

According to a manuscript which was hidden in the British Museum, and found only a few years ago, Jesse de Forest, under the auspices of the West India Company, led a small group called "Les Pères de Famille" or "The Fathers of Families," to Guiana, South America, where he died, and through this unfortunate circumstance he never came to Manhattan.

The Amsterdam Chamber—of the West India Company—which undoubtedly had its capital fully subscribed before that of the other Chambers, and in charge of the affairs of New Netherland, was now actively busy with the preliminaries to the sending of the Walloons to the new colony to be founded.

For the transportation of these Walloon families the company provided a vessel of great size for that day, having more than three times the dimensions of the "Half Moon," or a measurement of two hundred and sixty tons. It was, appropriately, christened the "New Netherland."

PETITION OF THE WALLOONS AND FRENCH TO SIR DUDLEY CARLETON, FEBRUARY 5, 1621.

(Translated from the French).

My Lord the Ambassador of the Most Serene King of Great Britain is most humbly supplicated to advise and reply to us on the following articles:

1. Firstly, will his Majesty be pleased to permit fifty or sixty families, as well Walloons as French, all

[1] Hol. Doc. 1, 118; Res. Holl. and West. Friesland; Brodhead History St. of N. Y., vol. 1, pp. 147-148.

of the reformed religion, to settle in Virginia, a country under his obedience, and will he be pleased to protect and defend them from and against all, and maintain them in their religion.

2. And as said families may consist of nearly three hundred persons, they would also wish to take with them a quantity of cattle as well for purposes of husbandry as for their support, and would therefore require more than one ship; would not his Majesty then accommodate them with one, supplied and equipped with cannon and other arms, on board of which they could make their voyage with whatever they might themselves be able to furnish, return in search of commodities for the places conceded by his said Majesty and at the same time export those of the country.

3. When arrived in said country, would he not please permit them to select a spot fit for their settlement, from the places not yet cultivated by those whom his said Majesty hath been pleased to send thither.

4. Might they not erect a town for their security in said selected places, provide it with necessary fortifications, elect therein a Governor and Magistrates for the administration both of police and justice under the fundamental laws which it shall please his said Majesty to establish in said countries.

5. Would his said Majesty please to furnish cannon and ammunition for the preservation of said place, and grant them, in case of necessity, the right to make powder, run bullets and cast cannon under his said Majesty's arms and escutcheon.

6. Would he not grant them a banlieu or territory

of eight English miles all round, i.e., sixteen miles in diameter, which they might cultivate as fields, meadows, vineyards and in other ways; which territory they should hold from his said Majesty, either conjointly or severally, in such fealty as his said Majesty may deem reasonable, without any other person being able to reside there unless by taking a patent (lettre de baillette) of the land therein contained, in which would be reserved Inferior Seigniorial Rights; and whether those amongst them who could live as nobles would not be permitted to declare themselves such.

7. Whether they might not hunt in said countries all game whether furred or feathered, (à poil et à plume) fish in the seas and rivers, cut trees of lofty and other growth both for navigation and other purposes according to their pleasure; in fine, make use of everything under and above ground at their pleasure and will, (royalties excepted) and trade in all with those permitted them.

Which privileges would extend solely to the said families and theirs, without any newcomers being able to avail themselves of them; which means, that they would concede to them according to and not beyond their power, were his said Majesty not to concede to them anew.

And as they understood that his said Majesty hath established a public warehouse in London, in which and not elsewhere are to be unloaded the merchandises coming from said countries, and considering that it is only reasonable that those who by their labor and industry have procured for the public the enjoyment of this country, should receive the first fruits thereof, they will submit to the constitutions established there, for that purpose, which for their better observance shall be communicated to them.

Under which conditions and privileges they would promise fealty and obedience such as faithful and obedient subjects owe their King and Sovereign Lord, submitting themselves, with all their power, to the laws generally established in said countries.

My Lord Ambassador will, if he pleases, give information on the preceding; likewise if it would be his pleasure to expedite said privilege in due form as soon as possible, in consequence of the shortness of the time to collect whatever is necessary from now to March, which is the convenient season for embarking. This doing he will oblige his servants to pray God for the realization of his holy designs and for health and long life.

(Signed) Jose de Forest.

(Endorsed by Sir Dudley Carleton)

"Supplicâon of certaine Walloons
and French who are desirous to
goe into Virginia."

CHAPTER X

The Walloons and the "New Netherland." The Dutch historian, Nicolaes Van Wassenaer, who was living in Amsterdam at the time of the sailing of the Walloons, tells us in his "Historish Verhael" under date of April, 1624, that the West India Company equipped in the spring a vessel of 130 lasts (260 tons) called the "Nieu Netherlandt," whereof Cornelius Jacobs Mey of Hoorn was skipper, with a company of thirty families, *mostly Walloons, to plant a colony in New Netherland.*

And he continues: "they sailed in the beginning of *March,* and directing their course by the Canary Islands, steered towards the wild coast (Guiana) and gained the west wind which luckily took them in the beginning of *May* into the River called Rio de Montagnes (now the Hudson River) lying in 40½ degrees."

Wassenaer says that the passengers were "mostly Walloons," and his statement is accepted and reproduced by all the authoritative writers on the early history of America; there is not one single dissenting voice on this subject. See, for instance, such well-known authorities as: John Romeyn Brodhead; E. B. O'Callaghan; Frederick Robertson Jones (in Lee's); J. Franklin Jameson; Benson Lossing; Charles W. Baird; George Bancroft; David Valentine; General James Grant Wilson; Martha J. Lamb and Burton Harrison; Mary L. Booth; William L. Stone, and many others.

Obviously, if the passengers on the New Netherland had been people of the country of Wassenaer, that is to say Dutch, he would not have presented them as Walloons.

But, on that boat, who were those representing the minority? If they were Dutch was it not worth while for Wassenaer to say so? They might have been Dutch at that.

Perhaps they were French, as Jesse de Forest had made, as we have seen, an application to Sir Carleton for fifty or sixty Walloon and French families to go to Virginia, and it appears that many names on his "Round Robin," for that destination were later on found in New Netherland. However, this voyage to America had only thirty families, mostly Walloons, instead of the fifty or sixty families desirous to go to the climate of Virginia. Did all the French withdraw from this trip which had a very different destination? They seemed to have a preference for the southern regions, as will be noted below.

On the other hand, there is a strong possibility that the minority, that is to say those who were not Walloons, was represented by Flemings(easily confused with the Dutch) for the Fleming William Usselinx was the founder of the West India Company which

THE SHIP NEW NETHERLAND.

took the emigrants to Manhattan, and therefore it is possible that this first voyage of settlers had only Belgian passengers.

Novi Belgi. It is very significant, however, that at this time the somewhat indefinite territory of New Netherland, where Wassenaer tells us that the Walloons had been sent "to plant a colony," was formally erected into a Province, and, says Brodhead, was "honored" by the States-General of Holland with a grant of the armorial distinction of a Count. This armorial distinction, as represented in the provincial seal of New Netherland, was a shield bearing a beaver, proper, surmounted by a count's coronet, and encircled by the words "Sigilum Novi Belgii," or "Seal of New Belgium."

We have seen that the Walloon and French petitioners, headed by Jesse de Forest, in 1621, had applied to England for permission to go to Virginia, and that the unacceptable conditions which they had themselves set forth prevented them from going there. From the following note it would appear that, at that time, settlements to the south of New Netherland appealed more to the French.

Six years after the landing of the Walloons in New Netherland, an application was made to the English Government, in behalf of a body of French Protestants, asking for encouragement to settle in Virginia. In June, 1629, Antoine de Ridouet, Baron de Sance, addressed such an application to the Secretary of State of England. (State papers, Colonial Series, Vol. V., No. 14. Public Record Office, London).

His proposal to form a colony of French Protestants in America was favorably entertained by the Government. Elaborate plans for the voyage and the settlement were drawn up by the leader, in consultation with the Attorney-General; and after many delays the French embarked. Their destination was Carolina, but they were landed in Virginia.[1]

The date 1623. It is interesting now to go to the dates as presented by Wassenaer.

At the beginning of this chapter, we have seen that the Dutch historian wrote under date of *April, 1624,* that the Walloons left Amsterdam in March, and that they arrived in May, in the river Mauritius, now the Hudson.

As he wrote in April, 1624, that they arrived in America in *May,* his narrative must appear to point directly to the year 1623. This is the logical interpretation made by numerous historians. Many writers do not see sufficient proof in the arguments set forth by those who claim that the Walloons arrived in May, 1624, and therefore do believe that Wassenaer narrated the events of his time as he knew them and as they happened, for he had made a specialty of this kind of writings.

His passage referring to the voyage of the Walloons is in part VII of his "Historish Verhael," and it is true that the preface to this part is dated December 1, 1624. However, it is a common practice among authors to write the preface to their work after the book has been completed.

Some writers in order to show that the voyage took place in 1624, have cited only the date of his preface

[1] Baird. Hist. of Hug. Em. to Am. vol. 1. p. 165.

(December 1, 1624), while others have simply mentioned that he wrote about those Walloons in 1624. Both parties have ignored the date at which Wassenaer wrote, that is to say, April, 1624.

Wassenaer's description is in the old Dutch language, and this probably accounts for the confusion; a translation of it into English will be found in "Narratives of New Netherland," edited by Franklin Jameson, Director of the Department of Historical Research in the Carnegie Institution of Washington. In this interesting work the date of the description of April, 1624, with its reference to the departure of the Walloons in March and their arrival in New Amsterdam in May, are all presented, and Mr. Jameson—in a special foot-note, on page 75—also assigns to this trip the date of 1623.

In the early part of the seventeenth century, newspapers were but just beginning to exist. News-pamphlets, not periodical, were more numerous. Annual or semi-annual volumes detailing the events or news of the year, after the manner of the "Annual Register" of our time, began with the "Mercure François" in 1605.

But one of the very earliest of such compilations was the "Historish Verhael alder ghedenck-weerdichste Geschiedenissen die hier en daer in Europa, etc. voorgevallen syn" (Historical Account of all the most Remarkable Events which have happened in Europe, etc.), which was first published, at Amsterdam, in 1622 by Nicolaes Van Wassenaer. It appeared in twenty-one semi-annual parts, covering the years 1621-1631.[1]

[1] Jameson.   Narratives of New Netherland, pp. 63-64.

Wassenaer, a learned scholar, son of a minister of the Reformed Church of Amsterdam, studied at Geneva, at the expense of the Amsterdam Magistrates. He wrote a history of the Turks, published a Greek poem on the siege of the city of Harlem, where for a while he was at the head of a school, and practiced as a physician at Amsterdam, where he published a medical work of some repute.

A list of the passengers of the boat "New Netherland," numbering perhaps 150, unfortunately does not exist, or at least has not been found as yet. It probably never will be, as Brodhead informs us that all the documents of the old East and West India Companies, of a date prior to 1700 were sold, in 1821, at public auction, as waste paper....

No records of the colony for the first fifteen years of its existence have been preserved. The earliest council minutes, and other historical documents, in the possession of the State of New York date only as far back as 1638, and the registers of the most ancient ecclesiastical body in the state, the Reformed Protestant Dutch Church of New York, commence in 1639.

While the names of those first settlers in New Amsterdam are not positively known, we are well informed by Wassanaer that they were "mostly Walloons," and through other reliable sources we are well informed also as to their scattering and settling elsewhere, as will be shown in this chapter.

But in the absence of such names, the list of petitioners, headed by Jesse de Forest and presented to the British Ambassador, in 1621, assumes a special interest. Among the sixty names of families desiring then to emigrate to Virginia it seems highly probable that some were with the thirty families who came to New York in 1623, as several names on the "Round Robin" of de Forest are found in the early registers of New York; that is to say, fifteen years or so after the landing of the first settlers.

Among such names were: De la Mot, Du Four, Le Rou, Le Roy, Du Pon, Ghiselin, Cornille, De Trou, De Crenne, Damont, Campion, De Carpentier, Gille, Catoir, De Croy, Maton, La Montagne, Lambert, Martin, Gaspar and other signers of the "Round Robin."

And, as to the year of that landing being 1623 or 1624, it does not change in the least the fact that the passengers on the "New Netherland" were "mostly Walloons," as the Dutch writer Wassenaer tells us, and as the origin of certain place names in Long Island, New Jersey, along the Hudson, and elsewhere, conclusively proves.

Great must have been the joy of those enterprising travelers when in the distance they perceived the Land of the Free. The wooded shores rising on each side of the Narrows, and receding to encircle the broad harbor; the beautiful expanse of the bay, over whose waters, teeming with fish, flocks of birds were seen darting in search of their prey.

But, as Wassenaer informs us, an unexpected sight awaited the voyagers as they approached the land. A French boat lay in the harbor. Her errand was to take possession of the country discovered by Verrazano (1524) and now claimed by France by virtue of that discovery.

The captain was about to set up the standard of the French King (Louis XIII) upon the soil of New Netherland. The company of peaceful immigrants could hardly have diverted him from his purpose, but there chanced to be a Dutch vessel of several guns, the "Mackerel," lying a short distance above; and the remonstrances of the colonists, seconded by a show of force from the Dutch ship, were effectual. The unwelcome visitor soon disappeared, and our Walloons were free to land upon Manhattan Island.

SOME PRESENTATIONS OF THIS VOYAGE OF THE FIRST SETTLERS:

1. (From Charles Baird's "History of the Huguenot Emigration to America," vol. 1. p. 171): "The settlers found a few huts standing near the southern end of the Island. A *'trading post'* had been maintained here for several years by the merchants of Amsterdam; and here Adriaen Block, a mariner, in their employ, passed the winter of the year 1613, building a ship to replace his vessel which had been burned.

"But the permanent occupation of the site of the City of New York dates from the arrival of the ship 'New Netherland' in May, 1623."

2. (From George Bancroft's "History of the United States of America" Vol. 1. p. 494, of the author's last revision): "The organization of the West India Company, in 1623, was the epoch of two serious efforts at colonization. In the spring of that year, the

'New Netherland' carried out thirty families. They were chiefly Walloons, Protestant fugitives from Belgian Provinces.''

3. (From Martha Lamb's "History of the City of New York," vol. 1, p. 49): "The Directors of the Amsterdam Chamber of the Dutch West India Company were: the historian John Delaet (from Antwerp), Kiliaen Van Renssalaer, Michael Pauw, Peter Evertsen Hulft, Jonas Witsen, Hendrik Hamel, Samuel Godyn, and Samuel Blommaert. They were all men of wealth and education. But there were none of them very deeply interested 'in the wild Indian country. However, they took measures to secure a party of Protestant Walloons to send over to their new possessions. These people were that portion of the Belgians who were of Celtic origin, and were ingenious as well as brave and industrious.''

4. (From "Narratives of New Netherland," p. 75, by Franklin Jameson, Director of the Department of Historical Research, in the Carnegie Institution at Washington): "This group of Walloons, or French-speaking Belgians, had in the spring of 1622 applied to the States of the Province of Holland for transportation to New Netherland as *colonists,* and the matter had been referred to the Amsterdam Chamber of the West India Company.''

5. (From Dr. John Romeyn Brodhead's "History of the State of New York," vol. 1, p. 150): "The spring of the year 1623 was the era of *the first permanent agricultural colonization of New Netherland,* under the authority of the West India Company.

Anxious to commence their colony with willing and active emigrants, the Amsterdam Chamber equipped the 'New Netherland' and embarked on board of it a company of thirty families. The greater part of these colonists were Walloons.''

Students of early American history are greatly indebted to the splendid research work of Mr. Brodhead. In 1841, the State of New York commissioned him as agent to search the archives of Europe for materials illustrating the colonial history of the State. Never did an American State send out a better recording agent. After four years of diligent search and labor he returned with eighty volumes of manuscript copies of documents procured in the Netherlands, France, and England (sixteen of them from the Netherlands), which were subsequently published as the series entitled: ''Documents Relating to the Colonial History of the State of New York.'' [1]

6. (From General James Grant Wilson's ''Memorial History of the City of New York,'' vol. 1. p. 144): ''The setting out of this *first colonizing expedition* to New Netherland cannot be regarded without interest. It left Amsterdam in 1623 and reached the mouth of the Hudson in May. Thirty of the Walloon families were on the 'New Netherland,' and it had been carefully planned in advance how these were to be distributed into various *settlements*.''

The little company of passengers soon dispersed. They brought with them, says Martha Lamb, ''a knowledge of the arts in which they were proficient, and were distinguished for their extraordinary per-

[1] Jameson. Narratives of New Netherlands, p. 99.

sistence in overcoming difficulties." They brought also with them the "Belgic Confession of Faith," which is still, today, the standard symbol of the Reformed Church in America. (See Chapter XI.)

General Settlements. The first Belgian passengers, and those who arrived afterward during the Dutch Administration, settled at: Manhattan, Albany, Long Island, Staten Island; along the Connecticut River, and the Delaware River; in New Jersey, Pennsylvania and Delaware; in the Hudson Valley, at Esopus, Wallkill, Kingston, Hurley, New Paltz, and along the banks of the Walloonsac River.

Settlements, details. Manhattan: Eight of those on the boat "New Netherland" were left at "Fort Amsterdam," now the lower part of Manhattan, to take possession for the West India Company.

At the beginning of the history of the Province of New Netherland, many of the place names included the word "fort," as one of the first buildings to be erected was a place capable of defending the traders and settlers against the Indians.

New Jersey. Four couples who had married at sea, and eight men were sent to form a settlement on the South River, now the Delaware, and selected a spot on its east bank, near the present town of Gloucester, four miles below Camden, N. J., and built a fort which they called "Fort Nassau."

Connecticut. Two families and six men were sent to the great fresh river, now the Connecticut, where a small fort was built; later on it became the "Fort Good Hope," on the site of the present city of Hartford.

Albany. Eighteen families remained on the ship, which now proceeded up the Hudson. Approaching the head of navigation in this river, the unusual size of the New Netherland, as compared with the class of "trading" ships that ordinarily visited these shores, proved to be of some inconvenience.

When opposite Esopus Creek it was found necessary to lighten her by transferring a portion of her cargo to boats that were left there by the Dutch, who had been there the year before trading with the Indians upon their own account, and who had gone back again to Holland.

Finally, the Walloons landed near the spot where the city of Albany now stands. A little further north, a new fort was immediately projected and called "Fort Orange," in honor of Prince Maurice of Orange (son of William of Orange), who was greatly beloved by the Belgians. These Walloons came to occupy the site of the present city of Albany, or that level part of it where its business is transacted.

Around this fort, huts of bark were hastily constructed by the settlers. Some friendly natives came with presents of peltry and a brisk trade was opened with the Mohicans and other nearby tribes. Such was the beginning of the capital of the Empire State of New York.

At the same time that the "engineers" of the expedition began marking out the angles of the fortress and digging the trenches, the Walloon colonists put their spades into the virgin soil and sowed their grain. So that when the fort was completed and Captain Mey,

Landing of the Walloons at Albany.
(After an old print.)

head of the expedition, leaving Adriaen Joris in command, was about to partake himself to the quarter assigned to his special jurisdiction, the grain and corn already stood high and promising.

Merchants from the Dutch Republic had formerly traded in that section, and for the greater security of the traders, says Wassenaer, a castle or small redoubt, then called "Fort Nassau," had been built in 1614 or 1615, on Castle Island, near where Albany now stands, but had been abandoned in 1617, on account of injury by freshets.[1] We have seen that later on the first settlers called "Fort Nassau," a place in New Jersey.

Under the English, the name Fort Orange was changed to Albany, after the Duke of York, whose Scotch title was Duke of Albany, afterwards James II of England. Before the arrival of the white man, the site of Albany was named "Chescodonta" by the Indians.

A ship that reached Holland in the following August carried letters from New Netherland making a cheerful report of the settlement. "We were much gratified," wrote the colonists, "on arriving in this country, where we found beautiful rivers, bubbling fountains falling down into the valleys; basins of running water in the flatlands, agreeable fruits in the woods, such as strawberries, walnuts, and wild grapes. The woods abound with venison. There is considerable fish in the rivers; good tillage land; here is, especially, free coming and going, without fear of the naked natives of the country. Had we cows, hogs, and

[1] Jameson. Narr. of New Netherlands, p. 67.

other cattle fit for food—which we daily expect in the first ships—we would not wish to return to Holland." [1]

The income from the fur trade of New Netherland, during the first year, amounted to 28,000 guilders, ($11,200), according to Wassenaer. Rich beavers, otters, martins and foxes, were found there. De Laet notes, for this year, 4000 beavers and 700 otters brought in by two ships, and selling for 25,000 to 27,000 guilders.

First Colonies in New Netherland. Thus, the first colonists had been established in New Netherland, and on this occasion the territory which had received the name of New Netherland by a charter dated October 11, 1614, was now, 1623, formally erected into a Dutch Province, and received from the States General of Holland a seal with the inscription "Novi Belgii," or New Belgium, as a compliment, apparently, to those Walloon settlers, and perhaps, also, to the Fleming Usselinx, promoter of the West India Company, under whose auspices the Walloons came to America.

But we need not suppose that the thirty families brought out by the first ship were the only ones to supply so many points with settlers. A few months after the sailing of the New Netherland, the project was pursued still farther, and, says General James Grant Wilson, more of the Walloon families were brought over in June by an expedition consisting of no less than three ships at once.

Boundaries of New Netherland. These were somewhat indefinite. However, in a "Report and advice on the condition of New Netherland, drawn up from

[1] Baird. Hist. Emigration of Huguenots to America, vol. 1. p. 171.

Documents and Papers placed by commission of the Assembly of XIX (the General Executive Board of the West India Company) in the hands of the General Chamber of Accounts, and dated December 15, 1644, we find this: "New Netherland, situated in America between English Virginia and New England, extending from the South River (the Delaware), lying in 38½ degrees, to Cape Malabar, in the latitude of 41½ degrees,..." While this fixes the line along the coast, the extent of the inland is not given, and very likely was never determined.

Directors and Governors of New Netherland. When the Walloons landed in Manhattan, Cornelius Jacobsen Mey, who was the captain of the boat "New Netherland," was appointed Director General for the Province of New Netherland. Here is the list of the Directors General and Governors, at the time of the Dutch:

Cornelius Jacobsen Mey	1623-1625
	(or 1624-1625)
William Verhulst	1625-1626
Peter Minuit	1626-1632
Sebastian Jansen Krol	1632-1633
Wouter van Twiller	1633-1638
Willem Kieft	1638-1647
Peter Stuyvesant	1647-1664

The Governors were Peter Minuit, Wouter van Twiller, William Kieft and Peter Stuyvesant.

Purchase of Manhattan in 1626. The little section of Manhattan Island which is now known as the Battery, was, on the 6th of May, 1626, the scene of one of the most interesting business transactions ever made.

It was the purchase of the site of the City of New York.

Peter Minuit, then Director General of New Netherland, had been instructed by the West India Company to conclude the deal. He made a superficial survey of the island, and estimated its area at about 11,000 morgens (22,000 acres).

Having assembled the principal Indian chiefs, the shrewd "middleman" offered them glittering beads and other trinkets in exchange for their valuable real estate. The "generous offer" was accepted and the bargain was closed at once. The value of the entire lot of trinkets, which secured the title to the whole of Manhattan Island, was about sixty guilders or $24.00!

Peter Minuit came from Wesel, Westphalia, Germany, but many historians claim him to be a Belgian, or of Belgian parentage. The Belgian historian, Baron de Borchgrave, says that he was the scion of a Flemish family who had taken refuge at Wesel, while the American historian, Charles Baird, tells us that Minuit was a Walloon, that his family, during the persecutions in the Southern Provinces, had taken refuge in Wesel, where Minuit was a deacon of the Walloon Church at the time of his appointment as Director of New Netherland.[1]

Wesel, so near the border of the Belgian Provinces, had been a "city of refuge" in the days of religious persecution. It is interesting to note that in 1627, Minuit wrote to William Bradford, Governor of New

[1] Baird. Hist. Hug. Em. to America, vol. I. p. 175.

Plymouth Colony, letters in "French" and in Dutch,[1] and that his Secretary Isaac de Rasières, was a Walloon.

Minuit arrived at Manhattan on May 4, 1626, on the boat "Sea-Mew," and by the middle of the month, it appears, grain of many kinds was already in the ground, and Wassenaer tells us that in 1628, the village lying close to the Fort on the southern part of Manhattan Island numbered two hundred and seventy souls.

During Minuit's term of office, two other interesting events deserve special mention.

First Minister. Manhattan was visited for the first time by a minister of religion, "Jonas Michaelius," a clergyman of the Reformed Church of Holland, who came over in the year 1628. A congregation was gathered and public worship was instituted.

On August 11, 1628, the Rev. Jonas Michaelius wrote, from Manhattan, to the Rev. Adrianus Smoutius, minister of the Reformed Church at Amsterdam: "We have had at the first administration of the Lord's Supper full fifty communicants—*Walloons* and Dutch —not without great joy and comfort for so many, of whom a portion made their first confession of the faith before us, and others exhibited their church certificate."

"Some had forgotten to bring their certificates with them, not thinking that a church would be formed and established here; and some, who brought them, had lost them unfortunately in a general conflagration, but they were admitted upon the satisfactory testi-

[1] James Wilson. Mem. Hist. N. Y., vol. I, p. 164.

mony of others to whom they were known and also upon their daily good deportment, since we cannot observe strictly all the usual formalities in making a beginning under such circumstances.''

''The Lord's Supper was administered to them in the French language and according to the French mode, with a preceding discourse, which I had before me in writing, as I could not trust myself extemporaneously.'' [1]

This revelation by the Rev. Michaelius that the communicants at the first adiministration of the Lord's Supper were Walloons and Dutch, and that the administering of the Sacrament and discourse were made in French, the language of the Walloons, and this by a Dutchman, not familiar with the French language, seems to prove, very conclusively, that in 1628 the inhabitants of the Island of Manhattan were still ''mostly Walloons'' as at the time of the arrival of the boat New Netherland, in 1623.

Greatest Boat in the World. There being a superabundance of timber, it occurred to two Walloon shipbuilders to utilize it in the colony instead of sending it to Holland.[2]

A practical exhibition of the excellence of the wood, and the remarkable length of the beams that could be obtained from the trees in this vicinity would be given, if these were constructed into a vessel larger than any that then floated on the seas. Gov. Minuit was speedily won over to the scheme, and encouraged

[1] Documents Colonial Hist. of N. Y., vol. 2, pp. 764-765.
[2] Wilson. Mem. Hist. N. Y., vol. 1. p. 168; Martha Lamb. Hist. of N. Y., vol. 1. p. 63.

it, pledging the funds of the West India Company for its execution.

Parties of men scoured the woods, even to the vicinity of Fort Orange, (Albany) encamping in the forests for weeks at a time, cutting timber for the great ship. As a result there was launched in the harbor of New York, in 1630, a vessel larger than any that had heretofore been produced in the shipyards of Holland or Zeeland, being of twelve hundred tons burden, according to some authorities, and carrying thirty guns.[1] It was proudly christened the "New Netherland" in remembrance of the name of the smaller boat that had brought the Walloons to Manhattan.

The fame of this extraordinary naval architecture was, as a matter of course, carried to the ends of the earth, and excited the envy of all the European powers.[2]

Wallabout and Long Island. Some Walloons headed by George Jansen de Rapalie—or Rapalje, according to the Dutch spelling—settled on Long Island at the "Waal-Bocht," where de Rapalie bought from the Indians three hundred thirty-five acres of land.

In Dutch "Waal" means Walloon, and "Bocht" bay, thus it was the "Walloon Bay;" the name has become Wallabout Bay. In that section are now the well-known Wallabout Market and the Brooklyn Navy Yard. The Wallabout was the mooring-ground of the Jersey and other British prison-ships during the American Revolution.

1 Wilson. Mem. Hist. N. Y., vol. 1. p. 168.
2 Martha Lamb. Hist. of N. Y., vol. 1. p. 63.

"These early colonists are not to be confounded with the 'Waldenses,' who subsequently emigrated from Amsterdam. The descendants of the Walloons soon spread themselves over the country in the vicinity of the 'Waal-Bocht,' and the names of many of the most respectable families on Long Island attest their Belgian and French origin." [1]   Later, in this chapter, the "Waldenses on Staten Island" are described.

George de Rapalie or Rapelje was the progenitor of the respectable family of that name on Long Island. [2]

The wife of George de Rapalie was Catelina Trico; these two persons are the only ones so far identified as having been on the first passenger boat—the New Netherland.

"In the Documentary History of New York, III, 49-51, are two depositions made in 1685 and 1688 by Catelina Trico, one of the company who came out in the first voyage. She gives interesting details respecting the distribution of the immigrants to the Connecticut River, Delaware River, and Manhattan, and concerning her voyage with the remainder, about eighteen families, up to Albany, where she lived three years, "all of which time the Indians were all quiet as lambs." [3]

Some historians say that it was at Wallabout, on June 9, 1625, that was born to the Rapalies, the first female child of European parentage in the Province.

[1] Brodhead. Hist. State of N. Y., vol. 1. p. 154; Benson's Memoir, p. 94.
[2] Clute. Annals of Staten Island, p. 15.
[3] Jameson. Narr. New Netherland, p. 75.

An event full of human interest as well as a purely historic one. The name of the little Walloon was "Sarah."

There have been various statements in regard to the residence of the Rapalies at the time of the birth of Sarah. But the depositions of the wife, Catelina Trico, made in New York, before Governor Dongan, the year prior to her death (she died in September, 1689), establish the time of her arrival in this country and her first residence.[1]

They went first to live at Fort Orange (Albany) where they remained about three years, and where Sarah was born. They afterwards removed to Manhattan and from there to the Waal-Bocht, and this explains the confusion as to the exact place of her birth.

Sarah de Rapalie, or Rapalje, who gave birth to fourteen children, was the maternal ancestor of several of the most notable families of Kings County, while old directories of Staten Island show also the name of Rapalje, under which the Rapalies were known.

At the age of twenty-nine, she was the widow of Hans Hansen Bergen, the ancestor of the Bergen family, with seven children. She afterwards married Theunis Gysbert Bogaert, the ancestor of the Bogaert family in this country.

Two travelers, Dankers and Sluyter, in 1679, visited Catelina Trico, who lived in Brooklyn in a little house by herself, "with a garden and other conveniences," and evidently regarded her as a dis-

1 Doc. Hist. N. Y., vol. 3. p. 49-51.

tinguished historical personage.[1] Her progeny numbered 150.

It will be observed that the statement calling her daughter Sarah "the first born Christian daughter in New Netherland", does not conflict with the statement of Jean Vigné that he was the first "male" born of European parents in the province. But of this other Walloon, more hereafter.

Gowanus. At Waal-Bocht (Wallabout) and "Gowanus" as well as at the Ferry, small settlements quickly sprung up.

Gowanus was that part of south Brooklyn called, today, the Gowanus Bay and Gowanus Canal sections. Here William Adriaen Bennet and Jacques Bentyn had bought nine hundred and thirty acres of land. Wallabout and Gowanus formed the nucleus of the present Brooklyn.

The Ferry. The early "ferries" were canoes or small boats. Later on big boats performed the "service" and the first ferry was naturally established between New York and Brooklyn, its earliest neighbor. To avoid as much as possible the labor of stemming the strong current, the narrowest part of the river was chosen, though this was far above the farthest limits of the city, being from a point below "Peck Slip," near Fulton Street on the New York side, to Fulton Street on the Long Island (Brooklyn) side of the river.

This ferry—the Old Ferry, as it afterward came to be called—was maintained as a private enterprise until about the middle of the seventeenth century,

[1] Memoirs of the Long Island Hist. Soc. vol. 1.

when a regular ferry was established, which provided a source of revenue to the city.

As a private venture, this first ferry was established in 1642 by Cornelius Dircksen, who kept a small inn near Peck Slip and owned a farm in the vicinity. Dircksen ferried passengers across the East River for the small price of three stuivers in wampum, meaning nine purple beads or eighteen white beads. (See wampum, Chapter XIX.)

Brooklyn. Between Waal-Bocht (Wallabout) and Gowanus lay a level stretch of territory which the Indians used for growing their corn. To this tract they gave the name of Mareckawieck; through it, lay the road or trail that led from the Ferry to Flatlands, and it was on this trail, and on this fertile tract, right between the present Court House and Flatbush Avenue, that the village of ''Breuckelen''—now the big borough of Brooklyn—had its beginning.[1]

The original name ''Breuckelen'' was derived, it is said, from that of the pretty village about eighteen miles from Amsterdam, (Holland) on the road to Utrecht.

Later on, we note the following political changes: the Act incorporating the Village of Brooklyn passed the State Legislature, April 12, 1816; the Act incorporating the City of Brooklyn passed the State Legislature April 8, 1834; on March 1896, a Bill for the consolidation of New York and Brooklyn, to be effective January 1, 1898, passed the State Legislature. The Charter was signed by Governor Levi P. Morton, May 2, 1897.

[1] Ross. Hist. of Long Island.

Flatbush. Its early name was "Vlacke Bosch" from the two Dutch or Flemish words "vlak" or flat, and "bosch" or woods.

New Utrecht. On the south side of the "Narrows," (fortified strait between Long Island and Staten Island, chief entrance to New York harbor) the lands which had been granted to Cornelius Van Werckhoven remained uninhabited for several years. After his death, Jacques Cortelyou, a surveyor and former agent for Van Werckhoven, laid out a town on those lands, with twenty lots of fifty acres each, and began a settlement, between 1657 and 1661, which was called "New Utrecht" in compliment of Mr. Van Werckhoven's place of birth.

It is well to note that the real name of Cortelyou was Jacques Cortelliau (a Walloon name), so written by himself.[1] He came to America in 1652; in some of the old records the name is spelled "Corteleau." The name was also known on Staten Island.

Bushwick. In 1660, between "Mespath Kill" and "Norman's Kill," Governor Stuyvesant chose a site for a new village. In a year the settlement contained twenty-three families.

The place was called "Boschwijck" from the two Dutch or Flemish words "bosch," or woods, and "wijck" or region, section. Two block houses were built, in 1663, for the defense of that village, now "Bushwick."

Midwoud was then called Middlewout."

Mespath. The little colony of Mespath was called

[1] Clute. Annals of Staten Island, p. 363.

"Middelburgh," but was more familiarly known as "Newtown."

Flatlands. This little town on Long Island was originally called "New Amersfoordt," after the birthplace of the celebrated Dutch statesman, Olden-Barnevelt.

Staten Island. On August 10, 1630, Staten Island was bought, for account of Michael Pauw, in about the same way Manhattan Island had been. For the entire Island, the Indians received some duffels, kettles, axes, hoes, wampum, drilling awls, and divers other small wares.

The duffel is a kind of shaggy woolen fabric usually referred to "Duffel," a Belgian city near Antwerp, where such clothes were made. "The clothing of the Indians, as well of men as of women, consists of a piece of duffels...around the body...which they obtain in trade from the Christians."[1]

Hoboken, Jersey City, Pavonia. The same Michael Pauw bought also Hoboken, so called after a Belgian village of the same name on the River Scheldt, opposite Antwerp.[2] He purchased also "Ahasimus," now Jersey City, and the Jersey shore opposite Manhattan, extending inland a considerable distance. To the latter he gave the name of "Pavonia." The origin of this name is quite amusing. Pauw, in Flemish and in Dutch means a peacock; and Mr. Pauw translating his own name into Latin, got "Pavonia!"

There is now the village of Pavonia, two miles N.E. of Camden, N. J., not far from Gloucester, where, as

[1] N. Y. Col. Doc. 1. 281.
[2] O'Callaghan. Hist. of New Netherland, vol. 1. p. 126.

mentioned previously, the Walloons had erected "Fort Nassau."

Communipaw. Pauw planted also, in New Jersey, a little colony that was called the "Commune." This name, as we have seen in the chapter "Antecedents of Belgium," was adopted in the Middle Ages by self-governing communities, and is still today in Belgium and in France a political division governed by a mayor and a council.

The place where those first colonists settled, is commemorated by the present romantic little village called "Communipaw," a word which bands "Commune" and "Pauw" together: the Commune of Pauw. Many persons mistake it for an Indian name...

Staten Island; Changes in Ownership. Pauw, apparently, never entered upon his purchase or did anything with his Staten Island property, and in 1637 the directors of the West India Company succeeded in purchasing his territorial rights as patroon, for which they paid him twenty-six thousand guilders ($10,400.00). By this arrangement, Pavonia and Staten Island became the property of the Company.[1]

Michael Pauw or de Pauw, died, it is believed, at Ghent, Flanders.

The first attempts at settlement on Staten Island were due to two men: David Petersen De Vries of Hoorn, Holland, and Cornelius Melyn of Antwerp, Belgium.

De Vries evidently did not have a very secure claim to Staten Island, for on July 3, 1640, the directors of the West India Company gave Cornelius Melyn per-

[1] Brodhead. Hist. State of N. Y., vol. 1. p. 268.

mission to establish a colony on Staten Island and acknowledged him as patroon,[1] and De Vries notes, on August 20, 1641, the arrival of Melyn who claimed that Staten Island belonged to him.

The location of this plantation or "Bouwerie" is said to have been at "Tompkinsville" at or near the "watering place" where vessels on their way to sea stopped for water and wood. The watering place is shown on the 1797 map of Staten Island; a copy of this map is in the Staten Island Institute of Arts and Sciences' collection. It is described as "the small rivulet called the watering place," and shown in detail on the Map of Quarantine Property, 1799 (filed in the office of the County Clerk as Map No. 1).

This rivulet (no longer in existence), fed, it is said, by a spring, was less than two hundred feet north of Arietta Street, Tompkinsville, and its outlet was a short distance east of the present railway. It is quite probable that the entire neighborhood of this outlet became known as the "Watering Place."[2]

Cornelius Melyn, the Fleming, who started his colony August 20, 1641, wrote, about 1661, that Staten Island had not been occupied by anybody else but himself, and those who received his permission.[3]

The Waldenses or Waldensians, in French "Vaudois," so called, it is said, after Petrus de Valdo or Waldo, in French Pierre de Vaux, a reformer of the twelfth century. He was born at Vaux, in the old Dauphiné, now forming the French Departments of

[1] N. Y. Col. Doc. 13, p. 200.
[2] George W. Tuttle. Proceedings of Staten Island Institute of Arts and Sciences. Issued August, 1922.
[3] Melyn's Papers in N. Y. Hist. Soc. Coll. 1913.

Isère, Hautes-Alpes, and part of the Drôme. He became an important merchant of the city of Lyons, a place renowned for its silks and, in recent years, attracting much attention by its annual commercial fair known as the "Foire de Lyon," promoted by Mr. Edward Herriot, Mayor of the city, and now the Premier of France.

Vaux or Waldo, after having given all his wealth to the needy, began, with some disciples, to explain the Bible to the people and to dogmatize; in 1136, he formed a brotherhood in which each member became voluntarily poor, and thus known as the "Pauvres de Lyon" (the Poor of Lyons).

They intended to re-establish the ways of the primitive church and to reform the customs of the clergy; they maintained the equal rights of the laity with the clergy to conduct the offices of religion. Their doctrine was condemned by the Roman Church in 1179.

This religious sect, very distinct from the Albigenses (after the name of the city of Albi, in southern France) had, as we have seen, its origin in Lyons, France. It spread over the nearby territory of the Dauphiné, one of the most beautiful sections of Europe, with magnificent scenery, high peaks covered with ice and snow, pleasant valleys, splendid lakes, charming little villages, and gorgeous waterfalls; an enchanting spot of France that all tourists should visit.

The immense amount of power supplied to the electric plants by those numerous waterfalls, induced Mr. Berges, the proprietor of a large factory devoted to the manufacture of wood pulp and paper, located at

Lancey, near Grenoble, to call such power "la houille blanche" or "the white coal," an appropriate name that has become part of the vocabulary of the electrical world.

The Dauphiné, an ancient province of France, now forming the French Departments here above mentioned, was annexed to the Crown, in 1349, under Philip IV, and had for capital the interesting city of Grenoble, now the capital of the Department of Isère, well known for her manufacture of gloves and allied industries, such as button making in which line the leader is the firm of Mr. Achille Raymond, with its model factory of modern machinery.

The Waldenses were terribly persecuted in 1332, 1400, 1478 and 1655, and those who escaped the massacres went to various parts of Europe. Many made their way to Holland, while others fled to the nearby mountains of Piedmont, in Italy, in which places they kept up the exercises of their own faith.

They were variously known as the "Cathares," meaning pure, in Greek; the "Poor of Lyons," on account of their voluntary penury; the "Leonisti," from Lyons their original place; the "Humilitati," an allusion to their humility; the "Sabotati," because they wore wooden shoes.

In December, 1656, the directors of the West India Company informed Governor Stuyvesant that they were about to send Waldenses to New Netherland, for colonization between the Hudson and the Delaware Rivers.

On Christmas Day, 1656, they embarked from Holland on three boats: the "Prince Maurice," the

"Bear" and the "Flower of Guelder." A severe storm separated the squadron, and after a long voyage the "Prince Maurice," with most of the emigrants on board, struck on the south coast of Long Island near Fire Island Inlet.

The shipwrecked emigrants, and most of the cargo, were brought in safety to New Amsterdam, where the other vessels had already arrived. A few weeks later, 1657, they were sent to the banks of the Delaware River, while some, it is believed, remained in Manhattan.

In the course of the following years, more Waldensian families came over from Holland, and most of them established themselves on Staten Island.

Cornelius Melyn, the Belgian, who began the colonization of Staten Island, in 1641, long before the arrival of the Waldenses, surrendered to the West India Company, in 1661, his claims to the Island, for which he received fifteen hundred guilders, an indemnity for his losses, the promise of certain privileges as a "free colonist and inhabitant" in New Netherland, and a "full amnesty with regard to all disputes." [1]

Grants of land on Staten Island, were presently made to various persons, among whom were several French Waldenses, and afterward many Huguenots from La Rochelle.

Harlem. In 1658, the village of "New Harlem" was laid out, on the northern end of Manhattan Island. Of thirty-two male inhabitants of adult age, in 1661, nearly one-half were Walloons and Frenchmen.

Among the early Walloon pioneers in Harlem were:

[1] Brodhead. Hist. State of N. Y., vol. 1. p. 692.

Isaack de Forest (son of Jesse de Forest), the founder of that family in America; his wife, Sara du Trieux, was the daughter of Philippe du Trieux, a worsted-dyer from Roubaix, then in Belgian Flanders; Jean Gervoe from Beaumont, near Avesnes; David du Four from Mons; Jean de Pré from Comines, near Lille; Simon de Ruine from Valenciennes; etc.

Conspicuous in the little colony of New Harlem was this de Ruine, familiarly called "de Waal" by the Dutch, and "le Wallon" by those who spoke French.[1]

The Belgian family Kortright, or Courtright, was one of the most wealthy in landed possessions in Harlem.[2] Kortryk (in French Courtrai) was and is still a city of Belgium, in Flanders, on the River Lys. It has a universal reputation for the manufacture of fine linen, and there, also, are made those beautiful laces known as "Valenciennes."

In history, Kortryk or Courtrai, recalls the famous battle of the "Golden Spurs," fought in 1302. In this terrible encounter, the noblemen of Philip IV, King of France, and their commander, Robert of Artois, were annihilated by the soldiers of the Flemish Communes. Seven hundred golden spurs taken from the battlefield were hung as trophies on the walls of the church of Notre-Dame, hence the name of this battle. It is also known as the battle of Courtrai, or the battle of Groeninghe.

Population in 1660. The little town of New Amsterdam, located in the section of what is now Wall Street and lower Broadway, had two hundred poorly con-

[1] Riker. Hist. of Harlem, page 111.
[2] Riker. Hist. of Harlem, page 74.

structed houses to give meagre comfort to some fourteen hundred people.

Other Walloons Arrive. For several years after
Stuyvesant's arrival, the ships of the West India
Company continued to bring colonists to New Amster-
dam, and at that time we find the names of Arnout du
Tois, of Lille; Jean le Clercq and Adrien Fournie, of
Valenciennes; Simon Drune, Bastien Clement and
Adrien Vincent of Tournai; Juste Kockuyt, of Brug-
es; Meynard Journeay, Walravens Luten, and Juste
Houpleine, from Flanders. (The French cities men-
tioned in this paragraph were still Belgian territory
at that time.)

Louis du Bois. In 1660, still another expedition of
the oppressed Walloons who had temporarily sought
refuge along the banks of the Rhine, came to America.
Under the leadership of Louis du Bois, they settled
at Esopus and began the towns of Kingston and New
Paltz.[1]

Louis was the son of Chrétien du Bois, an inhabitant of Wieres, a hamlet in the district of La Barrée,
near Lille, (then in Flanders), where he was born on
October 27, 1627.[2]

At that time, as we have seen, the provinces of
Belgium, including Flanders, were under Spanish
rule. The southern parts of Flanders and Hainault
became French territory only in 1678, after the treaty
of peace of Nimegue; the ceded territory was then
officially named French Flanders and French Hainault.

[1] Jones in Lee's Hist. of N. America, vol. 4. p. 181.
[2] Baird.   Hist. Hug. Em. America, vol. 1. p. 187.

But even before part of Belgian Flanders belonged to France, many called it "French Flanders" because good French was spoken there by the Belgians. The latter consideration makes the subject rather complicated. Many Walloons were living there, and, at one time, Lille had become to the Walloons what Ypres, its great rival, which lay but fifteen miles to the northwest, was to the Flemings—the chief emporium of their cloth manufacture.[1]

One should be careful in the use of the expression "French Flanders," which finds its correct application only after 1678. Before this date the territory was part of the county of Flanders, and belongs to the history of Belgium.

Louis du Bois left his native province in his early manhood, and removed, as many others were doing, to the Lower Palatinate.[2] This Calvinistic State, which had taken the lead among the Protestant powers of Germany, now offered a refuge to the oppressed Protestants of other lands.

A little colony of Walloons, flying before the troops of the Duke of Alva, had come to settle within the territory of the Palatinate, at Frankenthal, near Mannheim, its capital, where we find many families that later on removed to New Netherland: David de Marest, Frederic de Vaux, Abraham Hasbroucq, Chrétien Duyou, Mathese or Matthew Blanchan, Thonnet Terrin, Pierre Parmentier, Antoine Crispel, David Usilie, Philippe Casier, Bourgeon Broucard, Simon Le Febre, Juste Durie, and others.

[1] Riker. Hist. of Harlem, p. 67.
[2] In the old German empire, a political division ruled over by a Prince; the Lower or Rhine Palatinate.

There, at Mannheim, on October 10, 1655, Louis du Bois married Catherine, daughter of Mathese Blanchan, who was also from Flanders. Two sons, Abraham and Isaac, were born of this marriage.

Louis du Bois and some of his fellow refugees decided to emigrate to America, and in order to understand better the Walloon colonization along the River Hudson, a brief outline of the situation there, just previous to the arrival of du Bois, is presented as follows:

In 1655, the Indians attacked little settlements on the Hudson, and the few inhabitants at "Esopus" fled to other places; some of them returned after the conclusion of peace. But in 1658 the savages resumed their attacks, and the people, apparently, abandoned their homes and fields, as they were advised by Governor Stuyvesant to lay out another town spot which was called "Wiltwyck," and to "fortify" it.

Wiltwyck, however, did not long enjoy tranquility, for in the following year another outbreak of Indian ferocity occurred, and several hundred Indian warriors invested the little village, and again the small population was scattered. The intervention of Stuyvesant brought peace in July, 1660.

It was at this time that Louis du Bois and his countrymen arrived in New Amsterdam, just when lands in the fertile Esopus Valley were to be had for the asking, and when provision was made for the religious instruction of the settlers.[1]

The families forming the group of followers of du

[1] Baird. Hist. Huguenot Em. America, vol. 1. p. 192.

Bois came over early in 1660, by the Dutch ship "Gilded Otter," and more arrived soon thereafter.

Esopus. Their stay in New Amsterdam was short. Taking counsel doubtless of their Walloon countrymen, they soon decided upon a place of settlement, and by the latter part of the year 1660, Mathese Blanchan and Antoine Crispel, with their families, had established themselves in Esopus where Louis du Bois, and his wife and sons, joined them a few months later.[1]

A clergyman of the Reformed Church of Holland, Hermanus Blom, was sent over to minister at Esopus, and, says Baird, certain it is that among the persons admitted to the Lord's Supper, upon the occasion of its first celebration in Esopus, on December 7, 1660, were Mathese Blanchan with Madeleine Jorisse, his wife, and Antoine Crispel with Maria Blanchan, his wife.

To this section of the west side of the Hudson River, the Dutch "traders," before the settlement of New Amsterdam, went to traffic with the then friendly Indians. And here at Esopus Creek, in 1623, as we have seen, the ship "New Netherland" on her way to Albany, stopped to lighten her cargo.

A difference of opinion exists as to whether the Indian tribe "Esopus" took this name from the River Esopus or whether the river was named for the tribe. Schoolcraft gives "seepus" or "seepu," "river," as the word nearest like it in the Indian language.

Kingston. The territory where, after many wanderings, the Walloon refugees had finally found a home, was splendidly located near the romantic Hud-

[1] Baird.   Hist. Huguenot Em. America, vol. 1, p. 189.

son. The plateau upon which the village of Wiltwyck stood was skirted by the Esopus creeks and the beautiful valley of the Wallkill opened toward the southwest, while on the north the Catskill Mountains displayed their wooded slopes.

The familiar trio of Du Bois, Blanchan, Crispel, left their countrymen at Esopus and came to settle at Wiltwyck, where they were soon joined by a fourth Walloon family, that of Rachel de la Montagne, daughter of Jean de la Montagne, and now wife of Gysbert Imborch.[1]

Wiltwyck is frequently spelled Wildwyck, which, in Dutch, means "wild section" or "wild country." While under British rule, it got the name of Kingston, from the city in England, and is today the capital of Ulster County. It was incorporated as a city, in 1872, by the junction of the former incorporated villages of Kingston, and Rondout (also in existence at the time of the Walloon settlement) and the small village of Wilbur.

Wallkill. In the previous paragraph, there is mention of the beautiful valley of the Wallkill, now a famous dairy region.

The Wallkill River, a large and important mill stream, rises in Sussex County, N. J., flows north into New York State, crosses Orange and Ulster Counties and empties into the Rondout, after a course of about 115 miles.

The composition of the word "Wallkill" also bears testimony to the presence of the early Walloon settlers. The Dutch called "kil" (and still spell it

[1] Baird. Hist. of Huguenot Em. America, vol. 1. p. 193.

"kil" and not "kill"), a current of water, a stream;[1] and as for the word "wall"—English spelling—it stands for the Dutch word "Waal," meaning "Walloon," and so the "Wallkill" is in reality "Waalkil" or Walloon's Stream. The sound of this Dutch word is responsible for its customary English spelling. Near this river, is the Wallkill village, in Ulster County.

The origin of the names Wallkill and Wallabout (already explained) is of particular interest, in the consideration of first settlements.

Hurley. A mile or so west of Wiltwyck, our Walloons founded a settlement then called "New Village." Unfortunately, it was built upon lands claimed by the Indians, who, after a successful attack, burned every dwelling. The "New Village" was reduced to ashes, and eight women with twenty-six children were taken prisoners; they included the wife and three children of Louis du Bois, the two children of Mathese Blanchan, and Antoine Crispel's wife and child, who had just moved to the new settlement from Wiltwyck. The rest of the people had taken to the woods.

Wiltwyck was also attacked and sustained severe losses. Among the persons now taken away by the Indians were Rachel de la Montagne, and the wife and child of the clergyman Blom. Armed parties were organized to rescue the prisoners; Rachel de la Montagne escaped from the Indian camp and supplied the rescuing party with accurate informations.

[1] See the spelling "kil" in "Documents relating to the Hist. and Settlements of the towns along the Hudson," Vol. XIII, old series, by Fernow. Albany, 1881.

After much delay and difficulties the expedition, led by Krygier, having taken the Indians by surprise, routed them, and brought the captives back to the settlements.

The "New Village," first settled by the Walloons in 1662, was later on called "Hurley," after the Lovelace family, who were Barons Hurley. Col. Lovelace was appointed Governor of New York, in 1668, and was active in settling the County of Ulster, where he laid out the "town" of Hurley, so named after his ancestral seat in Berkshire, England.

New Paltz. Once more, war was over! In the terrific contests between the "Whites" and the "Reds," the Esopus Indians were almost exterminated.

> "All beside thy limpid waters,
>   All beside thy sands so bright;
> Indian Chiefs and Christian warriors,
>   Joined in fierce and mortal fight."
>
> *(Spanish Ballad, in Percy.)*

More colonists had arrived, and further expansion became necessary. Louis the Walloon, as du Bois was often called, and his companions, continued their favorite work of building up settlements. Remembering their days of exile in the Palatinate, they called their latest home and surroundings, 1663, "Le Nouveau Palatinat" (New Palatinate) and therefore their village is known as New Paltz.

All those localities: Esopus, Kingston, Rondout, Wallkill, Hurley, and New Paltz are in Ulster County, whose early records are first in French—the language of the Walloons—then in Dutch, and finally in English.

Walloomsac River and Valley. This name is a corruption of "Walloonsac." [1]

The Walloomsac River rises in Bennington County, State of Vermont, takes a northwest direction, leaves the State near the northwest corner of Bennington, and unites with the Hoosac River, near the border line between Washington and Renselaer Counties, in the State of New York. The Hoosac, called "Hoosick," in New York, empties into the Hudson fifteen miles above Troy.

The east branch of Hoosac River, known as St. Croix, was first settled by Walloons, from which arose the name "Walloonsac" or "Walloomsac." [1]

The clergyman Michaelius, whom we have seen as administering the first Lord's Supper to the Walloons of Manhattan, in 1628, recorded in 1630 that "The Hoosac and Mahicansac Tribes have fled," and "their lands are very fertile and pleasant."

The Walloons, in their quest for lands suitable for plantations, came across those abandoned fertile lands, and noted the ruins of Fort St. Croix built by the men of that Frenchman Jean Allefonsce, a fur trader, already mentioned in Chapter III as having come from Canada to the Hudson River in 1542. The lucky Belgian adventurers settling there, christened St. Croix River the "Walloon Creek"; the Schaghticoke Indians subsequently deeded the valley to them as the "Walloomsac Tract." [2]

[1] G. G. Niles. The Hoosac Valley, p. 519.
[2] G. G. Niles. The Hoosac Valley, p. 20.

As recorded in the Albany Archives, the name has fifty different spellings. Carlos Botta, the Italian historian, refers to the Battle of Bennington, directed by General Stark, in 1777, as won on "the banks of the Walloon Creek," now known as the Walloonsac.[1]

Ghent. This time, we have a true Flemish name.

The elaborate stage coaches, drawn by six and eight spirited horses, made between 1832 and 1874, the journey from Boston to Albany, over the Stone Post Road, in forty-eight hours. Relays of horses were made at several points along the line, namely at "Charlemont Inn," on Hoosac Mountain, and at "Walloonsac Inn."

On the southern road from Albany to Boston was another famous tavern, in the little town of "Ghent," in Columbia County, New York.

Waal-bocht or Wallabout, Waalkil or Wallkill, and Walloonsac or Walloomsac,—from Long Island to Vermont—are indelible marks of the early Walloon settlements in America.

Hellgate or Hellegat. Name given, in 1614, by Adriaen Block to the whole East River. It now applies only to the pass, seven miles from New York.

The name is after the branch of the River Scheldt, situated between Axel and Hulst, in Flanders.[2] One can well call it Belgian Flanders as it was only after the Treaty of Munster, in 1648, as we have seen in chapter VII, that Spain abandoned to the Dutch Republic northern parts of Flanders, Limbourg and

[1] Carlos Botta. Hist. War. Independence, book 8, p. 34. George Otis. Trans. 1826.
[2] O'Callaghan. Hist. New Netherland, vol. 1. p. 72.

Brabant such as Axel, Hulst, l'Ecluse, Breda, Bois-le-Duc, Bergen-op-Zoom, Maestricht, etc.

Governor's Island. The early settlers of New York took a foothold there, and used it also as a good place where to keep their cattle and sheep. They called it "Noten Island" (Island of the Nuts) because excellent nut trees grew there. In 1637, Governor Wouter Van Twiller bought it for himself, and from then on it was called Governor's Island. The Indians called it "Pagganck."

Coney Island, N. Y., now the rendez-vous of pleasure seekers, was called by the Walloons "Isle aux Lapins" or "Island of the Rabbits," from which it took its present English name of same meaning. Did the Walloons raise the Belgian hare there?

Pierre Le Moyne d'Iberville,[1] in his "Memoir on Boston and its Dependencies, 1701," wrote: "The entrance into the river at New York is difficult for the space of two leagues, as far as "Isle aux Lapins" where but sixteen to seventeen feet of water are to be found, following the sinuosities of the channel, and where tacking is impossible."

"It is four leagues from Isle aux Lapins to New York where there is plenty of water. The passage lies between Long and Staten Islands, which are half a league apart. Staten Island, which is fully seven leagues in circumference, may have four hundred and

---

1. A French-Canadian from Montreal, distinguished himself in many actions against the English. He commanded a vessel sent by the French Government to explore the mouth of the Mississippi, which he discovered in 1699, and established the first French colony in Louisiana.

fifty effective men, most of whom are Walloons, Dutchmen, with a few English." [1]

The Dutch translation for the Walloon or French word "lapin" is "konyn," and on Joan Vingsoon's Map of 1639, the Island is mentioned as "Conine Island"; the Labadists in the narrative of their voyage of 1679, call it "Conynen Island." As to the English translation of "lapin" it is rabbit, or cony or "coney," as in the expressions "cony-wool" or rabbit's hair, and "cony-burrow."

De Laet's Island, N. Y. On the "Map of Rensselaer's Wyck, Anno 1630," a copy of which is to be found in Dr. O'Callaghan's "History of New Netherland," vol. 1, one can see "De Laets Island," [2] and "De Laet's Burg" (a redoubt) opposite Fort Orange, now Albany; between De Laet's Island and the Burg was De Laet's Mill Creek and Waterfall.

Who was De Laet? He is often mistaken for a Dutchman but John or Jan De Laet was a Belgian, a Fleming, born in Antwerp, in 1582, who migrated to Leyden, like so many other Belgian Protestants, and in 1597, at the age of 15 was matriculated at the Leyden University.

He was a director in the Amsterdam Chamber of the West India Company founded by his countryman Usselinx, also from Antwerp as we have seen. De Laet was a well-known historian who published, in 1625, through the famous house of Elzevir, [3] in Ley-

---

[1] Paris Documents: VI, in N. Y. Col. Doc., vol. IX, p. 729.
[2] It was encircled by the Hudson and a creek; the latter having been filled in, the land is no longer an island, and has now no particular name.
[3] Elzevir, name of a famous family of publishers and printers, established in Holland during the 16th and 17th centuries. The best known

den, a large folio volume in Dutch, entitled: "Nieuwe Wereldt, ofte Beschryvinghe van West—Indien" (New World, or Description of West India, i.e., America), which at once took high rank among such publications.

A new edition of the book was published in Dutch in 1630. It contains some additional matter in the chapters devoted to New Netherland, and an interesting map of "Nova Anglia, Novum Belgium and Virginia," the middle part of which is reproduced in Windsor's Narrative and Critical History of America, vol. 4, p. 436.

In 1633, a Latin version, "Novus Orbis" was published in eighteen books, and in 1640 a French, "Histoire du Nouveau Monde." In both, the map above mentioned appears unchanged, nor are additional authorities cited in the preface. But both those later editions show signs of that increasing interest in natural history which marked De Laet's later years; they contain many excellent plates of American animals and plants.

In those editions of 1625 and 1630 is to be found a description of the voyage of Henry Hudson to America.

De Laet was also a man of science. In the medical garden of Leyden he cultivated plants sent to him from New Netherland. The botanical species "Laet-

are Louis Elzevir, born at Louvain, Belgium, in 1540, who went to Leyden and who founded the reputation of the firm; Bonaventure, his son, printer at Leyden from 1618 to 1653, and Abraham, brother and partner of the latter. They produced those masterpieces of typography which have immortalized the name of "Elzevir."

ia" was named after De Laet by the celebrated Swedish naturalist, "Linnaeus," himself.

De Laet died at Leyden in 1649. He seems never to have visited America, but his daughter, Johanna, is recorded as living in New Netherland from 1653 to 1673, at least, as the wife successively of Johan de Hulter and of Jeronimus Ebbingh.[1]

Pennsylvania. Peter Laurensen, a servant to the West India Company, who came to New Netherland in 1628, in his deposition made before Governor Dongan, on March 24, 1685 (Deed Book VII, and Doct. Hist. N. Y., vol. 3, p. 50) says that by order of his employers, he and seven more, were, in the year 1630, sent in a sloop to Delaware, and that upon an Island near the falls of that river, and near the "west side thereof" —meaning "Verhulsten Island" in the State of Pennsylvania, near the bend of the Delaware at Trenton—the said company, "some three or four years before", had a trading house where there were three or four families of "Walloons"; the place of their settlement he saw.[2]

Walloons and Swedes in the State of Delaware. We have just noticed a Walloon settlement on the Delaware in the State of Pennsylvania, and previously we have seen that four couples who had been married on board the "New Netherland" in 1623, went to form a settlement on the Delaware near Gloucester, New Jersey.

As to the colonization of the State of Delaware by the Swedes, it was due to Belgian initiative. Belgian

[1] Jameson. Narratives of New Netherland.
[2] Brodhead. Hist. State of N. Y., vol. 2, p. 160.

refugees in Holland, had, in great numbers, migrated to Sweden, where they duplicated the splendid work they had done in the Dutch Republic. Thus it was now the turn of Sweden to become wealthy and great through Belgian skill and co-operation.

It was mainly in metallurgy, in which the Walloons excelled—and are still masters today—that the exiles were showing their extraordinary ability which so greatly contributed to the improvement and expansion of the iron industry of Sweden.

In those days, about 1628, the Belgian Louis de Geer, from Liége, was as well known in the iron industry of Sweden as Carnegie and Schwab are now known in the steel industry of America. De Geer brought into Sweden thousands of Walloons, able iron and mine workers; hundreds of Belgians had enrolled in the Swedish army.

Official and public recognition of Belgian participation in the welfare of Sweden, was and is still alive in that country where the descendants of those Walloon immigrants of the 16th and 17th centuries thrive in great number.

As early as 1624, the Belgian William Usselinx from Antwerp, the original promoter of the Dutch West India Company, had drawn up a plan for the promotion of a similar company in Sweden.

Swedish West India Company. The above scheme from which originated the settlement of Delaware, was adopted by Gustavus Adolphus then King of Sweden, and confirmed by the Diet. A company called the "Swedish West India Company" was formed, and received a charter on July 2, 1626.

Usselinx's description created a perfect furor among all ranks in Sweden; subscription books were opened and there was great rivalry in securing stock. King Gustavus himself pledged the Royal Treasury to the extent of four hundred thousand Swedish dollars.[1] The King called the undertaking "the jewel of his kingdom."

The project was in a fair way to be executed when the Thirty Years' War, and then the death of the King, at the Battle of Lutzen, in 1632, became serious causes for postponement.

King Gustavus was succeeded by his daughter "Christina," a child of six years of age. The States entrusted the government, during her minority, to a regency, at the head of which was Chancellor Axel, Count of Oxenstiern; the Swedish Chancellor viewed the consequences of American colonization as "favorable to all Christendom, to Europe, and to the whole world." In consequence he published, 1633, the Nuremberg Proclamation, which Gustavus had left unsigned, and he appointed as first director of the company William Usselinx,[2] and the next year, 1634, the charter which Oxenstiern prepared for the Swedish West India Company, and containing extension of the privileges to the citizens of Germany, was confirmed by the Deputies of the German Circles at Frankfort.

Peter Minuit was no longer in the service of the Dutch West India Company, and having gone to Stockholm he offered to the Regency the benefit of his

---

[1] Jones in Lee's Hist. of N. America, vol. 4, p. 44; Brodhead. Hist. State of N. Y., vol. 1. p. 280.

[2] Jones in Lee's Hist. of N. America, vol. 4, p. 44.

colonial experience; it was Minuit, the Belgian, and not his countryman Usselinx who finally led the Swedes to the Delaware River.

This, however, did not take place until about the end of 1637, when Minuit sailed from Gottenburg with a commission from the infant Queen "signed by eight of the chief Lords of Sweden" to plant a new colony on the west side of the Delaware Bay, a region probably suggested by Minuit.

The emigrants, about fifty, very likely included some Belgians, then so numerous in Sweden, and so well known for their initiative and skill. They were on an armed ship "The Key of Calmar" and on a tender "The Griffin." The little expedition, led by Minuit, arrived in the Delaware Bay in the early part of 1638. A clergyman, Reorus Torkillus, accompanied the expedition.

Minuit, an expert buyer of lands, as proved when he bought Manhattan Island, in 1626, now bought from the Indians a stretch of land running from Newcastle and Wilmington up to the Schuylkill River, for the consideration of—a copper kettle and some trifles.

The fort erected by the newcomers was called "Fort Christina," the creek "Christina Creek," and the settlement "Christinaham" and later on "New Sweden."

Voyage of Labadists to America.[1] Two Labadists from Holland came to visit America in 1679, and the description they made of their voyage contains many

---

[1] Labadists, a Calvinistic sect or followers of Jean de Labadie.

interesting details about the Walloons they met in New York.

Here are a few of such impressions taken from their own narrative called: "Journal of a Voyage to New York and a Tour in Several of the American Colonies, in 1679-1680," by Jaspaar Dankers and Peter Sluyter, (the two Labadists). Their "Journal" was translated, from the original manuscript in Dutch, by Henry C. Murphy.[1]

De Lanoy. The two Labadists tell us that the commissary in the Custom House who examined their luggage, was Peter De Lanoy. This is a good old Belgian name! In the "Antecedents of Belgium" we have seen "Charles de Lannoy" of an old family from Flanders, taking the King of France, Francis I, as prisoner at the Battle of Pavia, 1525.

Peter De Lanoy became Collector of the Port of New York, and was Mayor of the City, 1688-1689, under Jacob Leisler, and a Member of his Council. He was the first Mayor elected by the popular voice, the city charter being suspended at the time in consequence of the Leislerian troubles.

"Abraham De Lanoy," the schoolmaster, was the brother of Peter.

Rombouts. Before De Lanoy, another Belgian had become Mayor of the City of New York in 1679. He was François Rombouts, born at Hasselt, in the Flemish section of Belgium. He resided in Broadway, south of Trinity Church, where he was a merchant; he died in 1691.

---

[1] This English translation is in "Memoirs of the Long Island Historical Society," vol. 1.

Cornelis Steenwyck, Mayor of New York from 1668 to 1670, and also in 1682-83, was of the old Belgian stock.[1] He had been appointed Governor pro tem, during the temporary absence of Governor Lovelace; he was wealthy, and under both Dutch and English administrations was extremely popular. He probably exercised a more healthful influence over the public mind than any other man of his time.[1]

A Walloon from Liége. In Brooklyn, wrote the two Labadists, "we came to a place surrounded with peach trees, from which so many fruit had fallen off that the ground could not be discerned, and you could not put your feet down without trampling them; and, notwithstanding such large quantities had fallen off, the trees still were as full as they could bear."

"This place belongs to the oldest European woman in the country. We went immediately into her house, where she lived with her children. We found her sitting by the fire, smoking tobacco incessantly, one pipe after another. We inquired after her age, which the children told us was an hundred years. She was from Liége, Belgium, and still spoke good Waalsche (Walloon) with us. She had been about fifty years now in the country, and had about seventy children and grandchildren. She saw the third generation after her."

Unfortunately, the Labadists do not mention the name of this old Walloon woman.

Van Helmont's Book, in Burlington. Our Labadists went to Burlington, on the Delaware, in New Jersey, opposite Matinakonk, or Chygoe's Island, and

[1] Martha Lamb. Hist. of N. Y., vol. 1. p. 234.

they tell us "that the Island, formerly belonged to the Dutch Governor, who had made it a pleasure ground or garden, built good houses upon it, and sowed and planted it and that the English Governor at the Manathans, now held it for himself and had hired it out to some Quakers,[1] who were now living upon it at present."

"We entered the ordinary exhorter's house, where we breakfasted with Quakers, but the most worldly of men in·all their deportment and conversation."

"We found lying upon the window a book of 'Virgil'[2] and also Helmont's book on 'Medicine,' whom, in an introduction, which they have made to it, they make pass for one of their sect, although in his lifetime he did not know anything about Quakers; but it seems these people will make all those who have had any genius in any respect, more than common, pass for theirs; which is certainly great pride, wishing to place themselves far above all others."

This finding, in 1679, among settlers on the Delaware, of a book on "Medicine" by "Helmont"—as our Labadists spell it—is of interest, for Jean-Baptiste "van Helmont"—correct spelling—was a celebrated Belgian physician, a Fleming, born at Brussels, in 1577. At the University of Louvain he occupied the chair of Professor of Surgery.

Van Helmont, says Dr. Hoefer, "is much superior to Paracelsus (professor of Medicine at Basle, in 1526) whom he took, in some measure, as his model.

[1] "The Society of Friends," a Protestant body commonly known as "Quakers"; but this name is not used by the Society.
[2] A Roman epic poet (70-19 B. C., author of the Æneid).

He had the durable glory of revealing scientifically the existence of invisible, impalpable substances, namely gases." He was the first who used the word "gas" as the name of all elastic fluids except common air.

Among his works are one on the magnetic cure of wounds, and one on "The Origin of Medicine," etc.

Van Helmont died at Vilvorde, near Brussels, in 1644. One of the streets of Brussels bears the name of this great physician.

Jean Vigné. To those two Labadist visitors, we are also indebted for information concerning this Walloon.

They wrote: "We conversed with the first male born of Europeans in New Netherland, named Jean Vigné. His parents were from Valenciennes, and he was now about sixty-five years of age."

No authentic record of his birth exists; some writers have made the Labadists say that Vigné was born in 1614, but the visitors did not write this as will be seen by their narrative reproduced hereabove; they did not mention the year 1614.

In 1679, they wrote that Vigné was "about" sixty-five years of age, and consequently he must have been born not in 1614, but about that time, if not many years later, for what is meant by "about 65 years of age" is not easy to determine exactly. Furthermore, the Labadists' narrative does not say whether Vigné himself told them that he was about 65 years old, or that they (the Labadists) judged him to be about sixty-five.

His physical condition might have given him the

appearance of a man about ten years older than his real age, and consequently he would have been about fifty-five years of age, and thus born in 1624, that is to say at the time of the first landing of the Walloons in Manhattan. In any event the Labadists did not mention the year 1614, and there is no authentic record of his birth.

It is well to recall that Jan Block who passed the winter of 1613-1614 on the lower part of Manhattan Island did not mention the Vigné family; and furthermore that there were no settlements of Europeans on Manhattan at that time. That Jean Vigné, born of Belgian Walloon parents, was in New Amsterdam, is well proved as we find him to be a schepen (official) of the city in 1655-56 and 1661-63.

Henry C. Murphy who translated into English the "Journal" of the Labadists was too hasty in taking for granted the year 1614 as the correct date of the birth of Vigné, and this error led him to believe that there was a Dutch settlement on Manhattan at that time.

Here is, exactly, what the Labadists wrote: "Syne ouders waren van Valencyn en hij was nu ontrent 65 jaer out." (His parents were from Valenciennes, and he was now 'about' 65 years old.) These sentences are as presented by Henry C. Murphy himself.[1]

Catalina Trico. The same Labadists tell us that Catalina Trico (the wife of George de Rapalie or Rapalje), with whom they had a conversation in Brooklyn, was also from Valenciennes, and that La

[1] Memoirs of Long Island Hist. Soc., vol. I., pp. 114-115.

Grange, who had a little shop in New York, was her nephew.

The Bouwerij. This was then a village which the Labadists visited on their way to New Harlem. A bouwerie was a farm with large tracts of cultivable lands.

The Bronx. One Jonas Bronck bought a valuable tract in West Chester "over against Haarlem," and from him the Bronx River and Section derived their names.

Yonkers. In 1639, Governor Kief secured for the Company from the Indian owners of "Kekesick" all the territory which lies over against the flats of the Island of Manhates, adjoining "the great kill." This purchase is supposed to have included the present town of Yonkers.

In 1646, Kief granted to Adriaen Vander Donck the privilege of a patroon over those lands. The new patroonship was soon afterward formally named "Colen Donck" or Donck's Colony. The Dutch, however, familiarly called the Vander Donck's estate "de Jonkheer's Landt." Jonkheer is a title usually applied in Holland to a young nobleman; it had a more extended significance in New Netherland. The English, afterward, corrupted the word "Jonkheer's" into Yonkers.

Vander Donck died in New Amsterdam, in 1655, leaving his estate of Yonkers to his wife, who subsequently married Hugh O'Neal.

Whale Island. Vander Donck, in his "Beschryvinge van Nieuw Nederlandt," speaks of two whales having swum up the North River, in March, 1647; one

of which grounding on an Island near "the great Co-
hoes' Falls," since known as Walvisch or Whale Island, afforded the colonists a supply of oil besides
causing the river to be covered with grease for three
weeks.

The second edition of his book, hereabove mentioned, contains a map of the Province, reduced from
the larger one of Visscher with the title: "Nova Belgica sive Nieuw Nederlandt" (New Belgium or New
Netherland). It is reproduced in Chapter XV of this
volume.

Pelham. Thomas Pell, an English gentleman,
in 1654 bought of Chief Annhook a tract of land in
Westchester, including the estate formerly owned and
occupied by Mrs. Anne Hutchinson, murdered by the
Indians; it included also the present township of New
Rochelle. Pelham derives from Pell, and ham, a
home or house. Hame (Scot.)=home.

Geographic names in the United States, connected
with Belgian settlements and memories:

Antwerp in the States of New York, Ohio, Michigan.
Belgium in the States of New York, Wisconsin.
Boistfort in the State of Washington.
Brussels in the States of Illinois, Wisconsin, Missouri.
Charleroi in the State of Pennsylvania.
De Smet in the States of Idaho, South Dakota. Named for
    the Belgian Jesuit Missionary, Peter John de Smet.
Flanders in the States of New York, New Jersey.
Fleming in the States of Georgia, New York, Pennsylvania,
    Ohio, Texas, etc.
Floreffe in the State of Pennsylvania.
Ghent in the States of New York, Minnesota, Kentucky,
    Pennsylvania.

Hennepin in the States of Minnesota and Illinois. Named for the Belgian Missionary, Louis Hennepin.

Hoboken in the States of New Jersey, Pennsylvania, Alabama, Georgia, Indiana.

Jeannette in the State of Pennsylvania. Named for the daughter of the Belgian director of the glassworks of that place.

Kortright in the State of New York. After the Kortright family, important landowners.

Leopold in the State of Indiana. Named for Leopold I, King of the Belgians.

Namur in the State of Wisconsin.

Ostend in the State of Pennsylvania.

Philipsville in the State of Pennsylvania. From Philippeville in the Province of Namur.

Pepin in the States of Wisconsin and Minnesota. A lake named for Pepin le Bref (Pepin the Short).

Rubens in the State of Kansas.

Saint Anthony in the State of Minnesota. Falls discovered and named by the Missionary, Louis Hennepin. Also a town named for the falls.

Solvay in the State of New York. For the Solvay Process Works located there.

Spa. In many compound place names.

Van Leuven Corners in the State of New York. Named for the Van Leuven family. (Leuven is the Flemish translation for Louvain.)

Wallonia in the State of Kentucky.

Waterloo in at least twenty States of the Union.

The above are taken at random. Besides Dutch names showing a Walloon origin such as Wallabout, Wallkill, Walloonsack, etc., and names of Flemish origin confounded with Dutch, there are other names apparently improperly spelled, approaching the names of Belgian localities, such as, for example, Danvers in Massachusetts, and Dardenne in Missouri.

CHAPTER XI

THE Bible, the "Belgic Confession," and the Heidelberg Catechism were the spiritual guides of the Protestants.

Now, what is the Belgic Confession? Many people do not know what it is though they are using it daily. It is simply that "Confession of Faith" based on Calvinistic doctrines, the recognized symbol of the Reformed Churches in Belgium and Holland, as well as *the doctrinal standard of the Reformed (Dutch) Church in the United States,* which holds to it even more tenaciously than the mother church in the Netherlands.

The Walloons proudly brought it with them to New York, for the author of this Confession—now the one professed by hundreds of thousands in the United States and other countries—was their own countryman "Guido de Bray," born at Mons, Hainault, in 1522, and this is why it has received the name of "Belgic Confession."

The Rev. William Elliot Griffis in his "Belgium: The Land of Art," says: "Not least among the honors of the Belgic people is this noble piece of literature, flowing out from the heart and intellect of a grand people, nor least worthy of renown, among the men of the ages is the Walloon Guido de Bray." And further, he adds: "It is acknowledged to be one of the clearest, as it is, in many ways, the best statement of the Reformed Faith."

For full details, see: Philip Schaff, "The Creeds of Christendom," vol. 1. pp. 502-508, and vol. 3. pp. 383-436; also "The New Schaff-Herzog Encyclopedia of Religious Knowledge," vol. 2. The Belgic Confession is also mentioned, but simply referred to, in "Ecclesiastical Records," published by the State of New York, under the supervision of Hugh Hastings, State Historian. See "Index" in vol. 7, of that work.

History. The Belgic Confession is a statement of belief written in French, in 1561, by Guido de Bray aided by H. Saravia (professor of theology in Leyden, afterward in Cambridge), H. Modetus (for some time chaplain of William of Orange), and G. Wingen. It was revised by Francis Junius of Bourges, a student of Calvin, pastor of a Walloon congregation at Antwerp, and afterward professor of theology at Leyden, who abridged the sixteenth article and sent a copy to Geneva and other churches, for approval. It was probably printed in 1562, or at all events in 1566, and afterward translated into Dutch, German, and Latin. It was presented to Philip II, in 1562, with the hope of securing toleration. It was formally adopted by synods at Antwerp (1566), Wesel (1568), Emden (1571), Dort (1574), Middelburg (1581), and again by the great synod of Dort, April 29, 1619.

Inasmuch as the Arminians had demanded partial changes, and the text had become corrupt, the Synod of Dort submitted the French, Latin, and Dutch texts to a careful revision, 1619. Since that time the Belgic Confession, together with the Heidelberg Catechism, has been the recognized symbol of the Reformed Churches in Holland and Belgium. It is also the doctrinal standard of the Reformed (Dutch) Church in the United States.

The Confession contains thirty-seven articles, and follows the order of the Gallican Confession, but is less polemical and more full and elaborate, especially on the Trinity, the Incarnation, the Church and the Sacraments. It is, upon the whole, the best symbolical statement of the Calvinistic system of doctrine, with the exception of the Westminster Confession.

The French text must be considered as the original. Of the first edition of 1561 or 1562 no copies are known. The Synod of Antwerp, in September, 1580, ordered a precise parchment copy of the revised text of Francis Junius to be made for its archives, which copy had to be signed by every new minister. This manuscript has always been regarded, in the Belgic Churches, as the authentic document. The Brussels edition of 1850 presents, in modern French, the ancient text of 1580, as revised at Dort.

Schaff, in "Creeds of Christendom," vol. 1. p. 503, makes the following remark: "It is strange that Motley in his great works on the Rise, and the History of the Dutch Republic, ignores the Belgic Confession and barely mentions the name of Guido de Bray."

John Motley, in his "Rise of the Dutch Republic," vol. 2, pp. 79-80, relates the arrest and the execution of the ministers Guido de Bray and Peregrine de la

Grange, and concludes: "so ended the lives of the two eloquent, learned and highly-gifted divines."

Thus the original Belgic Confession of thirty-seven articles was written in French, the language of the Walloons, and hereunder is presented Article 1. in French and in English. The French text is taken from the authentic manuscript of 1580, with the revision of Dort, 1619, as reprinted by the "Société Evangélique Belge," at Brussels, 1850, under the title "La Confession de Foi des Eglises Réformées Wallonnes et Flamandes." (The Confession of Faith of the Reformed Walloon and Flemish Churches.) The headings of the articles of the Confession are supplemented from the Latin editions.

ART. 1
De Natura Dei

Nous croyons tous de coeur et confessons de bouche, qu'il y a une seule et simple essence spirituelle, laquelle nous appelons Dieu éternel, incompréhensible, invisible, immuable, infini; lequel est tout puissant, tout sage, juste, bon, et source très abondante de tous biens.

ART. 1
There is one only God

We all believe with the heart, and confess with the mouth, that there is one only simple and spiritual Being, which we call God; and that he is eternal, incomprehensible, invisible, immutable, infinite, almighty, perfectly wise, just, good, and the overflowing fountain of all good.

Its Literature. The complete text of the thirty-seven articles, in both languges, is to be found in vol. 3, pp. 383-436 of Schaff's "Creeds of Christendom."

A Latin translation from the revised French copy of Francis Junius, probably made by Beza, or under his direction, appeared in the "Harmonia Confes-

sionum,'' Geneva, 1581, and in the first edition of the
"Corpus et Syntagma Confessionum,'' Geneva, 1612.

A second Latin translation by Festus Hommius,
Leyden, 1618, was revised by the Synod of Dort, 1619,
and from it was made the English translation in use
in America. It was reprinted (as revised) in the
second edition of the above "Corpus et Syntag.
Conf.,'' 1654, and (in its original form) with various
readings in Niemeyer's Collectio (pp. 360-389). It
appeared in Greek, in 1623, 1653, and 1660, at
Utrecht.

It is also given in the Oxford "Sylloge Confessionum'' and in Augusti's Collect. The Latin texts in
these editions differ considerably.

The English text written from Hommius' Latin
translation mentioned above is the one authorized by
the Reformed (Dutch) Church in America, and
printed in its Constitution.

An older English version is in the "Harmony of
Protestant Confessions,'' Cambridge, 1586, and a
more recent one by Owen Jones, in "Church of the
Living God,'' London, 1865 (incomplete and inac-
curate).

There are several Dutch editions, and German
translations in Beck and in Boekel. In the Greek edition by Jac. Revins, Utrecht, 1660, the Greek and
Latin are in parallel columns.[1]

In "Ecclesiastical Records of the State of New
York,'' vol. 1, p. 148, is a reference to a Spanish trans-

---

[1] The New Schaff-Herzog Encyclopedia of Religious Knowledge; also
Philip Schaff, The Creeds of Christendom, vol. 1.

lation which a Consistory desired to obtain, 1642, through the Directors of the West India Company.

Guido de Bray. (Guido de Brès; Guy de Brès). Reformer in the Netherlands; born at Mons, 1522, executed at Valenciennes, May 31, 1567.

He was brought up strictly by his Roman Catholic mother, but before his twenty-fifth year had become a thorough Protestant. When persecution broke out, in 1548, he fled to England, where he spent four years. Then he came back and settled at Ryssel (Liege), where he won great popularity as a preacher.

In 1556 his congregation was dispersed by a fresh persecution, and he was obliged to flee, going apparently for a while to Ghent, then to Frankfort, and probably to Switzerland.

Early in 1559 he returned to the Southern Netherlands, with Tournai for his headquarters, but serving also Ryssel and Valenciennes, and visiting Antwerp and Mons in the cause of his religion, often in disguise for safety's sake.

The public singing of Marot's psalms in September, 1561, gave rise to a judicial investigation which exposed Bray to fresh danger. Undaunted, he undertook to secure justice for his comrades by laying before the authorities his confession of faith (known as the Belgic Confession) in thirty-seven articles, on the model of that adopted by the French Reformed churches in 1559.

This modest, sober, positive statement, which he hoped would show the authorities that his friends were not revolutionary Anabaptists, failed to stop the persecution; but the frequent editions of it show that it met with popular approval; it won thousands to the cause of the Reformation, and was soon recognized as a standard formula. Once known, however, as its author, the Reformer was obliged to escape from Tournai to Amiens, and thence possibly to Antwerp.

In 1564 he was in Brussels for a conference with William of Orange, and took part in the negotiations at Metz for a union of the Lutherans and Calvinists. Then he found a refuge at Sedan with Henri Robert de la Marck, Sieur de Bouillon, but was called back to a post of danger in the summer of 1566 by the consistory of Antwerp.

In August he settled at Valenciennes, where by this time, more than two-thirds of the inhabitants were in sympathy with the Reformation. At first he preached in the open air, but after the iconoclastic outbreak of August 24th, took possession of St. John's church.

The governor's attempt to suppress the movement led to the siege of the city in December, and its surrender in the following March, 1567. Once more Bray was forced to flee, but he and his fellow preachers were captured a few hours later at Saint Amand, and sent as prisoners to Tournai and then back to Valenciennes. The letters that he wrote to comfort his wife and his aged mother give an insight into his faith and the nobility of his character. He was sentenced to be hanged in front of the town hall of Valenciennes, and thus ended a life of toil and peril, which is one of the glories of the Reformation in the southern Netherlands.[1]

[1] The New Schaff-Herzog Encyclopedia of Religious Knowledge, vol. 2.

CHAPTER XII

Dates in Belgo-French History. The complicated history of Europe during the sixteenth and seventeenth centuries has led many writers into grave errors, especially those who fail to take careful notice of the dates of events. Thus, people well intentioned have through carelessness, placed into the history of France facts belonging to the history of Belgium.

Taking, for instance, Jesse de Forest, de Rapalie (called Rapelje by the Dutch), the parents of Jean Vigné, and Louis du Bois, all names having one connection or another with the early settlements in the Province of New Netherland, such writers, as here above mentioned, have called those settlers ''French'' because de Forest was from Avesnes, the parents of Vigné from Valenciennes, de Rapalie presumably from Valenciennes also, and du Bois from Lille.

It is true that these cities are French to-day, but they were not French when the above personages were born. Then, and for a long time after their birth, those cities had not, as yet, been turned over to France.

We have seen in the Chapter ''Antecedents of Belgium" that this country was often transferred from one foreign domination to another, and that these changes transformed "momentarily" the Belgians into Romans, Franks, Austrians, Spaniards, Austrians again, French, and Dutch, till 1830 when they became independent as they were before the time of Cæsar. The presentation of this subject, cannot be made correctly without the strict observance of the dates at which such political changes took place.

This observance, several American writers have utterly neglected, and as a consequence have written in newspapers, pamphlets and books about the first settlers in New York many things contrary to history.

All the Walloons who came to settle here between 1623 and 1659 or 1678 were Belgians and not French people, for the simple reason that the cities from which they came, the places from which they originated, were annexed to the French crown only in 1659 and 1678. The transfers of territories took place under Louis XIV, who was King of France, from 1643 to 1715.

Louis XIV coveted the Belgian soil located north of his own domain, and having declared war on Spain, his Marshal—Henri de Turenne—won, in 1658, the Battle of the Dunes, near Dunkerque (then in the Belgian Flanders) and as a consequence of this victory, the next year, 1659, Mazarin,[1] minister of Louis XIV, imposed on Spain the "Treaty of the Pyrenees."

The provinces of Belgium, at that time, belonged to

[1] Giulo Mazarini, an Italian cardinal, naturalized as a French citizen in 1639; a friend of Richelieu, he became at the death of the latter first minister of Louis XIII, and later on of Louis XIV.

Spain and the above treaty of 1659 obliged the Spanish king, Philip IV, to give to France the province of Artois, part of the province of Luxembourg, and the "southern parts of Flanders and of Hainault." This, was the first time that France acquired Belgian territory, and the date of 1659 is interesting to note as the colonization of New York and vicinity by the Walloons, begun in 1623.

Later on, the Franche-Conté and part of the province of Namur went also to the French crown.

Then, came the "Treaty of Nimegue," in 1678, by which France, for the second time, received more lands of Flanders and of Hainault. What was left of the Belgian provinces remained under Spanish rule till 1713, when Belgium passed to the domination of Austria.

And now, 1678, Louis XIV with the new lands ceded to him through the two treaties just mentioned, organized:

(A) The "French Flanders" with the city of Lille as capital. To-day those old French Flanders are represented by practically the entire Department du Nord, of which Lille is still the capital.

It is interesting to note that before these territories became French they were already called "French Flanders" in some quarters, because many people spoke good French there, and this particularity has probably added to the confusion of certain students of history.

We have already seen, that at one time Lille had become to the Walloons what Ypres, its great rival, which lay but fifteen miles northwest, was to the

Flemings, the chief emporium of their cloth manufacture.

(B) The "French Hainault" with Valenciennes as capital, and such cities as: Avesnes, Condé, Maubeuge, Le Quesnoy, Landrecies, Givet, Charlemont, Philippeville, etc.

Thus there were the political divisions of: "Flanders" and "Hainault" on Belgic soil, but under Spanish domination, and "French Flanders" and "French Hainault." The intricacy of facts and the care required in their study are plain.

From the above chronologic presentation of events will be seen that Jesse de Forest, de Rapalie, the parents of Jean Vigné, Louis du Bois, and all those who came from Avesnes, Valenciennes, Lille, Roubaix, Tourcoing, or from any place of Hainault and of Flanders, before the new political organizations of Louis XIV, were people from Belgic soil and not from France. There can be no mistake on this point since we have noticed that before Louis XIV, France had never received Belgian territory.

In a certain work published in Boston, it is stated that "in 1559, Hainault was ceded to Spain by the French." This is a grave mistake; in 1559 the Belgian provinces, which included Hainault, belonged to the Spanish ruler Philip II, who did not receive them from the French, but from his father, Charles V of Spain, through the abdication of the latter, in 1555.

We have seen that it was Spain who ceded parts of Hainault to France, but only in 1659 and 1678.

The same authoress writes: "The grandparents of Jesse de Forest were Melchior de Forest and

Catherine Du Fosset of Mons. They were married in 1533 in Avesnes, which was situated in what was then France."

Again, the dates of territorial ownership in Europe were not observed, for Avesnes in 1533 does not concern France, but the vast possessions of Charles V, Emperor of Germany and King of Spain. Avesnes in 1533 belongs to the Austro-Spanish period of Belgian history.

—Mr. Lucian J. Fosdick in his book "The French Blood in America," also failing to observe the dates of transfer of Belgian territory to France, makes the mistake of writing in his chapter concerning "The Founders of New Amsterdam" that "The Walloons were French who had fled from the province of that name, on the northern boundary of France, to escape religious persecution..."[1] We have seen that those Walloons were not French, as their country had not, as yet, been ceded to France.

In the same book the chapter concerning "The French Church in New York" contains another error in the following sentence: "In 1628, when the first minister, Jonas Michaelius of the Reformed Church of Holland, came to New Amsterdam, services were conducted for both the French and the Dutch."[2]

The Rev. Michaelius who conducted those "services" wrote a very different story; he wrote, in 1628: "We have had, at the first administration of the Lord's Supper, full fifty communicants, *Walloons* and *Dutch.*" Those "services" of 1628 and the first ad-

[1] Fosdick. The French Blood in America, p. 212.
[2] Fosdick. The French Blood in America, p. 225.

ministration of the Lord's Supper by the Rev. Michaelius were not two different happenings as Mr. Fosdick makes them appear, but the very same religious affair, at which the Rev. Michaelius acknowledged the presence of the Walloons and the Dutch, and not the presence of French people. The gentle Dutch minister, at this first meeting of the Church, administered the sacrament and delivered a discourse in French, because the Walloons were in the majority and because their language was French. (See details page 165.)

We cannot change the wording of the letter of the Rev. Michaelius, which letter—written from Manhattan in 1628—is reproduced in full in "Documents Relative to the Colonial History of the State of New York," vol. 2, Appendix p. 763.

Henry C. Murphy, the historian and United States Minister at The Hague, in an introduction (page 759 of above "Documents Relative to New York") attracts special attention to the importance of the letter of the Rev. Michaelius, and says: "the nationality of the first adventurers, Walloons as well as Dutch, are stated" and the letter "possesses a peculiar interest independently of its importance in connection with the history of the Church."

On page 225 of his book "The French Blood in America," Mr. Fosdick omits an important word in the supposed "reproduction" of the letter of the Rev. Michaelius, who wrote that after the first Lord's Supper, the holy sacrament was administered once in four months. And then Mr. Fosdick makes the Rev. Michaelius say: "The Walloons have no services on

Sundays, other than in the Dutch language, of which they understand very little.''

The Dutch minister did not write such a thing. He wrote: ''The Walloons and...the French have no services on Sundays other than in the Dutch language...'' By omitting the word ''French'' Mr. Fosdick, who has mixed things up in the most regrettable way, leads us to believe that the Walloons—and not the French—had their service in Dutch, and seems to want to create the impression that the French had their services in their own language, and that they formed a separate group all by themselves.

The French must have been in such a small number, that the courteous Michaelius did not even mention them as having been present at that important religious ceremony of the first administration of the Lord's Supper in Manhattan, at which meeting the Church was now organized (1628).

It was after the revocation of the ''Edict of Nantes'' in 1685, that the great exodus of Huguenots or French Protestants began, and Mr. Fosdick himself, further in his book, states that ''during the earlier years of the colony the French had no church of their own.''

Dates in Belgo-Dutch History. The students of history should also remember that many so-called ''Dutch people'' who came from the European districts mentioned below, and who settled in America between 1623 and 1648 were not Dutch but Belgians.

Indeed, the treaty of Munster, concluded in 1648 between Spain and the Dutch gave to the latter Belgian territories of Northern Flanders, Brabant and Limbourg and consequently, before this treaty, the places called l'Ecluse, Axel, Hulst, Bois-le-Duc, Breda, Maestricht, Bergen-op-Zoom, etc., were Belgian towns and not Dutch, as is generally believed. Many people from Bergen-op-Zoom, when still Belgians, were early settlers in New Jersey, "Bergen County." Furthermore, as a consequence of the treaty of Munster, the Belgian province of Limbourg was not divided between the Belgians and the Dutch until 1661. In other words, these dismemberments of northern Belgium in favor of the Dutch were similar to the dismemberments of southern Belgium, 1659-1678, in favor of the French, as explained in this chapter.

Walloon and French Languages. As the Walloons spoke French (and they still speak it) this custom seems to have been another cause of confusion among some writers.

The fact that the Walloons who formed colonies in America spoke French does not make them Frenchmen. The French language is spoken in Belgium and in Switzerland by several million people who have never seen France. The people of the United States talk English but this does not make them English, not even pro-English!

Another mistake is to be found in the definition of the Walloon language, called by some persons an "old French dialect," that is to say, an inducement to believe that the Walloons were of French origin. They were not. It also induces the belief that the Walloon tongue is a derivative of the French, and consequently that the French language is older than Walloon, but in reality, it is just the opposite.

Walloon is an old Romance dialect, one of those languages spoken by the old Gallo-Roman populations, centuries before French was born.

Before Cæsar, the language of the Walloons, and of the other populations of Gaul, was "Celtic," except in Aquitania (Southwest of Gaul) where "Iberian" was spoken. After the Roman conquest, "Latin" was imposed upon the inhabitants of Gaul, and the use of Celtic gradually decreased, while Latin became the main language. The clergy, using it in their teachings and religious services, were the natural propagators of this language which, in the fourth century, was spoken from the Pyrenees to the Rhine. The natives of Gaul had practically abandoned their national language.

During the fifth century, the latest invaders of Gaul, the Visigoths and the Franks, brought from Germania their own Teutonic languages, as foreign to Latin as to Celtic, and this further modified the tongue of the population of Gaul. It is this mixture of Latin and Teutonic languages, and some Celtic words,—but with Latin dominating—that constituted the "Romance Language." Naturally, it could not be uniform all over the immense territory of Gaul, hence the appearance of dialects in several sections of the great country.

The French language was born from the fusion of those old dialects spoken in Gaul, including, of course, the Walloon dialect, which distinguishes itself from the French by a greater number of Latin words and Latin grammatical construction.

Thus Walloon instead of being an "old French

dialect'' contributed, even if its contribution was small, to the formation of a ''new dialect'' which through many changes, additions, and time, became the beautiful and elegant French language of to-day.

In Belgium, French is spoken not only by the Walloons, but also by all well educated Flemings. As to the old Romance dialect called Walloon, it has not disappeared, for it is heard all over the southern part of Belgium, which part is often called ''la Wallonie'' (Wallonia) or country of the Walloons. It is spoken also in Northern France, in those ancient Belgian territories which, as we have seen, were annexed to the French crown.

It is well to note that the French themselves do not claim the Walloons as being French people; all the French historians tell us that the Walloons are Belgians. The well-known French educators Littré, Larousse, Bouillet, Grégoire, Dezobry and Bachelet, in their standard dictionaries of history and geography describe the Walloons as Belgians.

Bescherelle, in his ''Nouveau Dictionnaire National de la Langue Française,'' vol. 4, page 2009, says: ''Walloon. Name given to the inhabitants of Belgium, of Gallic origin, who have ''adopted'' the French language.''

It is rather strange that some New York writers should call the Walloons ''French'' while the French historians and educators teach that the Walloons are Belgians of Celtic or Gallic origin who adopted the French language. But American historians such as Dr. Franklin Jameson, Director of the Department of Historical Research in the Carnegie Institution at

Washington, call the Walloons "French-speaking Belgians," fully agreeing with the French authorities on ethnographical and historical definitions.

Huguenots and Calvinists. The French and American writers tell us that "Huguenot" was a nickname given to the Calvinists of France in the sixteenth and seventeenth centuries. During the New York celebration, 1924, of the tercentenary of the first settlements, the name Huguenot received an unusual meaning, and was applied to the Walloons.

As the Walloons were Calvinists of Belgium, and not of France, and as part of their territory went to France only during the second half of the seventeenth century, that is to say long after the Belgian Walloons had arrived in New York, the name "Huguenot" is not correctly applied to the Walloons who settled in New York. However, this mistake can easily be explained; it is a natural consequence of the first error in calling the Walloon a Frenchman, and thus the Walloon is mistaken for a Huguenot.

In recent pamphlets the Walloons have been repeatedly called "French-speaking Protestant." Yes, they spoke French but were not French people; they were French-speaking Belgians, professing the Protestant religion.

—In volume 1 of "Collections of the Huguenot Society of America" is an "Introduction" by the Rev. Alfred Wittmeyer, which contains also mistakes in the presentation of the early settlers in New York.

This "Introduction" makes the following statements:

1. "According to the Labadist travelers who visited

New York in 1679, Jean Vigné, whose parents were Protestants from Valenciennes, in French Flanders, was born on Manhattan Island as early as 1614.''

It has already been explained, on page 199, that the Labadists did not mention the year 1614, but that from what they wrote of their voyage of 1679-1680, some have taken the year 1614 for granted, whereas the wording used by the Labadists in their ''Journal'' plainly shows that it was not that year. But my remark has not this point in view. Supposing that the date 1614 were correct, neither at that time nor at the time of the birth of the parents of Jean Vigné was Valenciennes in ''French Flanders'' but in Belgian Hainault, and consequently the parents of Vigné were neither French nor Huguenots, they were Walloon Protestants. This part of history has been fully explained in the present chapter.

2. The writer of that ''Introduction'' also speaks of ''the first French service'' of 1628—with which the reader is now familiar—but fails to explain that this was the first administration of the Lord's Supper by the Rev. Mr. Michaelius, and also fails to say that if this service was in French, it was because at this religious meeting the Walloons who spoke only French were in the majority.

We have already seen that this so-called ''first French service'' of 1628 was not a French affair, but a Walloon-Dutch gathering at which the French seem to have been absent, for the Rev. Mr. Michaelius did not mention them.

And, curious enough is the following information to be found in the ''Introduction'' written by the Rev.

Mr. Wittmeyer: "The former Eglise françoise à la Nouvelle York (French Church in New York) properly dates only from 1688."[1] This, is also the date of the foundation of New Rochelle by the Huguenots, among whom were now many Walloons who had become French as a consequence of the annexation of their native land in 1659 and 1678, as explained. Many Huguenots are of Walloon descent.

3. The Rev. Mr. Wittmeyer, though well aware of the difference between a Walloon and a Frenchman, makes, on the second page of his "Introduction," the following amazing declaration: "The Walloons are not here to be distinguished from the Huguenots. They originally belonged to the same general race, spoke the same language, and (those of them who became Protestants) professed and suffered for the same faith as the Huguenots."

There is no doubt that the Walloons and the French, and all the white people "originally belonged to the same general race"!

The Rev. Mr. Wittmeyer will have no difficulty in finding in the Bible that the father of the white race was Japheth, the third son of Noah, and consequently to be logical with his own personal views he might call the first settlers in New York "Japhethites"!

The question is not to what general race the first settlers in New York did originally belong to, but from what nationality they were. What would the Reverend gentleman say if his own argument were used by somebody else, and thus declared that the

[1] Collections of the Huguenot Society of America, vol. I, first page of Introduction.

Huguenots were Walloons because they originally belonged to the same general race, or because at one time or another they spoke the same tongue, or because they had suffered together? And what would he reply if, for the same reasons, one declared that the Walloons founded New Rochelle?

Dr. William Elliot Griffis says that the "Belgic-Walloons of 1624 were pioneers and pilots of the 'French Huguenots' who came numerously to America after 1685." And he adds: "The Walloons, like the Pilgrim Fathers, were forerunners of the larger (Puritan) immigration." [1]

Some persons in speaking of the first settlers in New York designate one group by the name of its nationality, and another group by the name of its religion. Why call the French "Huguenots" when one has in view a settlement by people engaged in trade, agriculture, and industry? Why not call them the French, and thus show plainly that French and Walloons were of two different nationalities.

Confusion of Family Names. The Walloons and Flemings sheltered in Holland, and who in 1623 and afterwards "came and settled" in New York, New Jersey, Pennsylvania, Delaware, and Connecticut, have been often—too often—mistaken for French and Dutch.

Many people in the United States with a name that "sounds" French like Lebon, for instance, believe that they are therefore of French descent, while many others bearing a name that "sounds" Dutch like Vandam, for instance, are under the impression that

[1] Griffis. The Story of the Walloons, p. 201.

therefore they are of Dutch origin. As a matter of fact, the sound and the appearance of those two names, taken as examples, do not necessarily make the first French and the second Dutch, for French and Walloon names sound and appear the same, while Dutch and Flemish names do likewise, and consequently genealogical research might prove that this Lebon was not French but Walloon, and that this Vandam was not Dutch but Fleming.

As French and Walloon names sound alike and have the same "physiognomy" and as Dutch and Flemish names are alike in this respect, one must not be too hasty in coming to a conclusion as to the true nationality of such names. Caution is all the more necessary, since it must be admitted that we know more about the French and the Dutch than about the Walloons and the Flemings.

And notice should be taken of the fact that many family names were translated from Walloon or from French into Dutch, or were given a Dutch appearance such as Rapalje for Rapalie; Baird calls this "Batavian disguises." Moreover, some settlers, for reasons of their own, changed their names entirely, adopting Dutch names or English names according to the period of European occupation here.

A family by the Walloon or French name Dumont, would become "Vanden Berg" or "Vanden Bergen" in Dutch; DuBois "Vandenbosch"; Dechamp "Vandevelde"; Legrand "DeGroot"; Leblanc "De Witte", etc. Of course, the same changes took place for all first names going with the last name, and Jean became Jan or Johan, etc. Names were also often misspelled by clerks in record offices.

Walloon Library. At Leyden, in the south of Holland, where the Belgian refugees lived in great number, many people in the United States could learn of their Belgian ancestry.

Indeed, at Leyden, in Klok Steeg (Bell Alley) is an old library called the "Walloonsche Bibliothek" containing numerous archives, rare historical manuscripts, valuable genealogic documents, and long lists of names of foreigners who came to Holland and remained there or emigrated to America and elsewhere.

There, many Americans will find out that their supposed "Dutch" name is Flemish, or that their "French" name is in reality Walloon. There, they will see that their real origin is not what they supposed.

The following list is a sample of what can be found in the old Walloon library at Leyden, and by carefully observing the dates at which certain parts of Belgium were ceded to France and to Holland, the true ancestry of numerous Americans will be established.

EXTRACTS FROM THE WALLOON RECORDS OF LEYDEN

De la Marlier. Jean de la Marlier was witness to the baptism of Philippe, son of Jesse de Forest and Marie du Cloux, in the Walloon Church of Leyden, September 13, 1620.

Damont. Francoise Damont, a native of Liége, was married, December 15, 1633.

Gille. Jean Gille, a native of Lille, was married to Cataline Face, of Leyden, October 17, 1615.

Maton. Philippe Maton, a native of Fourcoin, (Tourcoing), was married to Philippotte Caron, January 10, 1599.

Catoir. A child of Arnoul Catoire, was baptized September 23, 1618.

Desendre. Anthoine Decende witnessed the baptism of a child of Jean de Croi, March 28, 1621.

Crepy. Abel Crepy and Jaquemine de Lannoy presented their daughter Susanne for baptism, February 6, 1627.

Barbe. Adrien Barbe was witness to the baptism of Adrien, son of Jean Barbe, September 14, 1625.

Le Roy. Jerosme le Roy, a native of Armentieres, was married to Susanne le Per, of Norwich, England, November 1, 1620.

Ghiselin. Claude Gyselin was witness to the baptism of a child of Gregoire le Jeune, March 28, 1621.

Censier. Michelle, daughter of Michel Censier, was baptized September 29, 1624.

De Cranne. Jean de Cranne was a witness to the baptism of a child of Gregoire le Jeune, March 28, 1621.

Broque. Louis Broque and Chertruy Quinze presented their son Pierre for baptism, January 30, 1622.

Coinne. Jacues Coinne, a native of Ron, near Lille, was married to Christienne Baseu of Fourcoin, July 27, 1614. Their son Noe was baptized June 28, 1620.

Lambert. Henri Lambert, was received to the Holy Communion, at Pentecost, 1620, upon confession of his faith. Henri Lambert, born near Limbourg, and Anne Digan, of Noyelles in Hainault, were married November 1, 1620. (Another Henri Lambert, a native of Liége, was married November 10, 1621, to Marguerite Simon.)

Du Pon. Michiel du Pon, a native of Valenciennes, was married to Nicole Billet, of Herdeyn, July 5, 1597.

Campion. Jean Campion, a native of Artois, was married to Isabeau Cap, August 25, 1607.

De La Mot. Jean de la Mote and Marie Fache, his wife, presented their son Jean for baptism, November 10, 1622.

Martin. Antoine Martin, born near St. Amand, was married to Prudence Husse, of St. Amand, December 8, 1619.

Le Ca. Jean le Ca, a native of Halewyn, was married to Marie des Pre, of Monvau, January 7, 1617.

Du Four. Theodore du Four and Sara Nicaise, his wife, presented their daughter Madelaine for baptism, July 24, 1616.

Broque. Gillain Broque was a witness to the baptism of Pierre, son of Louis and Chertruy Broque, January 30, 1622.

Sage. Marie, daughter of Jean le Sage, was baptized in March, 1605.

De Lechielles. Jacques de Lespielle witnessed, with Jesse and Rachel de Forest, to the baptism of Henri Lambert's son Henri, August 1, 1621.

De Croy. Two children of Jean de Croi were baptized in the Walloon Church, April 12, 1615, and March 28, 1621.

Du Carpentry. Jean des Carpentry, a native of Landa (Landas, in Flanders), was married to Anna Chotein, from the neighborhood of St. Amand, March 10, 1619.

Farnarcque. Thomas Farvarque and Marie, his wife, presented their son Abraham for baptism, August 4, 1624.

Le Jeune. Gregoire le Jeune and his wife, Jenne de Merre, presented their son Zacharie for baptism, October 25, 1620.

Quiesnier. Pierre Quesnee, or Quesnoy, a native of Fourcoin, and Marie le Per, of Wacka, near Lille, were married, February 27, 1617.

Digand. Barthelemy Digand and Francoise Fregeau, his wife, presented their son Isaac for baptism, March 1, 1620.

"The Walloons rather than the Dutch, first made homes in New Netherland, and, with the Flemings, furnished so large a contribution to the American composite. Thousands of Americans who say and believe that their ancestors were "Huguenots" are, in reality, descended from the Walloons." [1]

[1] William E. Griffis. Belgium: The Land of Art, p. ix.

CHAPTER XIII

REFUTATION OF CLAIMS OF SETTLEMENTS BEFORE THE ARRIVAL OF THE WALLOONS IN 1623

THE Belgian Walloons who arrived in America aboard the New Netherland, were the first "settlers" in New York, New Jersey, Pennsylvania, Delaware, and Connecticut.

That the Walloons came here at that time and settled here, is universally recognized. That they were the first settlers is questioned by the Holland Society of New York, who claim the honor for their own people.

Their claims, however, show a lack of thorough knowledge of the real situation as well as a lack of study of events, and, what is worse, are based on the confusion in which certain travelers and writers had fallen. That the Dutch did not settle in New York and vicinity before the Walloons, will be proved, in this chapter, through Dutch and British official documents, Dutch historians, and the Holland Society of New York itself.

The Dutch were Trading and Exploring. The discoveries in America by the Englishman Henry Hudson became known in the Dutch Republic in 1610, and from then on several voyages from Holland to Man-

hattan were undertaken by Dutch traders, as the commodities—mainly furs,—which abounded among the
Indians, were objects of great demand in Europe.

Those "traders," naturally, had to set up some
primitive constructions as a temporary residence
where they kept their merchandise. These primitive
constructions were "trading posts," sometimes called
"forts."

Some of the Dutch traders in quest of Indian settlements where they could secure furs, found many
creeks, inlets, and bays, and thus became "explorers."
In March, 1614, the States General passed an Ordinance conferring on those who should discover new
lands, the exclusive privilege of "making four voyages thither, before others could have admission to
the traffic."

This Ordinance excited considerable animation, and
a number of merchants of Amsterdam and Hoorn,
where at that time, 1614, Belgian refugees were living
in great numbers, fitted out and dispatched five ships
to Manhattan under the command of Adriaen Block,
Hendrick Christiaensen, and Cornelis Mey.

On a previous trip, Block had the misfortune, soon
after his arrival here, of losing his vessel "The
Tiger" which was accidentally burned. This incident
obliged him to remain, for a while, on Manhattan Island where he constructed a yacht 38 feet keel, 44½
feet long, and 11½ feet wide, which, when completed
he called the "Onrust" (The Restless), significant of
his own untiring industry. Of this forced and temporary sojourn of Block on the Island, some writers
have fabricated and presented to the public a Dutch

settlement on Manhattan in 1613-1614! This cannot properly be called a "settlement."

In his "Restless" Block proceeded to explore the east cost of Manhattan. He sailed along the East River and gave to the entire river the name of "Hellegat," after a branch of the River Scheldt in Flanders. This, was the first time that a Belgian geographic name was applied to New Netherland. Why did Block, in 1614, give a Belgian name to the East River? He must have had a serious reason to do so. There were and are, in Belgium, many families by the name of Block....

That branch of the River Scheldt, then in Belgium, is located, as we have seen in a previous chapter, between Axel and Hulst, two localities among those ceded to Holland only in 1648, in accordance with the treaty of Munster.

Leaving Long Island, and proceeding eastwardly, he found the Connecticut River, which he named "Fresh River." Passing out of the Sound, and ascertaining the insular character of Long Island, he gave his own name to one of the two islands off its eastern extremity.

While exploring Narragansett Bay, he went on to Cape Cod and there, unexpectedly, met his partner Hendrick Christiaensen. After some discussion they finally exchanged vessels, and Block "sailed for Holland" in the larger and safer craft of his comrade Christiaensen who continued to make "explorations," along the coast, in the "Restless." [1] It is plain that Block did not "settle" on Manhattan nor in New Netherland.

[1] Martha Lamb. Hist. of N. Y., vol. 1. p. 35.

While these navigators were thus engaged in the east, Captain Cornelius Mey was actively employed in "exploring" the Atlantic Coast farther south. He reached the great Delaware Bay...and two capes commemorated his visit, one, the most northward, being called after him "Cape Mey," and the other "Cape Cornelis," later on called "Hindlopen," after one of the towns in the Province of Friesland.

Intelligence of the discoveries made by skipper Block and his associates having been transmitted to Holland, was received there early in the autumn of 1614. The merchants by whom those skippers had been employed, lost no time in taking the steps necessary to secure to themselves "the exclusive trade" of the territories thus discovered which was guaranteed to them by the Ordinance of March, hereabove mentioned.

New Netherland. They sent deputies immediately to The Hague, who laid before the States General a report of their discoveries, as required by law, with a figurative map of the newly explored countries, which now for the first time received the name of New Netherland. A special grant dated October 11, 1614, in favor of the interested parties taking the name of "United New Netherland Company" was forthwith accorded..."to visit and trade" with the countries in America, lying between 40° and 45° north latitude, of which they claimed to be the first discoverers.[1]

[1] O'Callaghan. Hist. of New Netherland, vol. 1, bk. 1. ch. 4;
Doc. Rel. to Colonial Hist. of N. Y., vol. 1. pp. 4-12;
B. Fernow. New Netherland (Narrative and Critical Hist. of Am. vol. IV, ch. 8.)

Those merchants who had obtained from the States General the exclusive rights of "trading" to New Netherland, though united together in one company to secure the grant of their charter, were not strictly a corporation but rather "participants" in a specific, limited, and "temporary monopoly," which they were to enjoy in common.

On the first of January, 1618, the exclusive charter of this United New Netherland Company expired by its own limitation, and the trade to the Manhattes was, in a manner, thrown open, and thus competition was again excited among all who were acquainted with its value. This New Netherland Company petitioned the States General for a renewal of their charter for a few years more, or at least for permission to "trade" to the "Island" of New Netherland. Their High Mightinesses seemed unwilling to renew the grant.

Then, Hendrick Eelkins, Adriaen Engel and associates, "owners and partners in the New Netherland Company," sent in a memorial setting forth that they had already fitted a ship named the "Scheldt" for a voyage to the Manhattes, and requested permission to prosecute that voyage; this request was granted.

Other licenses were granted, namely to the group of Claes Jacobsen Haringcarpsel, "Petrus Plancius," the Belgian minister of the gospel (already mentioned), Lambrecht van Tweenhuyzen, Hans Claessen and Company, "traders to certain countries by them discovered between Virginia and New France, situated between the latitudes of 40° and 45° and called New Netherland, and to the adjacent territories, together with a great river lying between 38° and 40°."

This group got a license to send two ships fully freighted, one to the New Netherland and the other to the aforesaid new river, which must doubtless be the Delaware, to "truck and trade" with the natives of those parts, 1621.[1]

Thus, before the arrival of the Walloons not only Dutch people sent representatives to Manhattan for the purpose of "exploring and trading" but Belgians, such as Plancius, did the same.

The States General anticipating the commencement of business by the West India Company, inserted a special proviso in each of the above mentioned licenses, obliging the several parties interested to "return" on or before the next first of July, with their respective vessels and goods.[2]

Then, in the middle of 1621, the long-pending question of a grand commercial organization—the project of the Belgian William Usselinx—was finally settled, and an ample charter gave the West India Company almost unlimited powers to "colonize," govern, and defend New Netherland, and the powerful company started its operation in this territory in 1623.

Such is, in brief, the history of "exploration and trade" by the Dutch, between 1610 and 1623. Nothing can be said about settlements during that period, for there were none, as will now be shown through official documents.

[1] O'Callaghan. Hist. of New Netherland, vol. 1. p. 94.
[2] Hol. Doc., vol. 1. pp. 107, 109, 111-114.

Proof No. 1. Dutch Official Report of 1644

A Dutch official report of 1644 shows that there were no settlements in New Netherland before the dispatching of the boat "New Netherland" in 1623.

This report is of the greatest interest for it was written by the "Assembly of the XIX," [1] which Board, as we have seen in Chapter VIII, represented the highest officials of the Dutch West India Company.

It will readily be admitted that none could have been better informed on such a subject than the high officials of the Dutch West India Company, whose business it was to supervise the New Netherland colony. Furthermore, the date of the report of those Dutch officials, 1644, was only a few years later than the first Walloon settlement itself. It reads as follows:

"Report and Advice on the condition of New Netherland, drawn up from documents and papers placed by commission of the Assembly of the XIX, dated 15th of December, 1644, in the hands of the General Chamber of Accounts, to examine the same, make a digest thereof, and to advise the Assembly how the decay there can be prevented, the population increased, agriculture advanced, and that country wholly improved for the benefit of the Company."

Then the report begins with the following description: "New Netherland situated in America between English Virginia and New England, extending from the South River, was first *frequented* by the inhabitants of this country (meaning Holland) in the

[1] Or "College of the XIX."

year 1598, and especially by those of the Greenland
Company, but *without making any fixed settlements,*
only as a shelter in the winter.   For which purpose they erected there two little forts on the South
and North Rivers against the incursions of the
Indians.''

"A charter was afterwards, on the 11th of October, 1614, granted by their High Mightinesses to
…(follows a list of names, some already mentioned
in the present chapter), and associates, to 'trade' exclusively to the newly discovered lands, now called
New Netherland; to sail thereto exclusively for the
term of three years, without 'any other persons being
allowed to sail out of this country to' or 'frequent
that place during that time,' on pain of confiscation
of ships and goods, and a fine of fifty thousand Netherland ducats." [1]

And the official report continues: "In the years
1622 and 1623, the West India Company took possession, by virtue of their charter, of the said country,
and *conveyed thither in their ship, the 'New Netherland,' divers colonists* under the directorship of Cornelis Jacobs Mey." [2]

Then are presented a series of advices for the betterment of the colony.

The report thus sets forth that there were no
settlements, only a shelter in the winter; that charters
allowing to "trade" were granted to a few privileged,
and this only for a fixed period; that all other persons
were forbidden to sail from Holland to New Nether-

[1] Gold ducat was worth 11.82 francs; silver ducat, 5.38 francs.
[2] O'Callaghan.   Hist. of New Netherland, vol. 1. p. 418.

land or to frequent the latter, on pain of the most severe penalties—in other words that colonization was
strictly forbidden; that the West India Company took
possession of the new land in 1622 and 1623, and that
it was then, by the ship New Netherland, that colonists were conveyed thither.

These colonists, as we have seen at the very begin-
ning of Chapter X, were described, in 1624, by the
Dutch historian Van Wassenaer as being mostly
Walloons.

The above report by the highest officials of the
Dutch West India Company, in itself, would be suffi-
cient to establish that there were no settlements in
New Netherland before the arrival of the Walloons.

Proof No. 2. British Official Report of 1622

This is a report of Sir Dudley Carleton, British
Ambassador at The Hague. No settlements in New
Netherland (February, 1622) said the report.

The English ever maintained the right to the whole
American coast, from the Spanish possessions in the
South to those of the French in the North, on the
triple grounds of first discovery, occupation and possession, as well as by charters and letters patent obtained from their own sovereigns. When intelligence
was received that preparations were being made in
Holland, 1621, to send a fleet of ''merchant vessels'' to
Virginia and New Netherland, a formal complaint against the so-called Dutch occupation of
New Netherland, where Hollanders were exchanging
furs with the Indians, was presented to James I,

King of England, by the Earl of Arundel, Sir Ferdinando Georges, Sir Samuel Argall, superseded Governor of Virginia, and Captain John Mason.

The King accordingly directed the Lords of his Council to instruct Sir Dudley Carleton, the British Ambassador at The Hague, to bring the subject to the special notice of the States General of Holland. The Council at once addressed a dispatch to Carleton, in which the English Government, for the first time, 1621, distinctly asserted the unlawfulness of the Dutch "occupation" of New Netherland.

The remonstrance had to be based on something, and calling the Dutch "trading posts" a colony—for Carleton found out that there was no colony—the dispatch of the Lords read: "We understand that the year past the Hollanders have been entering upon some part of the land, and have left a colony, and given new names to the several parts of the country."

Carleton, on the receipt of the Privy Council's dispatch, proceeded to inquire from the best informed personages in the Dutch Republic before entering the complaint with the States General of Holland.

Result of Ambassador Carleton's Inquiries. This high British official learned, either from such important merchants as he was acquainted with in Amsterdam (the seat of the traffickers with New Netherland), or from the Prince of Orange, or from such of their High Mightinesses with whom he was on friendly terms, that about four or five years previously, two "particular companies of Amsterdam merchants" had begun "a trade" to America, and had ever since continued to send their vessels of sixty or eighty tons burden, at most, to fetch furs, which was "all their trade," and for this purpose they had continually agents there, who "truck" with the Indians.

But Sir Carleton could not learn that the Dutch had, as yet, planted any colony there, or intended to do so,[1] and the British Government dropped the matter, as no sign of a Dutch colony in New Netherland could be found by the British, in 1622.

Proof No. 3. Journal of New Netherland, 1647

In "Narratives of New Netherland" by Dr. J. Franklin Jameson, Director of the Department of Historical Research in the Carnegie Institution, are to be found many extracts from the "Journal of New Netherland, 1647," an important document found by Brodhead in the Royal Library of The Hague, where it is designated as No. 78 H. 32.

Dr. Jameson writes: "That it was either inspired by Governor Kieft or emanated from one of his supporters, is plain not only from its general tone but from its citations of documents. Of the documents to which its marginal notes refer, some of those that we can still trace are noted in the archives of the Netherlands as from a copy-book of Director Kieft's."[2] The piece was first printed in 1851 in the Documentary History of the State of New York, vol. IV, pp. 1-17.

And now will follow some extracts of the Journal of New Netherland, 1647:

[1] Brodhead. Hist. State of N. Y., vol. 1. pp. 140-142;
O'Callaghan. Hist. of New Netherland, vol. 1. pp. 96-97.
[2] Jameson. Narr. of New Netherland, pp. 267-268.

"By Whom and How New Netherland was Peopled."

"The subjects of the Lords States General had for a considerable time frequented this country (New Netherland) solely for the purpose of the fur trade."

"Then, in the year 1623, the chartered West India Company caused four forts to be erected in that country—two on the River Mauritius and one on each of the other (rivers); the biggest stands on the point where the Mauritius River begins, and the other one (East River, apparently) mentioned heretofore, which their Honors named New Amsterdam; and six and thirty leagues upwards another called Orange. That on the South River (the Delaware) is called Nassau and that on Fresh River (the Connecticut), the Good Hope."

"The company has since continually maintained garrisons there. In the beginning their Honors had sent a certain number of settlers thither, and at great expense had three saw mills erected." [1]

This "Journal of New Netherland" states that before 1623 the subjects of Holland had frequented New Netherland "solely for the purpose of the fur trade;" that in 1623, the West India Co. caused four forts to be erected, and that at the beginning their Honors (the Company) had sent a certain number of settlers there. Van Wassenaer in his "Narrative" dated 1624, tells us, as has several times been stated, that those settlers were "mostly Walloons."

---

[1] Extracts of the Journal to be found in Jameson's Narr. of New Netherland, p. 271.

Proof No. 4. Brochure of Charles M. Dozy, Archivist of the City of Leyden, inserted in the "Year Book of the Holland Society of New York, 1888-1889"

In 1888, about fifty members of the Holland Society of New York made a trip to Holland, and among the cities they visited was Leyden, and here "a two-story house had been specially procured for the occasion, and cleared of its contents, and all the riches of the libraries and collections of Leyden, which related to the connection between Leyden and America, and *the early settlements in North America,* were laid out for our benefit, with learned attendants to point out their beauties. A printed book of twenty-eight pages, inserted facing page 80 (of the Year Book) containing a catalogue of the treasures, had been especially prepared for the occasion." [1]

Now, in that book or brochure of twenty-eight pages especially prepared for the representative members of the Holland Society of New York, we read, on page 21, the following categoric declaration: "In 1622, Jesse de Forest sent a petition to the States General of the United Provinces; he speaks in it for himself and asks to be allowed to enroll Walloon families for emigration to the West Indies, as America was commonly called in that time. The permission was granted, a ship was equipped, and in March, 1623, the 'New Netherland' left Holland with thirty Walloon families aboard. In May, the mouth of the River Hudson was reached and the Dutch flag hoisted on the Isle of Manhattan."

[1] Year Book Holland Society of N. Y., 1888-1889, pp. 74-75.

"A Dutch sailor had passed a winter there[1] and sometimes Dutch vessels had taken in fresh water. But, *the permanent occupation of the emplacement of New York dates from the arrival of the 'New Netherland.'* In May, 1623, New Amsterdam was founded by one division of the colonists whilst another went on further and built the Fort Orange, the origin of the present Albany."[2]

The above plain statement is signed by Mr. Charles M. Dozy, Archivist of the City of Leyden, and is, as said above, reproduced in the Year Book 1888-1889 of the Holland Society of New York.

Mr. Dozy states that the permanent settlement of New York dates from the arrival of the boat "New Netherland" in 1623, which he says carried Walloon families who founded New Amsterdam (now New York) and Albany.

The Holland Society of New York forgot the above information contained in its own official organ or Year Book of 1888-1889! But after so many years this "oversight" can be excused, for after sixty-five years, Catalina Trico—the heroine of the Treatise of the Holland Society—had forgotten the name of the boat which brought her to Manhattan.... (See Chapter XIV, No. 4).

[1] Probably alluding to Adriaen Block.
[2] Year Book Holland Society of N. Y., 1888-1889, p. 21 of the Brochure inserted between pp. 80-81 of said Year Book.

Proof No. 5.   Mr. George W. Van Siclen, of the Holland Society, communicates with the Archivist of Leyden, 1895

This is practically a confirmation of Proof No. 4, by the same Dutch gentleman. In the Year Book of 1895 of the Holland Society of New York, is a chapter entitled "Who founded New York?"

The question was opened anew by a letter of a Mr. Burrows, published in the New York Tribune, in January, 1895; it gave no credit to Jesse de Forest, but erroneously stated that Peter Minuit had purchased Manhattan Island in "1623," and that he had founded New Amsterdam the same year! In that letter dates and facts are mixed up.

Mr. George W. Van Siclen, a prominent member of the Holland Society, wrote to Mr. Charles M. Dozy, archivist of the city of Leyden, Holland, in order to get the historical facts on this subject, and now will follow some "extracts" from the long reply given by Mr. Dozy to Mr. Van Siclen:

Leyden, 24th of February, 1895.
"Dear Sir:

You ask my opinion about a letter that Mr. Burrows wrote some weeks ago. You are right in thinking that the question does interest me, as I made researches about Jesse de Forest at Avesnes and Sedan.

I can assure you that all authorities agree that Peter Minuit arrived only in 1626. This is important as the whole question depends on dates.

In August, 1622, Jesse sent a petition to the States

General of the United Provinces asking to be allowed to enroll Protestant families for emigration, and in March, 1623, the "New Netherland" left the Dutch shores, and reached the Hudson river in May.

One division of the colonists went on and built Fort Orange, the origin of the present Albany. But the other part settled on Manhattan Island, and the name Walenbogt or Walloon Bay, the Wallabout of to-day, bears testimony to their being Walloons. It cannot be denied that from that fact, the arrival of the New Netherland in May, 1623, dates the permanent occupation of the site of New York.

(Signed) CH. M. DOZY."

To Mr. George W. Van Siclen,

This entire proof No. 5 is a summary of the chapter "Who Founded New York?" presented in the "Year Book of the Holland Society of New York" for 1895, pp. 119-124.

And, for the second time, Mr. Dozy, the archivist of Leyden, informs his friends of the Holland Society, that the founders of New York and Albany were not Dutch, but Walloons.

Proof No. 6. Dr. Thomas De Witt, Dutch Minister

The Board of Publication of the Reformed Protestant Dutch Church (in America) issued, in 1857, a book entitled: "A Discourse delivered in the North Reformed Dutch Church (Collegiate) in the City of New York, by Thomas De Witt, D. D., one of the Ministers of the Collegiate Reformed Dutch Church."

Here is an extract from said discourse: "After the

discovery of Manhattan Island, by Hudson, in 1609, commercial adventures were made by Holland merchants, and small trading-posts were formed at Manhattan and Fort Orange, as early as 1613, connected with the fur trade.''

''But it was not till after the formation of the West India Company in 1621, that measures were taken for an agricultural settlement in New Netherland, which took place in 1623.''

Conclusion. The proofs set forth in this chapter, based on statements by reliable and well-informed Dutch and British authorities, conclusively show that there were no settlements in New Netherland before the arrival of the Walloons; and that the Dutch who temporarily visited this country, before the landing of the Walloons, were not ''settlers'' but ''traffickers'' in furs, who returned to Holland as soon as their commercial transactions were concluded.

CHAPTER XIV

Refutation of its main claims

The proofs of "Dutch settlement" presented by the Society, are based on errors and unjustified interpretations, and in most cases on imagination, whereas the proofs of "no Dutch settlement" are, as we have seen in the previous chapter, based on official documents.

1. *The claim of a visit by Argall in 1613.*

The "Treatise" of the Holland Society says: "In 1613, Argall with an English ship from Virginia reported the Dutch settled at Manhattan with four habitations already constructed, which little settlement he professed to overawe and subdue before he sailed away."

Why stop right there, and not give also the pleasant end of that tale? This story mentions not only four Dutch habitations, but also a Dutch Governor, for the complete original story says so!

But, here is what the historian Brodhead has to say: "Plantagenet's New Albion, Heylin's Cosmography, and Stith's History of Virginia, are the au-

247

thorities for this story of Argall's visit to Manhattan.''

"Plantagenet, after stating Argall's expedition of 1613 against the French at Nova Scotia, adds that said expedition on the return voyage landed at Manhattan Isle, in Hudson's River, where they found four houses built, and a pretended Dutch Governor, under the 'West India Company of Amsterdam,'[1] share or part, who kept trading boats and trucking with the Indians.''

And Dr. Brodhead continues: "In New York Historical Society Collections, vol. 2, p. 326, the American historian Henry Murphy asserts that it is *a pure fiction, unsustained by any good authority.*"

"Singularly enough, the only authorities which affirm the fact of Argall's visit to Manhattan are printed English works. The earliest of these, from which the extract given above is taken, is the 'New Albion' of 'Beauchamp Plantagenet, Esq.' published in 1648. This imposing pseudonym was used probably by Sir Edmund Plowden, who, as grantee of an Irish patent of 1634 for New Albion,[2] had an obvious interest adverse to the Dutch title to New Netherland.''

"Almost the whole of Plantagenet's work, in fact, *is now generally held to be a mass of absurd and inconsistent errors.* Heylin, in his 'Cosmography,' which was published in 1652, seems only to have adopted and embellished Plantagenet's fanciful ac-

---

[1] The Company did not come into existence until eight years later!
[2] Under a vague and imperfect description, seems to have been meant to include most of the territory between Cape Mey, Sandy Hook, and the Delaware River, now forming the State of New Jersey.

count, and as to Stith's History of Virginia, published in 1747, the author has copied Heylin almost word for word."

"It is extraordinary that *no English or Dutch State Paper corroborates the story.* Smith, who speaks of Argall's foray in 1613 against the French missionaries who had been sent to America by the pious Madame de Guercheville, to convert the savages to Christianity, does not allude to his entering New York harbor. Dermer, who came directly from Virginia to Manhattan in 1620, does not allude to any previous visit of Argall."

"Bradford, in his Correspondence, in 1627, though he alludes to Argall's surprise of the French missionaries in 1613 says nothing about his alleged visit to Manhattan, and Argall, himself, never made such a statement. This silence of all these authorities upon this point is very significant and, to me (Brodhead) *conclusive against the truth of the story.*"

"The original authority—Plantagenet—which other writers have followed, is thus very suspicious, and the absence of official documentary evidence increases distrust to such a degree that I (Brodhead) cannot help *rejecting the whole story of Argall's proceedings at Manhattan as fabulous.*"

(All the above paragraphs concerning Argall represent the opinion of the well-known State historian John Romeyn Brodhead,[1] who cites also the opinion of the American historian Henry Murphy.)

More Refutations of Argall's Visit in 1613, by Dr. Edward Hagaman Hall in the "Nineteenth Annual

[1] Brodhead. Hist. State of New York, vol. 1., note E. pp. 754-755.

Report of the American Scenic and Historic Preservation Society," transmitted to the Legislature of the State of New York on March 24, 1914, by its President, Dr. George F. Kunz, of New York.

Dr. Hall says, in part: "But there was one alleged event ascribed particularly to the year 1613, which requires separate consideration, for the reason that upon it has been predicated the claim that Manhattan Island was settled in that year by the Dutch; that the infant settlement at that time dwelt in four houses which were at what is now No. 39 or No. 41 Broadway; and that it was governed by a Dutch Governor."

"The *sole basis for this claim* is a 32-page pamphlet which was published in London in 1648 and purported to have been written by 'Beauchamp Plantagenet.' It is entitled: 'A Description of the Province of New Albion, and a Direction for Adventurers with small stock to get two for one, and good land freely: And for Gentlemen, and all Servants, Laborers, and Artificers, to live plentifully, etc."

"The pamphlet is in the nature of a prospectus designed to promote a colonizing scheme. In phrases often incoherent, the author indulges in some high-flown metaphors; tells something of his alleged genealogy and alleged travels, gives extravagant descriptions of conditions and affairs in New Albion, and at length comes to the following passage containing the reference to Manhattan Island:

"Then Virginia being granted, settled, and all that part now called Maryland, New Albion, and New Scotland, being part of Virginia, Sir Thomas Dale

and Sir Samuel Argall, Captains and Counsellors of
Virginia, hearing of divers Aliens and intruders and
Traders without license, with a vessel and forty soldiers landed at a place called Mount Desert, in Nova
Scotia, there killed some French, and in their return
landed at Manhatas Isle in Hudson's River where
they found four houses built and a pretended Dutch
Governor under the West India Company of Amsterdam, share or part, who kept trading boats and trucking with the Indians; but the said Knights told him
their commission was to expell him and all aliens and
intruders on His Majesty's Dominion and Territories, this being part of Virginia, and this river an English discovery of Hudson, an Englishman, the Dutchman (the pretended Governor) contended them for
their charge and voyage, and by his Letter sent to
Virginia and *recorded,* submitted himself, company
and plantation to His Majesty and to the Governor
and Government of Virginia....."

"It will be noted that no date is given for the visit
of Argall to Manhattan Island; but as his excursion
to Mt. Desert was made in 1613, it is implied that 1613
was the date of his visit to Manhattan."

"All claims that Manhattan Island was settled in
1613 and that four houses built by Europeans were
standing there in that year, are traceable to this
pamphlet and their validity depends upon the reliability of its assertions."

"At the outset, the pamphlet lacks the credibility
of a reliable author, for the writer either discredits
himself by false statements concerning his genealogy
or else he is hiding behind a pseudonym *to escape re-*

sponsibility for his loose statements.''   And Dr. Hall
continues:

"On February 3, 1840, Mr. John Pennington read
before the Pennsylvania Historical Society a paper
entitled 'An Examination of Beauchamp Plantagenet's description of the Province of New Albion,' in
which he points out discrepancies in Plantagenet's
genealogy, assuming that Plantagenet was a real person.   On the other hand, Alexander Brown, in his
'Genesis of the United States' concludes that Beauchamp Plantagenet is a pseudonym covering the authorship of Sir Edmund Plowden, the patentee of
New Albion.''

"But quite aside from the question of authorship,
and without considering the numerous departures
from truth in other parts of the pamphlet, the passage
already quoted *supplies obvious evidence of un-
reliability.''*

"In the first place there was no Dutch West India
Company in 1613, and no Dutch Governor as alleged
in the pamphlet.   This allegation alone is sufficient to
shake confidence in the accuracy of other statements,
especially in the significant absence of corroborative
evidence.   In fact, there is nothing outside of this
pamphlet to support the claim that Argall and Dale
visited Manhattan in 1613.''

"The written and *recorded* submission alleged to
have been made by the Dutch Governor in 1613, *of so
much importance if a fact, has never come to life.* And
that no such transaction occurred at that time is
strongly indicated in the generous treatment after-

ward accorded by the States General to Captain Dale.''

Here is the interesting story of Captain Dale, who, with Argall, is alleged to have forced the submission of that mythical Dutch Governor of the four imaginary Dutch houses of Manhattan: ''In 1603, Dale, an Englishman, was commissioned Captain in the *Netherlands Army*. In 1611, the British Ambassador at The Hague requested that Dale be granted a leave of absence in order that he might be employed in Virginia on His Majesty's Service; and the petition was granted. Dale subsequently became Governor of Virginia. In 1618, he applied to the States General for pay during his absence from the Netherlands and the sum of one thousand pounds was granted to him (Brown's Genesis of the U. S.). If Dale, five years before had—with Argall—been a party to forcing the Dutch occupants of Manhattan to surrender their claims thereto, it is highly improbable that the States General would have rewarded him so liberally.''

It is well to note that the Holland Society of New York, in its ''Treatise,'' omits to say that this Captain Dale was with Argall in that supposed visit of 1613, and this is significant since Plantagenet's tale cites first Sir Thomas Dale, and second Sir Samuel Argall. And it is well to note also that Captain Argall was not knighted until 1622.

Dr. Hall after having attracted attention to the inaccuracy of Plantagenet as to dates concerning the voyage of Hudson, the administration of Stuyvesant, etc., says: ''The rest of the phamplet is an equally hopeless jumble.''

And Dr. Hall continues: *"The evidence of the unworthiness* of the 'Plantagenet' pamphlet appears so obvious in the light of what we have already stated that it seems unnecessary to strengthen the case against it by quoting Murphy, Pennington, and others. We may add, however, this single sentence from a letter of Mr. Victor H. Paltsits, of New York, formerly State historian, who has recently made a fresh and critical examination of the pamphlet. He says: 'I have examined this tract critically, noting its *general unworthiness,* and the *impossibility of its assertions* about Dale and Argall *finding Dutch at Manhattan* and under circumstances therein set forth.' "

All of the above paragraphs under the title "More Refutations of Argall's Visit," represent the argument of Dr. Edward Hagaman Hall.[1]

Thus, the claim made by the Holland Society of New York is without the slightest serious foundation.

2. *The Claim of More Dutch Settlements in 1614.*

The Holland Society of New York states: "By this year, 1614, habitations for settlers had increased in numbers on Manhattan in commemoration of which settlement on Manhattan, the Holland Society of New York erected a tablet, some years ago, on the lower part of Broadway." This statement carefully avoids giving any explanation.

On what this is based, who were the settlers, and where the Society got such information, they do not

[1] Dr. Hall. Nineteenth Annual Report, 1914, of the American Scenic and Historic Preservation Society, App. D. pp. 469-474.

say, and nobody knows! I have read all the best authorities, and others of less importance, on this subject and could find not one single item of information on, or allusion to habitations for settlers in Manhattan in 1614. I have already set forth, and at some length, through Dutch and British official reports, that there were no settlements here before the arrival of the Walloons on the boat "New Netherland," in 1623.

Block. There is a possibility that the above claim is an allusion to Block. During the winter of 1613-1614 the "Tiger"—the boat of Adriaen Block—had been destroyed by fire just off the southern point of Manhattan Island. Adriaen Block seeing no hope of any assistance from white men before spring [1] resolutely built shelter for himself and for his men. Martha Lamb writes that those constructions were "doubtless of the wigwam family."

Now, if in 1613 (a claim of the Holland Society) there were on Manhattan four houses and a Dutch Governor, and if in 1614 (another claim of the Holland Society) habitations for settlers had increased in numbers on Manhattan, why could Block not expect any assistance from white men before spring, and why did he need to put up "Indian huts?" Simply because Manhattan had no habitations at that time.

If the claim in the "Treatise" refers to Block, there is a Dutch statement which flatly contradicts the Holland Society. It is reproduced, in Brodhead's History of the State of New York, vol. 1. page 48.

Dr. Brodhead says: "The very rare tract—Breeden Raedt aen de Vereeinghde Nederlandsche Provintien,

[1] Martha Lamb. Hist. City of New York, vol. 1. p. 34.

etc.—for the use of which I am indebted to the kindness of Mr. Campbell, the Deputy Librarian at The
Hague, is now for the first time quoted in our history.
The statement in the 'Breeden Raedt,' of the Indians
themselves, is that 'when our people (the Dutch) had
lost a certain ship there, and were building another
new ship, they (the savages) assisted our people with
food and all kind of necessaries, and provided for
them until the ship was finished.' "

This authoritative Dutch statement conclusively
shows that there were no settlements of white people
on Manhattan Island in 1613 and 1614.

And when in the late spring, Block had finished the
construction of his little yacht, he started out on some
exploration, and meeting his comrade Christiaensen
with whom he exchanged his small craft for a larger
vessel, he returned to Holland, and Manhattan, again,
was left in primeval solitude, waiting till commerce
should come and claim its own.[1]

Of this incident, the forced and momentary sojourn
of Block on Manhattan, some persons have also tried
to make a "settlement" but the facts as officially
known[2] do not permit this "visit" to be called a
settlement....

Vigné. Perhaps, the above claim alludes to Vigné.
I have already explained, in Chapter X, how some
people made the visiting Labadists erroneously say
that Vigné was born on Manhattan Island in 1614.
But of this the Holland Society of New York appar-

[1] Martha Lamb. Hist. of New York, vol. I. p. 35.
[2] A record of the burning of "The Tiger" exists in the Royal archives
    of The Hague under date of August 18, 1614.

ently takes no advantage, probably because the Labadists stated that his parents were from Valenciennes, then in Belgian Hainault.

I must recall that those Labadist visitors did not mention the year 1614 but that they reported, when they met Vigné in 1679, that he was then "about" sixty-five years old. The word "about" is vague, and we do not know whether the age of sixty-five was what Vigné himself claimed to be, or if it was the guess of the Labadists. There is no authentic record as to the exact date of his birth, and under such circumstance there can be no proof of date of settlement with Vigné as a factor. Block, who spent on Manhattan Island the winter of 1613-1614, does not mention the Vignés. (See page 199.)

3. *The Claims of Dutch Settlements in 1619 and 1620.*

As will be seen, the first is based on an English private statement or rather on an English pretext or quarrel to prevent the Dutch from sending more trading ships to New Netherland, and the second is based on the "belief" of a group who never came to or touched New Netherland!

The "Treatise" of the Society tells us that "in 1619 an English Captain, Derner, on his voyage from the North to Virginia, passed through Long Island Sound and by Manhattan and reported that the Dutch had settled there."

His name was Captain Thomas Dermer, and passing through Hellegate, 1619, he lost his anchor by the strength of the current, which hurried him on through

the East River with such swiftness, that, without stop-
ping at Manhattan, he passed, "in a short space" into the lower bay which gave him "light of the sea."[1]

Dermer put to sea again, early the next Spring,
1620, and on this trip, and not on the one of 1619, he
had a talk with the Dutch "traders" of Manhattan
and warned them not to continue their occupation on
what he claimed as English territory.[2]   Yes, the Dutch
were there but as "traders."

Dermer was employed by Sir Ferdinando Gorges
and other Englishmen who, as we have seen in the
previous chapter (Proof No. 2, British Official Report
of 1622) addressed to King James 1, in 1621, a complaint having for purpose the prevention of the Dutch
from sending more trading vessels to New Netherland, which territory the English claimed to be their
own.

The complaint alleged that the Dutch had "settled"
there the year before, 1620, and this bold assertion,
already related, had for result, the dispatch of an
order to Sir Carleton, English Ambassador at The
Hague, to remonstrate with the States General of
Holland.   We have seen that Sir Carleton, before
getting in touch with the Dutch authorities, made
inquiry and could not find that such "settlement" as
alleged by the interested Englishmen, did really exist
or was contemplated, but that the Dutch had been
"trading" with that section of America.   We have
seen, also, that the British Government dropped the
case.

[1] Brodhead.   Hist. State of N. Y., vol. 1. pp. 92-93.
[2] Brodhead.   Hist. State of N. Y., vol. 1. p. 93.

And it is on this subtle trick of Dermer and his employers that the Holland Society of New York bases its claim of a Dutch settlement!

The other claim of the Holland Society is as follows: "In 1620, when the English Pilgrims sailed from Holland for America, as one of their diaries relates, they hoped to reach Manhattan, 'where the Dutch were,' but touched Amreica at Cape Cod, and there remained."

When, in 1620, the Pilgrims sailed from Plymouth for America they did not hope to reach Manhattan, for such was not their destination, and what was found in "one of their diaries" can certainly not be taken as a proof of Dutch settlement on that island, for the Pilgrims did not visit it.

Official papers tell us that the Dutch "were there" as fur traders.

4. *The arrival of the boat "De Eendraght."*

The "Treatise" of the Society states: "In 1623 we have an authentic record, all originals on file at Albany, of the arrival of a Dutch ship, "De Eendraght" (The Union), at Manhattan with entire families, as appears by the affidavit of Catalyntie Tricot, wife of Joris de Rapalje. The record about the arrival of the ship 'De Eendraught,' Captain Arien Joris, at Manhattan, in the spring of 1623, sets forth that of the passengers eight men were left at Manhattan, two men and six families were sent to the South River (the Delaware), two men and six families were sent to the Fresh Water (Connecticut) River, and sixteen families, mostly Walloons, were taken to Fort Orange, near the site of Albany of today."

To begin with, those names Catalyntie and Rapalje are Batavian disguises as Baird calls those clever transformations, for those people were not Dutch but Walloons, as we have seen.

As to the authentic record appealed to, it is surprising that the Society should change the date of arrival and the name of the boat set forth in said authentic records, filed at Albany.

Those official records, photographic copies of which can be seen at the New York Historical Society, plainly state that Catelina Trico made depositions before Governor Thomas Dongan, in 1685 and 1688, in which latter year the deponent was eighty-three years old.

She stated that: "She came to this country either in the year 1623 or 1624 to the best of her remembrance." This, word for word, is what the official records show.

She stated also that she came into this country with a ship called "ye Unity." There, are the exact words of the official records.

She further stated that of the boat "The Unity" Arien Joris, belonging to the West India Company, was commander, and that her ship was the first that came here for the said Company.

Brodhead has this to say concerning the error of Catelina Trico in naming the boat: "There is a slight discrepancy between Trico's testimony and Wassenaer's account, which states the name of the ship as the 'New Netherland.' Wassenaer's account was contemporaneous and it is *confirmed by Holland Documents, vol. 2, page 370.* On the other hand, the depositions of Trico were sworn to when she was eighty-three years old, and they described events which happened sixty-five years before."

Dr. Jameson makes this remark: "But in details where she differs from the contemporary account by Wassenaer, we are not to place much reliance on recollections stated sixty years later."

All the official reports call that first boat the "New Netherland," carrying the first Walloon settlers, of which ship Cornelis Mey and not Joris, was commander. It is well established that the superintendence of expedition was intrusted to Mey, who was to remain in New Netherland as the First Director of the colony, while that same Joris—mentioned by Cateline Trico as Commander—went out, at this very same time, as Second in Command! It is evident that in her deposition, the old lady, who died one year after said deposition, at the age of eighty-four, made a mistake, and under the circumstance none should try to take advantage of an error of that kind.

The Holland Society adds: "This is the first authentic mention of the arrival of Walloons in New Netherland." While there is nowhere any authentic mention of a boat "De Eendraght" carrying Walloons to New Netherland, one may well ask: Is it possible that the Committee on History and Tradition of the Holland Society of New York does not know that the first authentic mention of the arrival of the Walloons was already made, in 1624, by the Dutch historian Van Wassenaer? In his well-known "Historisch Verhael'' he tells us that the Walloons arrived by the boat ''New Netherland,'' a fact confirmed by Official Dutch documents mentioned in the previous chapter, and by the brochure of 1888, especially prepared for the Holland Society of New York by Mr. Dozy, Archevist of the City of Leyden. This brochure, as we have seen, is inserted in the 1888-1889 Year Book of the Society.

Further in the ''Treatise,'' the boat ''New Netherland'' is mentioned, but the explanations of the ''Treatise'' lead the incautious reader to believe that the ''Unity'' and the ''New Netherland'' were two different boats, whereas the name Unity was simply a confusion on the part of the old Catelina.

Madame Trico's age, probably, afflicted her with many confusions. For instance, in her deposition before Governor Dongan she stated that she was from Paris, whereas to the two Labadists who visited her, in 1679, she had declared that she was from Valenciennes.

5. *Population in 1623.*

The ''Treatise'' sets forth: ''Although *no accurate record* has been found of the number of Netherland citizens who were not mere temporary fur traders, but had settled permanently at Manhattan and elsewhere in New Netherland, during all these years down to 1623, one record in that year mentions that the colonists must then have numbered more than two hundred souls.''

If such a record exists, why not give the source of it? Is it another story by ''Beauchamp Plantagenet"? The Society carefully avoids to present any explanation as to such a record, and gives no consideration to its own statement that "no accurate record has been found" on this subject!

There is, of course, no record of the population of Manhattan in 1623! But the historians who have specialized in the History of New York tell us that in 1626 (and not 1623), the population of the Island had increased to nearly two hundred[1] and that in 1628 the colony at Manhattan numbered two hundred and seventy souls, including men, women, and children.[2]

6. *Walloons or Dutch?*

I will now close my analysis of the "Treatise" by answering the following paragraph: "So it appears to be clear that of those sixteen families (on the boat called "De Eendraght" by the Society, but called the "New Netherland" by the Dutch officials) mostly Walloons, and of those of French or Walloon blood who stayed later on Manhattan, most of them were born Netherlanders, many of them being women and children and citizens of the Dutch Republic, if of age."

First of all, one notices that the "Treatise," this time, applies to these settlers the expression "mostly Walloons," using the words of Van Wassenaer when he described the passengers of the "New Netherland," and not the passengers of a boat "De Eendraght."

But after having recognized them as "Walloons,"

1 Martha Lamb. Hist. of New York, vol. I, p. 55.
2 Brodhead. Hist. State of N. Y., vol. I, p. 183.

the "Treatise" immediately tries to make Dutch people of that very different Walloon race, by stating that "most of them" were born Netherlanders, and that others, through some legal technicality if they were of age, had become citizens of Holland!

However, nothing proves that they were born Netherlanders, or that they had a "certificate of naturalization." On the contrary, the Dutch gentleman Van Wassenaer tells us that they were Walloons. While the Walloon colonists in the Dutch Republic acquired, to a certain degree, the language of that country, they retained their own, and preserved for many generations a character distinctly that of their original country.

In 1628, the Dutch minister Michaelius, as before stated, wrote from Manhattan: "The Walloons and the French have no services on Sundays, otherwise than in the Dutch language, *of which they understand very little.*" Thus, the Walloons of Manhattan could not understand Dutch, but the Holland Society can see Dutchmen in them!

The periods after 1623, touched by the "Treatise," are fully presented throughout this work.

I have reviewed the claims of Dutch settlements as set forth by the Holland Society of New York, and we have seen that they lack reliability. They are not based on authentic reports, but on stories such as the one of "Beauchamp Plantagenet," and the notation in the diary of a Pilgrim, or are they based not on true facts, but simply on imagination.

All the official reports have made a very plain distinction between "trading" and "settling." And through such authentic documents we positively know that the Dutch were the "first traders" in New Netherland, but not the "first settlers."

Most of those Dutch traders were employed by rich merchants of Holland, came to Manhattan, attended to their business transactions and went back home; a few of them came several times, for the same purpose, during the period of the licenses granted to their employers.

But such was not the case with the Belgian Walloons who came as "settlers." Their coming marks the real founding of New York as plainly stated, in 1888 and 1895, to the Holland Society of New York by Mr. Dozy, the Archivist of the City of Leyden.

"They were of good stuff those Colonists—mostly Walloons. They were the first Europeans who came to dwell upon this Island of Manhattan with the intention of spending their lives here; and, in the end,— though that part of their intention was understood rather than stated—of making themselves permanently a part of it by being buried in its soil." [1]

[1] Thomas Janvier. The Dutch Founding of New York, p. 57.

CHAPTER XV

WHEN the Walloons landed on Manhattan Island, in 1623, the entire indefinite territory under Dutch rule, was called "New Netherland," a name which seems to have appeared for the first time in 1614, when the discoveries of skipper Block had become known, and when the merchants who had employed him sent to The Hague their deputies who laid before the States General a report and a "figurative map" concerning those discoveries. On those documents was based their application for "exclusive trade" in the said newly discovered territories.

Until the time of the arrival of the Walloons there was no permanent settlement in New Netherland, as we have seen, and consequently the Dutch officials had not given to their new territorial acquisition any particular standing in the State, nor had they found any necessity for a special seal. But with the arrival of the Walloon settlers, all these hitherto unnecessary steps became imperative.

The States General now granted a seal for New Netherland so as to place it on a level with the provinces of the Dutch Republic. As it will be remembered, these United Provinces had all originally been separate suzerainties: Duchies, Counties, Baronies, Lordships, and as such each had possessed its appropriate armorial bearings, which were still retained on their provincial seals.

Thus, New Netherland was formally erected into a Province, and "honored" by the States General with a grant of the armorial distinction of a Count. The Provincial seal was a shield bearing a beaver, proper, surmounted by a Count's coronet, and encircled by the words "Sigillum Novi Belgii," or "Seal of New Belgium."

Why was the armorial distinction that of a Count, and why that inscription of "Sigillum Novi Belgii"?

As in armorial bearings and coats-of-arms every detail has an appropriate meaning referring to something that it recalls, the States General must have had a good reason to choose a Count's coronet preferably to any other coronet, and to inscribe the words "Novi Belgii" preferably to any other name.

Naturally nobody in the Dutch Republic could have been better informed than the Dutch officials themselves, as to the true nationality of the first settlers to whom a seal was about to be given, nor was anybody better informed than those same officials as to the land whence those settlers originated.

Basing my opinion on such facts, I am inclined to believe that the preference was given to a Count's coronet because those Walloon settlers, who had taken refuge in Holland, originated from the "Comté de Hainaut" (County of Hainault) for a long time governed by rulers having the title of a "Count." And, it seems that among those first settlers some originated from Flanders, then called "Comté de Flandre" (County of Flanders) also governed by Counts.

And as to the inscription "Seal of New Belgium" it appears to me as logical, natural, and appropriate, for the Dutch officials knew that those settlers were from Belgic soil.

The inscription, besides having been a mark of official recognition of the settlers, might, furthermore, have been a compliment to William Usselinx, a Belgian Fleming from Antwerp, who was the founder of the Dutch West India Company under whose auspices the Belgian Walloons came to America. This company had also for its purpose the crushing of Spain, the bitter enemy of the Dutch Republic.

I have read three different opinions as to the inscription in the seal, and will present them for comparison with my own:

1. "Belgium in seventeenth century Latin meant Netherland, and Novum Belgium or Nova Belgica was a translation of New Netherland."

But "Belgium," the word standing by itself, certainly meant the Belgic soil. Therefore, when the Latinists had in mind the Dutch provinces of the Netherlands they did not call them simply "Belgium" but "Belgium Hollandicum" in order to avoid confusion; and this name for the Dutch provinces is recalled by the same writer who explains that Novum Belgium (New Belgium) was simply a translation of New Netherland.

Consequently, the inscription "Novi Belgii" was not, so it seems, in the mind of the Dutch officials or

Seal of New Netherland, 1623.

Seal of New Amsterdam, 1654.

Seal of Governor Stuyvesant.

in the mind of the Latinists who helped them, a simple translation of "New Netherland." If they had had in view to recall Holland instead of Belgium, they would have used the word Holland in one Latin form or another, just as it was the custom of those Latinists to call the Dutch Provinces "Belgium Hollandicum." Thus, it strongly appears that the purpose of the States General was, in this particular instance, to honor the Belgians alone, just as the old Dutch geographers, on their maps, had for Cape Cod the name of "New Holland" in honor of their own fatherland.

The name New Netherland—of the Dutch province in America, given before the arrival of the Walloons, and the inscription in the seal, when the Walloons arrived, were two different considerations.

The "Nieuwe Wereldt" of the historian Jan De Laet, published in Latin as "Novus Orbis" and then in French, 1640, as "Histoire du Nouveau Monde," translates "Novum Belgium" by "Nouvelle Belgique" and not by "Nouvelle Néerlande" or "Nouvelle Hollande."

But De Laet made a mistake in his previous work of 1630. "In this year, he had published a book 'Belgii Confederati Respublica' (The Republic of United Belgium) in which he described the Provinces of Gelderland, Holland, Zeeland, Utrecht, Friesland, Overyssel and Groningen."

Those provinces formed the Republic of the Seven Dutch United Provinces; there was no Republic of United Belgium.

"It is surprising that he made such a mistake, as

certainly he must have known the important report transmitted, in March, 1610, by Hugo de Groot (Grotius) to the States General, entitled "De Antiquitate Reipublicae Batavicae" published in numerous pamphlets, and translated into Dutch under the title of "Tractaet van de Oudtheyt van de Batavische nu Hollantsche Republique" (Treatise relative to the Period of the Batavian, *now Dutch,* Republic), which left no doubt as to the name to apply to the north of the Netherlands."

"Said treatise was reprinted in 1630, in a set of brochures published in Leyden by Johannis Maire, and entitled 'Respublica Hollandiae et Urbes' or 'The Republic and Cities of Holland.' " [1]

2. Another writer sets forth that "the words Novi Belgii, in the seal, recall the time when the Belgian and Dutch Netherlands were politically united."

This is hardly probable, for after they had become politically divided, Dutch and Belgians were, and for a long time, enemies. While the Dutch were most friendly towards the Belgian refugees who not only had made their republic great, but were of the same new religion, their feelings were bitter against the Belgian Provinces which had remained loyal to Spain and to the Catholic Church, and therefore the inscription does not seem to relate to the time of political union, but rather to the Belgian refugees who left Holland for America, their new country, or New Belgium.

3. Another view is as follows: "It recalls that earlier period when Caesar, referring to the peoples

[1] The explanations concerning the mistake of De Laet, are on pages 8-9 of Novum Belgium, by Senator Henri La Fontaine.

of Gaul, wrote—of all these, the Belgae are the bravest."

This is very doubtful, for it is difficult to find any
connection between the words of the Roman con-
queror and the inscription in the seal. Caesar referred, very plainly, to the Belgian tribes he had
fought for several years, and not to the Dutch then
called the "Battae," or Batavians, who did not fight
the Roman but who made an alliance with him instead,
54 B. C.

None of the above writers makes any suggestion as
to why a Count's coronet was chosen. The coronet and
the inscription complete each other, and are a correct
reflection of the events of that time.

SEALS WITH "NEW BELGIUM" INSCRIBED.

1. *The Seal of the Province of New Netherland,
1623.*

This was the first governmental seal used in the
entire territory or province of "New Netherland."
New Amsterdam, like all the other places, used the
seal of the Province.

This Provincial seal consists of a shield upon which
is represented, diagonally, a beaver. Before and after the permanent settlements, the trade in furs was
very important, and the beaver played the main rôle
in this kind of transactions. The beaver skin, like
wampum[1], was also used in the Dutch and early
English periods as money, a beaver, in 1658, being
reckoned as 16 guilders (a guilder = 40 cents).

[1] A full description of the wampum is presented in Chapter XIX.

In 1624, two ships returning to Holland took 4000 beavers and 700 otter skins, which sold for 25,000 to 27,000 guilders. In 1626, 7,258 beavers, 857 otters, 81 minks, etc., returned to the importers 45,050 guilders. By 1671, the Province furnished full 80,000 beavers a year.

There were beavers on Manhattan Island at the time of the first settlements, and Beaver Street (formerly the Bever Paatje and Bever Graft) marks the site of a little stream where we may conclude they had built a beaver dam.[1]

For such good reasons, the industrious little animal took a prominent place in the shield whose crest is represented by a Count's coronet between single stars, the Province having the armorial rights of a Countship, as already explained.

The beaver is surrounded by a string of wampum, and around the shield is the legend "Sigillum Novi Belgii" (Seal of New Belgium). The whole is surrounded by a wreath.

2. *The Seal of the City of New Amsterdam (New York) 1654.*

On December 24, 1653, the Burgomasters and Schepens of New Amsterdam asked the Dutch West India Company, for "a city seal different from the seal of the Province," as up till that date the city had been obliged to make use of the seal of the Province.

On May 18, 1654, the Directors of the Company wrote to Peter Stuyvesant: "We have decreed that a

[1] Dr. Hall, in "Seal and Flag of the City of New York," pp. 25-27.

seal for the City of New Amsterdam shall be prepared and forwarded.''

The painted coat-of-arms, with the seal of New Amsterdam arrived by the boat ''Peartree,'' and on December 8, 1654, the Director General delivered them to Martin Cregier, then presiding Burgomaster.

This seal of 1654 contains reminiscences of the coat-of-arms of old Amsterdam, in Holland, and the seal of New Netherland. It consists of a shield charged with a pale or vertical band in the center, upon which are arranged in a vertical row the three saltire crosses—not conventionalized windmills, as is sometimes supposed—which appear in the arms of the old city of Amsterdam.

The crest of the new arms is a beaver, taken from the seal of New Netherland. Above the crest are a mantle and a small escutcheon bearing the monogram G. W. C., standing for ''Geoctroyeerde West Indische Compagnie'' or ''Chartered West India Company.'' Below the coat-of-arms is the legend ''Sigillum Amstelodamensis in Novo Belgio'' (Seal of Amsterdam in New Belgium). The whole is surrounded by a wreath.[1]

Thus, in 1654, the name ''New Belgium,'' in an official seal, was inscribed once more.

3. *The Seal of Governor Peter Stuyvesant.*

Peter Stuyvesant, the last Dutch Governor of New Netherland, was born in Holland in 1602. He received his commission, and took the oath of office before the

[1] Dr. Hall, in ''Seal and Flag of the City of New York,'' pp. 23, 28, 29.

States General, July 28, 1646, and reached New Amsterdam, May 11, 1647.

He served in the West Indies, was Director of the Dutch colony Curaçao, and lost a leg in an attack on the Spanish Island of St. Martin. His lost leg had been replaced by a wooden one with silver bands, which accounts for the tradition that he wore a silver leg.

His administration was vigorous and rather arbitrary. New Amsterdam was attacked by an English fleet, to which Governor Stuyvesant surrendered in September, 1664. He died at New York in 1682.

Peter Stuyvesant forms a conspicuous character in Irving's humorous work entitled "History of New York, by Diedrich Knickerbocker."

His seal contains armorial bearings and emblems of his own, and are surrounded by the words "S. Pet: Stuyvesant: N: Belgii: Et Curaso: Ins: Gubernator" (Sigillum Petri Stuyvesant Novi Belgii Et Curaçao Insular Gubernator) or "The Seal of Peter Stuyvesant Governor of New Belgium and of the Island of Curaçao."

When Stuyvesant began to use this seal, bearing the inscription of New Belgium, is not known; but he was Governor of New Netherland from 1647 to 1664.

EARLY MAPS CALLING THE PROVINCE "NEW BELGIUM"

That the Dutch geographers also recognized that "New Netherland" had another name, is evidenced in their works. Among their maps, though entirely in the Dutch language, there are such titles as "Nova Belgica sive Nieuw Nederlandt" (New Belgium or

New Netherland) instead of simply "Nieuw Nederlandt."

Such a map, of 1656, mentioned hereunder as No.
8, by Adriaen Vander Donck, a Dutch Patroon along
the Hudson and at Yonkers, in 1646, is reproduced in
this chapter.

The Italian map, mentioned hereunder as No. 4,
taken from Dudley's well-known atlas "Dell' Arcano
del Mare," published in 1648, does not use the Latin
name, but presents the country as "Nuoua Belgia."
Reproduced in "Documentary History of the State
of New York," vol. 1, 1849, it is presented as depicting
"New Belgium" in 1631, and Lucini as engraver.

List of some Old Maps.

Copies of the maps mentioned below, will be found
in the important work entitled "The Iconography of
Manhattan Island," by I. N. Phelps Stokes.

1. Nova Anglia, Novum Belgium et Virginia. 1630
(New England, New Belgium, and Virginia, by Jan
De Laet, 1630).

2. Nova Belgica et Anglia Nova. 1635. (New Belgium and New England, by W. Jz. Blaeu.)

3. Nova Anglia, Novum Belgium et Virginia, 1636.
(New England, New Belgium, and Virginia, by Johannes Janssonius, 1636.)

4. Carta particolare della Nuoua Belgia, 1648.
(Special map of New Belgium, in Dudley's atlas "Dell'
Arcano del Mare," 1648.)

5. Belgii Novi, Angliae Novae, et partis Virginae
Novissima Delineatio, 1651.

(The newest map of New Belgium, New England,

and part of Virginia.   The Jansson or Janssonius Prototype, 1651.)

6. Novi Belgii Novaeque Angliae nec non partis Virginae Tabula multus in locis emendata per N. Visscher, 1655.

(A map of New Belgium and of New England as well as of a part of Virginia, by Nicholas J. Visscher, 1655).

7. Same title as No. 6. Early issue of the Danckers' map, 1655.

8. Nova Belgica sive Nieuw Nederlandt, 1656.

(New Belgium or New Netherland, by Adriaen Vander Donck, 1656.)

9. Recens edita totius Novi Belgii, in America Septentrionali siti, 1673.

(A recent map of the whole of New Belgium, situated in North America. The Seutter Map, 1673.)

10. Totius Neobelgii Nova et Accuratissima Tabula. 1673.

(A new and very accurate map of the whole of New Belgium. The Restitutio-Allardt Map, 1673.)

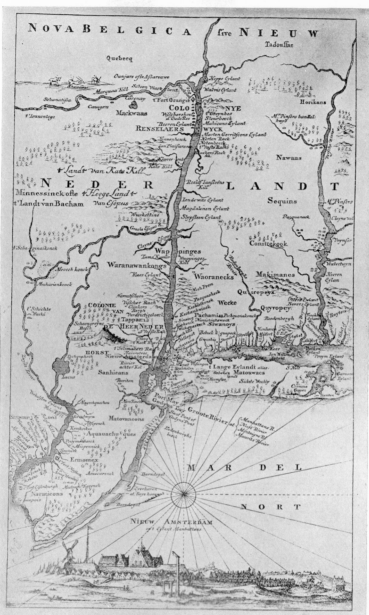

ADRIAEN VAN DER DONCK'S MAP, 1656.

CHAPTER XVI

PARTICIPATION OF THE BELGIANS IN THE GENERAL DEVEL-
OPMENT OF THE UNITED STATES. BELGO-AMERICAN MEM-
ORIES AND ASSOCIATIONS. THE WALLOON MONUMENT
IN NEW YORK.

Their Participation

OWING to the small population of little Belgium, her number of emigrants to the United States, is, by far, less than that of other nations. Yet the participation of her people in the development and progress of the Great Republic is notable, and finds leaders or important representatives in every branch of human activity.

In many instances, their useful contributions are overlooked, though we find them employed in a variety of occupations both in the present and during past generations.

Industry. Indeed, for years, the American artisans followed the "ways and methods" of the Belgian craftsmen of old, took as models their skillful works, found inspiration in their achievements and as a result themselves produced the many useful and practical American articles now used in all parts of the world.

Immigrants from Belgium, familiar with tapestry weaving; glass, rug and leather making; house furnishings, mainly those of wood; the art of the potter and of the goldsmith; wood and stone carving; diamond cutting (a specialty of the artisans of Antwerp frequently found in the state of New York); cutlery and cigar-making; the textile industry in which the Flemings are masters, and metallurgy in which the Walloons excel,—all such Belgian immigrants have largely contributed to the prosperity of the United States through their experience and co-operation, and their practical teaching in those professions.

And still to-day, in all the important industrial and commercial centers of the United States such as Detroit, Chicago, Boston, Rochester, New York, etc., their great skill and thoroughness are highly appreciated.

The Belgian methods of sugar manufacturing, as well as the chemical processes of Solvay, a Walloon, have been of the greatest utility to many branches of American industry, while the inventions of Dr. Leo Baekeland, a Fleming, now President of the American Chemical Society and an honorary Professor of Chemical Engineering in Columbia University, have rendered immense service to the chemical industry and to photography, now so important throughout the States.

"Dr. Baekeland's crowning work," said Dr. C. F. Chandler Mitchell, Professor Emeritus of Chemistry in Columbia University, "is the solving of the mysteries involved in the action of formaldehyde upon phenols, and giving to the world a new material: bakelite." He invented, also, the photographic paper "Velox."

He undertook direction of the works preliminary to the industrial development of the newly invented electrolytic cell for producing caustic soda and chlorine from salt. The result was the establishment at Niagara Falls of one of the largest electro-chemical plants in the world.

Radium. I believe it to be of interest to set forth another recent Belgian invention which will greatly benefit humanity. In a newly erected plant at Oolen, near Antwerp, the Belgians have been able to reduce the cost of radium to nearly half its former price. It will thus be more available for the cure of cancer and other ills of the human race.

Radium is brought to Antwerp from the "Congo," which rich Belgian colony possesses the largest deposit of high-grade radium that has thus far been discovered.

Washington Charles De Pauw, a manufacturer born at Salem, Indiana, in 1822, was a grandson of Charles de Pauw, that Fleming from Ghent who accompanied Lafayette to America and fought in the War of the American Revolution. With that perseverance which characterized his Belgian ancestors, Washington De Pauw, after ten years' study and the expenditure of half a million dollars, succeeded in making plate glass equal to any in the world, and thereafter engaged in its manufacture in New Albany, Indiana. He became wealthy, and used his means freely to develop that city.

Agriculture. Belgian farmers and horticulturists,

with their well-deserved universal reputation, are to be found in many sections of the country, constantly busy with their crops, the improvement of their lands, the increase in production, the creation of new varieties, and the free giving of advice.

Those humble people of the farm have rendered invaluable service to America, and from their native land they have imported great numbers of those splendid draft horses, intelligent dogs, and wonderful carrier pigeons, so useful in many ways.

Landscape Gardening. The people of Brooklyn (New York), justly proud of their splendid botanical garden, should remember the Walloon André Parmentier, born at Enghien, Belgium, in 1780.

Refusing the superintendence of the once famous Botanical Garden of New York, which was urgently pressed upon him by Dr. Hosack and others, he selected Brooklyn as his residence.

He is said to have exercised a more potent influence in landscape gardening in the United States than any other person of his profession up to that time. He was the first to introduce into this country the black beech tree, and several varieties of shrubs, vegetables and vines.

His beautiful gardens of twenty-five acres, lying between the Jamaica and Flatbush roads, (1825) attracted large numbers of visitors from all quarters.

Adèle Bayer. The daughter of André Parmentier, Madame Adèle Bayer, also born in Belgium, was revered by the seamen of the world as an angel and friend. She spent thirty years of her life caring for the spiritual and temporal wants of the sailors of the Brooklyn Navy Yard.

The Parmentier-Bayer Centenary will be celebrated in Brooklyn during the spring of 1925.

Commerce. The vast amount of commercial transactions between the United States and Belgium, especially before the Great War, is so well known that no special comment on this subject has, here, to be set forth.

But of equally great importance, though generally unknown, is that The Commercial Museum of Philadelphia, which since 1897, when it was inaugurated by President McKinley, has been of great service to thousands of American manufacturers and merchants, was organized on the plan of the "Commercial Museum of Brussels."

Dr. William Powell Wilson, the founder and able Director of "The Commercial Museum of Philadelphia," has had the extreme kindness of preparing an article for reproduction in this book. The statement of the venerable Dr. Wilson is as follows:

"The influence of the Brussels Commercial Museum upon the founding of the Philadelphia Commercial Museum."

"I was in Europe two or three times in early days and at the present moment I cannot remember when I went to Brussels and visited the Commercial Museum there.

"The first real impulse which I ever had in the direction of attempting to make useful to American manufacturers previously unknown products, and the first strong impulse I had which led to the study of methods through which the manufacturers of a country might gain commercial help of importance in another country, was in the study of this very wonderful Commercial Museum in Brussels.

"The method had then been thought out and was in operation in Brussels, to go into foreign countries, study what their competitors were sending into those countries, buy up and secure said material and exhibit it at home in their museum to the manufacturers of their own country. This was a remarkable exhibition of what Belgium had to compete with in England, France, Germany, and possibly the United States.

"This method was so well carried out in many lines of manufacture that I never lost from my mind the visual pictures of the actual products in this museum which had emanated from the manufacturers in other countries.

"This was really the starting point in my mind of doing a similar piece of work in the United States.

"Furthermore, at a little later date, in Philadelphia, I had made the acquaintance of the remarkable man, Consul General Paul Hagemans, who in his earlier days was a man who conceived and organized this Commercial Museum in Belgium. In later days I had often talked with him about his work there, at the time when I was organizing the Commercial Museum in Philadelphia."

(Signed) W. P. WILSON, Director,
The Philadelphia Commercial Museum.
"Philadelphia, November 16, 1923."

The services rendered by Mr. Paul Hagemans, the Belgian Consul General at Philadelphia, recall the unusual and remarkable consular careers of the "Malis" in New York.

The first Belgian Consul in New York, about 1835, was Mr. Henry W. Mali, who was succeeded, in 1867, by his brother, Mr. Charles Mali.

Mr. Pierre Mali, who had been appointed Vice Consul in 1899, succeeded his uncle, Mr. Charles Mali, on the death of the latter in 1899. And, Mr. John T. Johnston Mali, who was appointed Vice-Consul in 1922, succeeded to his father, Mr. Pierre Mali, on the death of the latter in 1923. For generations, this well-known Walloon family has been of the greatest service to New York manufacturers and traders, as well as to the Belgian residents.

The Belgian Chamber of Commerce, the steamship company "Lloyd Royal Belge" and the "Banque Belge pour l' Etranger, have headquarters in New York.

Education. The thoroughness and precision of the Belgian educators, who are well represented in many universities and colleges throughout the States, constitute a valuable contribution to the development of education in America.

Through that excellent system of "exchange professors" their methods of teaching continue their work of usefulness. The educational world remembers the high scholarship of Prof. Maurice de Wulf, of the University of Louvain, who teaches philosophy at Harvard and at Princeton; Prof. Henri Pirenne of the University of Ghent, who lectured on history at Columbia, and Prof. Albert Sauveur, of the School of Mines of Liege, who teaches metallurgy at Harvard.

The University of Georgetown, at Washington, D. C., the oldest Catholic educational institution in America, had many famous Belgian professors; its founder, Archbishop Carroll, spent several years at Bruges, in Flanders. The Catholic University of Louvain inspired the idea of the Catholic University of America.

Before the founding of the important University of Georgetown, Belgian Jesuits had been teaching in Maryland. The Provincial Seminary of Troy, N. Y., with its Belgian Faculty, enjoys a great reputation of learning, and Cardinal Mercier's works on philosophy are textbooks in many schools of higher education.

Washington Charles De Pauw, already cited, established and largely endowed "De Pauw University," located at Greencastle, Indiana, to which he bequeathed $1,500,000.00. He also endowed DePauw Female College at New Albany, Indiana, and expended large sums in building churches and in endowing benevolent institutions throughout Indiana and the adjoining States.

He gave, largely, for the support of superannuated clergymen of the Methodist Church. During the last ten years of his life his benefactions amounted to more that $500,000.00.

Literature. The French-speaking Belgians are generally mistaken for French people, and thus their personal contribution to the teaching of French and the study of French literature, of beneficial influence upon American literature and the theater, as well as upon international relations, has often been unnoticed.

However, Belgian teachers of French, as well as textbooks written by them, are to be found in the American public and private schools, for instance, the highly appreciated books by Dr. Victor E. François, Professor of French in the College of the City of New York.

The literary works of the Belgian writers Emile Verhaeren and Maurice Maeterlinck (author of "Blue Bird") are well known throughout the United States.

The French themselves have, of course, largely and splendidly contributed to the diffusion of their language through their own educators, literary men, and well organized societies.

Music. In the orchestras of our numerous theaters, and among the teachers of music, there are many Belgians. Their exceptional ability on the organ has been admired in all the great cities of the United States, and in recent years the organist Charles Courboin has been greatly applauded in New York.

Every American music lover has heard the great violinist Eugene Ysaye, a Walloon, who studied at the Royal Conservatory of Liege. He directed, with the greatest efficiency, important American musical societies such as that of Cincinnati. The old music master and splendid violinist Ovide Musin, of the same Conservatory of Liege, undertook the musical education of hundreds of pupils in the State of New York.

From that famous institution—the Royal Conservatory of Liege—have come such masters as Vieuxtemps, Leonard, Marsick, and Thomson. Among their pupils are: Fritz Kreisler, Wieniawski, Urso, and Jacques Thibaut, teacher of Albert Spalding.

At times, the Metropolitan Opera House of New York and the Opera Houses of other American cities, counted famous Belgian singers. Among them was Ernest Van Dyck, who died, recently, in his native city of Antwerp. His splendid voice attracted the notice of several musicians, including Massenet, who personally coached him for a part in his cantata "Gladiator." Cosima Wagner invited him to Bayreuth, where he became famous as Parsifal. Grau brought him to New York, and introduced him in "Tannhauser" with Emma Eames, Lilli Lehman, and David Bispham. Madame Delaunois and Madame Lardinois (Belgians) of the Metropolitan Opera, are well remembered by the New Yorkers.

Painting. If the paintings of the masters of the celebrated old Flemish school were of inspiration to the artists of every country, the works of the modern Belgian masters exercised also a beneficial influence upon the studies of the young American artists. They also excel in water colors. Commercial and decorative art here, saw their development through the co-operation of Belgian artists. Well known in the artistic world of America, is Pierre Nuytens.

The beginning of the Metropolitan Museum of Art of New York, 1871, was represented by a collection of paintings acquired from a Belgian nobleman, through Mr. Etienne Le Roy, the expert of the Royal Museum of Belgium. In every museum in the United States, Belgian art is well represented.

The public museums and American collectors

proudly show priceless Flemish tapestries, leather, and carvings; Belgian sculptures, engravings, porcelain, cabinets, chests, artistic carved and decorated furniture, laces, bookbindings, etc., of exquisite beauty.

Last year (1923) Mr. John D. Rockefeller, Jr., unveiled, at the Park Avenue Baptist Church in New York, a set of antique Flemish stained windows with sixteen panels, illustrating scenes from the life of Christ. These windows, dating from the early part of the sixteenth century, came originally from Flanders, and were probably removed from a church threatened or dismantled during the French revolutionary period.

It is the custom of the Mint of Philadelphia to stamp a medal of every President of the United States. The first of these medals, the one of George Washington, was designed by a Walloon, Pierre Simon du Vivier, grandson of Jean du Vivier, known as Du Vivier "le père," the first of a distinguished family of metal engravers who, at the beginning of the seventeenth century, lived in Liege.

Architecture. Belgian masons, stone cutters, workers of the building trades, architects, and the draftsmen of the St. Luke's School, an organization most proficient in the Ecclesiastical Art, have largely contributed to the erection here of public and private buildings, churches, and city halls.

A sumptuous construction, undoubtedly one of the most beautiful in the United States, is the office building of the Delaware and Hudson Company at Albany, N. Y. It is a somewhat modernized and amplified reproduction of the famous "Cloth-Hall" of Ypres, in Flanders, that wonderful edifice of the thirteenth century which was wantonly destroyed during the last war.

In every branch of human activity, in every profession, be it humble or prominent, the Belgian immigrant is to be found. Of good habits, he is naturally inclined towards thrift, and even on small earnings he succeeds in becoming prosperous; laborious and gifted with initiative, he does not know idleness; reliable, he is trusted by his employer; disciplined, he is absent from turbulent meetings and avoids dangerous associations; a law abiding citizen, his name is very seldom connected with crime or infringement of the rules of his adopted country. In spirit and in deed he shows himself a most desirable addition to the great American Republic.

Religious Welfare. Hundreds of highly educated and devoted Belgian priests came from the American College of Louvain to this country, and did most useful pioneer work in many states such as Michigan, Washington, Minnesota, Montana, Oklahoma, Missouri, Illinois, Ohio, Kentucky, etc., while Belgian missionaries were actively engaged in Christianizing, educating, and pacifying the Indian tribes.

Some of those priests occupied the highest ecclesiastical offices. Among them we find:

Bishop De Neckere of New Orleans, who during the yellow fever epidemic which broke out in New Orleans in 1833, helped the sick despite his own physical weakness, himself contracted the terrible disease and died. He was a native of Flanders.

Archbishop Seghers of Oregon. His field of labor extended to Alaska, where his extreme devotion deserved for him the appreciative appellation of "Apostle of Alaska." He was from Ghent.

Bishop Lefevre of Detroit, was born at Roulers, Flanders, in 1804. He and Bishop Spalding, of Louisville, were instrumental in founding the American College at Louvain.

Bishop Vande Velde of Chicago, was born at Termonde, Flanders, in 1795. He was, successively, a professor, vice-president, and president of St. Louis University.

Bishop Brondel of Montana, and Bishop Lootens of Idaho, were natives of Bruges.

Bishop Glorieux of Idaho, who succeeded Bishop Lootens, had been president of St. Michael's College of Portland, Oregon. He was from Flanders.

Bishop Maes of Kentucky, came from Courtrai. He wrote on early Catholicity in this country and compiled a "Life of Father Nerinckx."

Bishop Schelfhaut of the Virgin Islands, was from St. Nicholas, in Flanders.

Bishop Van de Vyver of Richmond, Virginia, came from Flanders.

Bishop Henry Gabriels of Ogdenburg, N. Y., was also from Flanders. He had been a professor in the Provincial Seminary of Troy, N. Y.

Bishop Meerschaert of Oklahoma, was the first Vicar Apostolic of Indian Territory. He was a native of Roussignies.

Father Charles Nerinckx, founder of the Order of the "Sisters of Lorette at the Foot of the Cross."

After pastoral and literary work in Belgium, he came to America and was assigned to Kentucky by Bishop Carroll, in 1805.

His district was more than two hundred miles in length. He is known as the "Apostle of Kentucky." The Holy See appointed him Bishop of New Orleans, but he declined the honor. He was instrumental in bringing from Belgium the first group of Jesuit missionaries in the West.

Several of the priests mentioned above did most useful missionary work before reaching their high ecclesiastical offices. Of the greatest importance were the services rendered by Father De Smet.

Father Pierre-Jean De Smet, S. J., born at Termonde, Flanders, in 1801, was admitted to the full order of priesthood at St. Louis, in 1823.

During the forty-seven years of his mission in America he is said to have travelled 250,000 miles among the Indians. Throughout the immense regions of the west and northwest he was the great pacifier of the red man. Writers, not of his faith, declare him the sincerest friend the Indians ever had.

He won the respect and confidence of both the White Man and the Red-Skin, and frequently acted as intermediary between the American authorities and the various Indian tribes, notably with the Sioux.

The utility of Father De Smet's efforts was borne witness to both by the Government at Washington and by the American officers in command of troops in the West. An eloquent tribute to this Belgian missionary priest was paid by the beloved President Harding, during his last and fatal journey in the Northwest, when he took occasion, in a speech, to extol the merits of Father De Smet and his co-workers, of any Christian creed, whose devoted efforts had contributed so materially to the opening up and development of the entire district, from the Mississippi River to the Pacific Coast.

Last year, 1923, the town of Termonde, in Belgium, celebrated the centenary of her renowned son, and Father De Smet's statue was unveiled in the presence of the American Ambassador to Belgium, the Honorable Henry P. Fletcher.

Father De Smet died at St. Louis, in 1873. It was from the latter city, as a base, that he carried on his work, extending over the whole of the region from the Mississippi to the Rocky Mountains, and even to the regions beyond. A town in Idaho and a village in South Dakota bear his name.

Father Hennepin, a Walloon from Hainault, already mentioned in a previous chapter, was the first white man to set foot on the site of Minneapolis. A street of the latter city, a village in Illinois and a county in Minnesota bear the name of Hennepin. He was the discoverer both of Niagara Falls, N. Y., and of the Falls of St. Anthony, Minnesota.

Father Adrian Croquet of the Grand Ronde Reservation, ministered for forty years to that reservation and also to the Seletz Reservation on the coast line of Oregon. He is referred to as "the Saint of Oregon." He was an uncle of the venerable Cardinal Mercier, of Belgium.

Father August Brabant, a secular priest, labored for thiry-four years among the Indians of Vancouver's Island, notwithstanding the greatest privations and numerous attempts on his life. He succeeded in converting to Catholicism the entire tribe of Indians among whom he labored.

Father Charles Van Quickenhorne, S. J., a native of Flanders, undertook in 1828, the construction of the St. Louis University.

Father Joseph Damien, of Louvain, worked among the lepers of Hawaii, contracted the terrible malady and died. His eulogy has been written by Robert Louis Stevenson.

Rev. Pierre Malou, born at Ypres, Belgium, in 1753. Most interesting and unusual was his career. At first he experienced no vocation to the ecclesiastical state, and by his marriage had two sons.

Belgium was then under the domination of Austria, and when he saw that the ruler, the dangerous despot Joseph II, aimed at nothing less than the destruction of Catholicism, Malou took a most active part in the "Brabant Revolution" of 1789; he organized an army, and became a general. He had given his estate and his person in defense of the cause of his country and church.

He also opposed the French invasion, and on the approach of the armies he had to become an exile. He came to America in 1795 to prepare the way for the emigration of his family, purchased land in Cherry Valley, near Princeton, and erected a mansion whose magnificence was the pride of the Princetonians.

His wife died and he returned to Europe. In 1801 he resolved to embrace the ecclesiastical state, and in 1805 became a Jesuit. In 1811 he was sent as a missionary to America, and when the Jesuit Fathers opened a school at the corner of Fiftieth Street and Fifth Avenue, a portion of the present site of St. Patrick's Cathedral, which was called the "New York Literary Institution," Father Malou was one of the staff.

He was afterwards one of the priests of St. Peter's Church, New York. An exemplary ecclesiastic, loving poverty, and devoting himself to the service of the sick to whom he gave all that he had, Father Malou also took a great interest in the schools, which he often visited. He was buried in St. Patrick's in 1827.

Monseigneur John Baptist Malou, Bishop of Bruges, universally known by his solid and learned works, and Mr. Jules Malou, several times the Premier of Belgium, were the grandsons of Father Pierre Malou.

Many other Belgian priests and missionaries such as: Father Duerinck, who was drowned while descending the Missouri River; Father de Theux, d' Hoop, Smedts, Van Assche, Verhaegen, John and Louis Elet, etc., labored among the Whites and the Indians.

The sufferings which those zealous pioneers endured must have been great! Their difficulties and sacrifices were constantly renewed, and their labors were without compensation or personal profit.

Those benefactors of humanity had in view only the good of the country they had voluntarily adopted. As Ministers of the Gospel they found their happiness in the spiritual welfare and betterment of the people, and their efforts and perseverance—which we cannot appreciate to their full extent—have had for result the establishment of a peaceful, honest and moral society from which emerged the contentment, comfort, and prosperity of the nation.

Belgian priests, to-day, follow the footsteps of their illustrious predecessors. Among them, most devoted, is Monsignor Joseph Stillemans, head of the Belgian Bureau and of St. Albert's Church in the City of New York.

His activities run both ways: spiritual and moral help to his countrymen residing here, and their moulding into good American citizenship. When the Great War broke out he founded the "Belgian Relief Fund" which, through the great generosity of the people of the United States, helped Belgium so splendidly. Later on, when this country entered the war, the great work of Monsignor Stillemans was continued by Mr. Herbert Hoover.

Religious Institutions for Education. Among the religious communities devoted to education, and in whose foundation and management Belgians had a part, we find: the Xaverian Brothers, the Brothers of Our Lady of Lourdes, and the Brothers of Charity, with colleges, academies, parochial and industrial schools, and homes for boys, scattered all over the United States.

There are also the Brothers of the Christian Schools whose devotion to their pupils, and excellent methods of teaching, deserve admiration, impose respect, and command support by all friends of humanity.

And among the sisterhoods for which America is grateful to Belgium, are the Sisters of Notre-Dame, of Namur, numbering 1854 Sisters who direct five colleges, fifteen academies, seventy-three parochial schools and one orphanage, with an attendance of 80,-000 pupils. The sisters of Saint Mary, who have also their mother-house in Namur, educate some 7,000 children. The Sisters Servants of the Immaculate Heart of Mary, organized by Belgian priests, have over 80,000 pupils in their schools which range from the elementary parochial to the college, comprising fifty-one parochial high schools.[1]

Such were, in brief, the contributions of the Belgians in the making of America.

BELGO-AMERICAN MEMORIES AND ASSOCIATIONS.

First Lord Baltimore. George Calvert, born in 1580, at Kipling, Yorkshire, England, was graduated at Oxford, and became a Secretary of State.

When, in 1624, he publicly avowed himself a Roman Catholic, he resigned his office but King James retained him in the Privy Council, and a few days before that Monarch's death he was created Baron of Baltimore in the Irish peerage. In 1632 he obtained, from King Charles I, a Charter of the territory on the Chesapeake, now forming the State of Maryland.

Among the most celebrated names connected with the early settlement of America, the position of Lord Baltimore ranks with the best.

It is not generally known that he was of Belgian descent. His ancestors belonged to the noble and ancient family of the name of Calvert, in the Earldom of Flanders, their principal and ancient seat being at Wervicq (one of the oldest cities of Belgium) in the

[1] Catholic Builders of the Nation, vol. 2, pp. 28-29.

said Province, where they had been living in great honor, for a long time, and where they had great possessions.[1]

Two brothers of that family had remained in Belgium, and when the Belgian and Dutch Provinces (forming The Netherlands) separated, one of the brothers, Jacques Calvert, Lord of Sonore, two leagues from Ghent (Flanders), remained loyal to the King of Spain, then the ruler of Belgium. Jacques had a son who became a Member of the House of Lords of the Seigniory of Mechelen, in the Province of Antwerp.[2]

The other brother, Lenius Calvert, sided with the Dutch Provinces, and was by them employed as their agent with Henry IV, King of France, who was a Huguenot. Later on, this King became a Catholic (1593) and it was he who, in 1598, signed the Edict of Nantes, which assured to the Calvinists the free exercise of their religion; this Edict was revoked by Louis XIV in 1685.

This Lenius Calvert left a son in France, whom King Henry IV entertained as a gentleman of his bed chamber.

The confirmation of the Calvert Arms, the original of which is in the archives of the Maryland Historical Society relates the above presentation concerning the origin of George Calvert, the First Lord Baltimore.

Nicholas Martiau and George Washington. Captain Nicholas Martian, called also Martiau (a word belonging to the Walloon language and meaning a "ham-

---

[1] Hester Dorsey Richardson.   Side-Lights on Maryland Hist., pp. 41-43.
[2] Hester Dorsey Richardson.   Side-Lights on Maryland Hist., pp. 41-43.

mer"), Martue, Martieu, Martien, Martain, Martier, etc., was born in 1591, and the several ways of spelling his name well indicate a Walloon origin.

He received his denization papers from the King of England, and must have come to Virginia about 1620, for soon thereafter he became, and continued for many years, a member of the House of Burgesses of Virginia, and later on a Justice of York from 1633 to 1657.[1] Martiau was one of the speakers at the meeting held at the House of William Warren at York, to oppose the misgovernment of Harvey, the first organized resistance in Virginia to the oppressions of government.

The York record shows that Captain Nicholas Martiau owned the site of the present Yorktown, and on this land once owned by him, his "descendent" General George Washington gave the final blow to English ascendancy.[2]

The relationship of George Washington and the Walloon Martiau is as follows: Lawrence Washington, the grandfather of George Washington, married the great granddaughter of Martiau. The latter was also the ancestor of Governor Thomas Nelson, who was an active and useful assistant in the siege of Yorktown.

Dr. Egan. Dr. Maurice Francis Egan, who died recently, was one of the foremost writers in America. After having been a professor at the Universities of Georgetown and Notre-Dame, and at the Catholic Uni-

---

[1] McIlwaine. Journals of the House of Burgesses in Virginia; Collins. Genealogy of the Washington Family.
[2] Collins. Genealogy of the Washington Family, p. 8.

versity at Washington, he became United States Minister to Denmark.

Dr. Egan claimed Belgian ancestry, and relationship with the Caloens of Bruges (Flanders).

American Revolution of 1775-1781. The history of Begium is full of struggles for independence and liberty. No people ever felt more the discomfort and oppression of foreign domination than the Belgians, and therefore their sympathies in the revolt of the Thirteen American States against Great Britain, were fully assured.

Among the officers of Belgian origin we note: Ensign Thomas Van Gaasbeck of New York; Captain Jacques Rapalje (de Rapalie) of New York; Captain Anthony Van Etten, of New York; Captain Johannes Van Eetten of Pennsylvania, etc.

Some left their native country to help the American States gain their independence, among them Charles De Pauw, from Ghent, who came over with the Marquis de Lafayette. This De Pauw was the grandfather of Washington Charles De Pauw, the benefactor of New Albany, and the founder of De Pauw University, already mentioned.

According to the Acting Chief Bibliographer of the Library of Congress at Washington, there is no separate work on the Belgians in the Revolution. This regrettable gap in the history of the United States prevents the writer from going deeper into this interesting subject.

But, numerous must have been the patriots, of Belgian origin, who participated in that great struggle for liberty, either as officers or privates, if we consider that one single family or branch,—the de Forests—had the names of twenty-five of its members on the rosters of New York, Connecticut, and Massachusetts forces alone.

The War of 1812. Peace signed at Ghent. The United States, under Thomas Jefferson, had felt the necessity of enacting laws restricting commerce with England and France, culminating in the famous "Long Embargo." These countries, but especially England, as a retaliation seized American ships and impressed the sailors of those ships into their own ranks.

As story after story was told of native Americans carried away into the service of the British navy, the popular ire rose higher and higher, while still other irritating incidents occurred. Finally, in May, 1812, the United States declared war on Great Britain, and a long and costly campaign on land and sea ensued.

When the cessation of hostilities was proposed, the Commissioners began their labors early in August, 1814, in the old Flemish city of "Ghent," in Belgium, where the Treaty of Peace was signed on December 24, 1814. It was ratified on February 17, 1815, by President Madison, and the Senate.

Neither side gained nor lost. The Treaty provided for the cessation of arms, the restoration of conquests and a commission to settle the long-disputed Canadian boundary. For the first time since the Constitution was adopted the United States faced the future without anxiety about their foreign relations.

The Great War of 1914-1918. The first American

soldiers to fight as one unit on Belgian soil, were New York troops, the 27th Division.

On July 4, 1918, brigaded with British troops they were only a few miles to the right of the position held by the Belgian Army, commanded by King Albert. At all times the most splendid spirit of brothers in arms existed between the American and Belgian regiments.

Belgium well remembers the brilliant work of the American troops around Ypres, and at Dickebush, Wyschaete, Mount Kemmel, and their splendid drive in September and October, 1918, when they broke the Hindenburg Line and brought victory in sight.

Poppies and the American Legion. The wild poppy of Flanders, that beautiful flower of a bright scarlet color, which the Flemings call "de kollebloem" or "de roode heul" and the French-speaking Belgians "le coquelicot," has become the emblem of that great and patriotic organization "The American Legion."

Everyone is familiar with that awe-inspiring lyric of Lieutenant-Colonel John McCrae, one of the greatest, if not the greatest, of the shorter pieces of literature produced in the World War, entitled "In Flanders Fields:"

> In Flanders Fields the poppies blow
> Between the crosses, row on row,
>   That mark our place; and in the sky
>   The larks, still bravely singing, fly,
> Scarce heard amid the guns below.
>
> We are the Dead.   Short days ago
> We lived, felt dawn, saw sunset glow,
>   Loved and were loved, and now we lie
> In Flanders Fields.

Take up our quarrel with the foe;
To you from falling hands we throw
   The torch; be yours to hold it high.
   If ye break faith with us who die
We shall not sleep, though poppies grow
In Flanders Fields.

THE WALLOON MONUMENT IN THE CITY OF NEW YORK

On May the 20th, 1924, in Battery Park,—near the place where the Walloons landed three hundred years ago, a memorial was dedicated in their honor.

The modest monument was fashioned from the granite of Hainault—from which Belgian province the first settlers in New York and in the Middle States, originated—and carved, in Belgium, by Walloons. The design is the work of the American architect Henry Bacon.

It is a plain shaft of stone, with the coat-of-arms of the Province of Hainault. In the upper part, runs a garland of sculptured oakleaves, and below an inscription reads:

PRESENTED TO THE CITY OF NEW YORK
BY THE
CONSEIL PROVINCIAL DU HAINAUT
IN MEMORY OF THE WALLOON SETTLERS
WHO CAME OVER TO AMERICA IN THE
"NIEU NEDERLAND" UNDER THE
INSPIRATION OF JESSE DE FOREST OF
AVESNES THEN COUNTY OF HAINAUT
ONE OF THE XVII PROVINCES.

The monument, unveiled by a charming young girl, a Walloon descendant, Miss Priscilla Mary de Forest, was presented to Mayor John F. Hylan, for the City of New York, by the Ambassador Baron Emile de Cartier de Marchienne, representing King Albert and the Belgian Government.

An iron casket, containing earth from the soil of Hainault, was embedded in the massive stone of that severely simple little mounment. Simplicity of life, hardship and resignation, had been the lot of these courageous, firm and unyielding first settlers.

A silver medal, a token of friendship of the City of Mons (capital of the province of Hainault) to the City of New York, was presented to Mayor Hylan, by the Reverend Leonard Hoyois, a Belgian.

In the presence of officials of the city and the Mayor's Committee on Receptions to Distinguished Guests, officials of Belgium, and of representatives of the Huguenot-Walloon New Netherland Commission, members of the Belgian colony, and numerous New Yorkers, addresses were delivered by the Belgian Ambassador, Baron de Cartier (who read, also, messages he had received from King Albert and from Mr. Hymans, the Belgian Minister for Foreign Affairs); Mayor Hylan; Mr. Francis Gallatin, President of the Park Board; Mr. Robert W. de Forest, a descendant of Jesse de Forest, and by Mr. Frank L. Polk, representing the Society of the "Friends of Belgium."

The One Hundred and Sixth Infantry (23rd Regiment, N. Y. N. G.) stationed at Brooklyn, and of which Colonel Thomas Fairservis is the Commander, stood at attention, while the band of the regiment played the national anthems of Belgium and of the United States.

Inauguration of the Walloon Monument, New York, 1924.

(*Left to right: Baron E. de Cartier, Rodman Wanamaker, F. Gallatin, Lt. Quinn, Mayor Hylan, Priscilla de Forest.*)

Coin. A silver coin of fifty cents, intended to commemorate the tercentenary of the arrival of the Walloons in America, was put in circulation early in the spring of 1924. The design of it was criticized by historians and the press, as not in accordance with the historical event of this commemoration.

Stamps. The United States Government issued, also, in honor of the first settlers, three postal stamps of one, two, and five cents values, respectively. The two cent stamp represents the landing of the Walloons in Albany.

Other Celebrations. More celebrations, under the auspices of the Huguenot-Walloon New Netherland Commission, took place in colleges and churches, and in Albany, Staten Island, along the Hudson river, etc.

CHAPTER XVII

CONCLUSION

WHO were the first settlers in New York and the Middle States? After having cited so many Dutch and American writers, official documents and books, I think it best to let the reader come to his own conclusion...

In writing this book, my purpose was to present historical facts as they are related by the best authorities and the most reputed historians. I have simply gathered and reproduced their statements; my work is their own.

Discussions on historical subjects and others occur every day, and in such controversies the opponents are not animated by animosity towards each other, but desire to find enlightenment and to reach a satisfactory conclusion as to the subject in which they are interested. My sole aim has been to be useful, not to antagonize or to provoke, and therefore I sincerely hope that I have offended none.

I fully recognize the real and important services rendered by the laborious Dutch people, and the Dutch officials, in the colonization, administration, and development of New York and vicinity.

In this gradual development, of considerable value

also was the participation of the French, and that of other European nations. The many geographic French names to be found throughout the United States attest the great work done by the diligent citizens of France.

And, as the well-informed Dutch officials and Dutch and American historians tell us that the first settlers in New York and environs were Belgian-Walloons, why should not full credit be given to these people as well? Their deeds cannot be suppressed; they will live forever!

"Observe good faith and justice toward all nations."—George Washington.

PART TWO

---

*She is a Mart of Nations...The crown-
ing city, whose merchants are princes,
whose traffickers are the honorable of the
earth.—Isaiah, xxiii.*

CHAPTER XVIII

FOR a long time the English had claimed New Netherland as part of Virginia, priorly discovered by Cabot. In 1664, Charles II, King of England, granted a charter of all the lands lying between the Hudson and the Delaware (the territory of New Netherland) to his brother, the Duke of York, who, later on, became James II.

An expedition against the Dutch in America was ordered, and the Duke of York, who had been appointed Lord High Admiral of the British Dominions, was to manage the enterprise. He borrowed of the King four war vessels on which he embarked four hundred and fifty well-trained soldiers, under the command of Colonel Richard Nicolls, who was also commissioned as Governor of the yet unpossessed territory. The fleet sailed from Portsmouth about the middle of May, 1664.

Suddenly came the news that the English squadron was actually on the way from Boston to New Amsterdam. The latter was ill prepared to stand a siege. Furthermore, the English inhabitants were already numerous in New Amsterdam, and would aid the King's forces; and the latter, before casting anchor, had cut off all communication between the city and Long Island.

Governor Stuyvesant regarded the situation with dismay. On August 30, 1664, Sir George Cartwright and three other gentlemen, all delegated by Nicolls, came to the city and presented to Stuyvesant a formal summons to surrender the Province of New Netherland, at the same time promising to confirm his estate, life, and liberty to every man who should submit without opposition to the authority of the King of England.

Stuyvesant was determined upon defending his post to the last, and withheld the paper which contained the terms of surrender, lest it should influence the people to insist upon capitulation. The City Magistrates were strongly in favor of non-resistance, but thought it well to bring the city into as far a state of defense as possible, in order to obtain "good terms and conditions."

The Dutch Governor sent delegates to argue the matter with Nicolls who refused to enter into any discussion, saying that if the reasonable terms he offered were not accepted he should proceed to attack.

On September 5, Nicolls came up under full sail, and anchored between the fort and Governor's Island. New Amsterdam, with its population of fifteen hundred souls, was "encircled round about" without any means of deliverance, and soon the white flag waved above the fort.

Arrangements were immediately made for a meeting to agree upon articles of capitulation. The time was

eight o'clock (September 6, 1664); the place Stuyvesant's country-house at the farm.

The proclamation and the reiterated promises of
Nicolls formed the basis of the twenty-four articles
which were carefully and intelligently discussed on
that momentous occasion. The Dutch citizens were
guaranteed security in their property, customs, conscience, and religion. Intercourse with Holland was
to continue as before the coming of the English. Public buildings and public records were to be respected,
and all civil officers were to remain in power until the
customary time for a new election.

The articles of capitulation were to be ratified by
Nicolls and delivered to Stuyvesant. On Sunday af-
ternoon, after the second sermon, the conciliatory
terms by which New Amsterdam was surrendered were
explained to the anxious community.

The next day, September 8, Stuyvesant and his
Council affixed their names to the articles of capitulation, and exchanged them with Nicolls. All things
being ready, the garrison marched out of the fort,
carrying their arms, with drums beating and colors flying, and embarked on a vessel about to sail for Holland. The English had finally succeeded in their long
cherished project of expelling the Dutch from their
American possessions.

The English flag was raised over the fort, which was
to be called "Fort James" and New Amsterdam was
henceforth to be known as "New York," after the
name of the Duke. But this invasion of the Dutch
possessions caused a war between England and Holland, and led to the Treaty of Breda, 1667, by which

New Netherland was now ceded to the English Government in exchange for the British possessions of Surinam and Nova Scotia.

New Orange. In 1672, Charles II proclaimed war against Holland and in July, 1673, a hostile Dutch fleet appeared off Sandy Hook, and dispatched a messenger requesting the Governor to surrender, and this not having been done within the time prescribed, the Dutch, who had already landed, again took possession of the Fort and of New York. The name of the city was changed to "New Orange," while the fort now became "Fort William Hendrick."

Gotham. The nickname of the city of New York was Gotham.[1]

The news of so easy a capture occasioned the deepest mortification to the English Government. But the days of Dutch rulers were numbered, for on the 9th of February, 1674, a Treaty of Peace between England and Holland was signed at Westminster, which restored the country to its former possessors. It was not, however, until November of the same year that the city was finally ceded to the English, and once more became New York, and the Dutch definitively dispossessed of the beautiful province of New Netherland.

[1] A village near Nottingham, England, noted in stories for the simplicity of its inhabitants.

CHAPTER XIX

I. *The Red Men.*

WE, THE busy people of New York, so familiar with our thoroughfares, tall buildings, big stores, important banks, splendid churches, institutions of learning, hotels, restaurants and theatres; we, so accustomed to swift means of communication and great display of electricity, and so fond of fashion, sports and games, do not appear to take much interest in the past—that glorious past of the great and rich metropolis of today, so charmingly described in many profusely illustrated books.

Washington Irving went so far as to say: "I was surprised to find how few, if any, of my fellow citizens were aware that New York had ever been called New Amsterdam, or had heard of the names of its early Dutch governors..."

The early history of New York presents numerous pages of the greatest interest, full of romance, sweet remembrances, amusing incidents, patriotic deeds, religious events, and deep tragedies.

Three hundred years ago, when the Walloons first landed in Manhattan, then a land of woods and marshes, with here and there a few huts and little fields of corn, they met the primitive people of a very different race. Wassenaer, describing the Indians, whose origin is uncertain, says: "They live in summer mostly on fish. The men repair to the river and catch a great quantity in a short time, as it is full and furnishes various sorts. The arrows they use are pointed with little bones, iron or copper, with which they, being good marksmen, shoot deer, fawns, hares, and foxes and all such. The country is full of game: hogs, bears, leopards, yea lions, as appears by the skins which were brought on board. Oxen and horses there are none.

"In the woods are found all sorts of fruits: plums, wild cherries, peaches; yea, fruits in great profusion. Tobacco is planted in abundance, but much better grows in the wild parts of Brazil; it is called Virginian. Vines grow wild there; were there wine-growers who understood the pressing, good wine could be brought hither in great quantity.

"Their trade consists mostly in peltries, which they measure by the hand or by the finger. It happened that a woman who had seen a skipper's lace shirt, fell sick; finding she should die she gave her husband three fine peltry skins to present to the skipper for the shirt, which he willingly gave her, for she wished to be buried in it, imitating the Christians in the sumptuousness of their burials. In exchange for peltries they receive beads, with which they decorate their persons;

t' Fort nieuw Amsterdam op de Manhatans.

First view of New Amsterdam, now New York.
(About 1630.)

knives, axes, chopping-knives, kettles, and all sorts of iron work which they require for house-keeping.

"In their waters are all sorts of fowls, such as cranes, bitterns, swans, geese, ducks, wild geese, as in this country. Birds fill also the woods so that men can scarcely go through them for the whistling, the noise, and the chattering. Whoever is not lazy can catch them with little difficulty. Turkey beans[1] is a very common crop. Pigeons fly wild; they are chased by the foxes like fowls. Tortoises are very small, and are not eaten, because there is plenty of other food. The most wonderful are the dreadful frogs, in size about a span, which croak with a ringing noise in the evening, as in this country. 'Tis surprising that storks have not been found there, since it is a marshy country. Spoonbills, ravens, eagles, sparrow-hawks, vultures are numerous and are quickly shot or knocked down by the natives.

"Respecting religion we as yet cannot learn that they have any knowledge of God, but there is something that is in repute among them. What they have is transmitted to them by tradition, from ancestor to ancestor. They say that mention was made to their forefathers many thousand moons ago, of good and evil spirits, to whose honor, it is supposed, they burn fires or sacrifices. They wish to stand well with the good spirits; they like exhortations about them. The ministry of which their spiritual affairs is attended to by one they call Kitzinacka, which, I suppose, is priest. When anyone among them is sick, he visits him; sits by him and bawls, roars and cries like one possessed.

[1] French beans.

If a man die, he is laid in the earth without a coffin, with all his finest garments of skins. This priest has no housekeeping of his own. He lodges where he pleases, or where he last officiated; must not eat any food prepared by a married woman. It must be cooked by a maiden or old woman. He never cohabits with them, living like a capuchin. When a child arrives at the age of twelve, then they can determine whether he shall be a Kitzinacka or not. If he says so, then he is brought up to such office. Becoming of age, he undertakes the exercise of it.

"All the natives pay particular attention to the sun, the moon, and the stars, as they are of as great interest to them, as to us, having like summer and winter. But geographers are aware that the length and shortness of the days differ, on account of situation. The first moon following that at the end of February is greatly honored by them. They watch it with great devotion, and when it comes, they compliment it with a festival; then they collect together from all quarters, and revel in their way, with wild game or fish, and drink clear river water to their fill. They have nothing with which they can become intoxicated. It appears that the year commences then, this moon being a harbinger of the summer. Shortly afterwards the women, who in that land provide the food, as respects both planting and gathering, begin to make preparations, and carry their seed into the field. They allow the succeeding moons to appear without any feasting; but they celebrate the new August moon by another festival, as their harvest then approaches, which is very abundant in consequence of the great mildness of the climate. The summers are frequently very hot, and the land moist, which produces abundance of fruits and grain. Turkish wheat[1] is abundant there, and is pounded by the women, made into meal, and baked into cakes in the ashes, after the olden fashion, and used for food.

"As they care nothing for the spiritual, they direct their study to the physical, closely observing the seasons. The women there are the most skillful star-gazers; there is scarcely one of them but can name all the stars; their rising, setting; the position of the Arctos, that is the Wain, is as well known to them as to us, and they name them by other names. But Him who dwells above they know not; affording all us Christians an argument to thank Him, that He hath so beneficently granted us knowledge of Him, leaving these in darkness; so that what the apostle says is found to be true. It is not of him that willeth, nor of him that runneth, but of God that sheweth mercy.

"There is little authority known among these nations. They live almost all equally free. In each village, indeed, is found a person who is somewhat above the others and commands absolutely when there is war and when they are gathered from all the villages to go to war. But the fight once ended, his authority ceases. They are very much afraid of death; but when they perceive that they must die, they are very brave and more ferocious than beasts. When a lad desires a wife, he buys her generally in a neighboring village, and she, being a maiden, is then delivered to him by two or three other women, carrying on the

[1] Indian corn.

head, meal, roots, corn or other articles, to the young man's hut, and he receives her. The dwellings are commonly circular, with a vent hole above to let out the smoke, closed with four doors, and made mostly of the bark of trees which are very abundant there. They sleep on the ground covered with leaves and skins. At their meals they sit on the ground. Each highly esteems his own children, bringing them up very much spoiled. The women sew skins into clothing, prepare bread, cook the meat which the men hunt and kill with arrows, especially in the winter when all is bare in the fields and but scanty forage is to be picked off the snow; then the animals approach the villages and are shot.

"It is very common among them for one man to buy and to have many wives, but not in one place; when he journeys five or six leagues he finds another wife who also takes care of him; five or ten leagues further, he again finds another wife who keeps house and so on to several, constantly buying up peltries through the country. But as those inland find that furs sold too cheap among them, they come down themselves to the rivers and trade with the nations as best they can. Also those who will trade with them must furnish them food at an inhabitant's in the village—let them cook their meat and fish there, as much as they like, and then they thank the trader. In other respects, they are extremely hospitable; the one lodges with the other without thought of compensation.

"'Tis worthy of remark that, with so many tribes, there is so great a diversity of language. They vary [extend] frequently not over five or six leagues; forth-

with comes another language; if they meet they can
hardly understand one another. There are some who
come sixty leagues from the interior, and can not at
all understand those on the river. All are very cunning in trade; yea, frequently, after having sold everything, they will retract the bargain, and that forcibly,
in order to get something more; and then they return
upwards, thirty and forty strong, all clothed in skins,
with the fur outside.

"It appears by the statements of the highlanders,
there are larger animals in the interior. On seeing the
head of the Bull, one of the signs of the heavens, the
women know how to explain that it is a horned head
of a big, wild animal which inhabits the distant country, but not theirs, and when it rises in a certain part
of the heavens, at a time known to them, then is the
season for planting; then they begin to break up the
soil with mattocks and to throw in seed.

"The science of foretelling or interpreting of events
is altogether undeveloped and unknown to them; de-
livering no oracles or revelations of the one or the
other sort, as they have very little knowledge of future or past things.

"It is somewhat strange that among these most
barbarous people, there are few or none cross-eyed,
blind, crippled, lame, hunch-backed or limping men;
all are well fashioned people, strong and sound of
body, well fed, without blemish.

"In some places they have abundant means, with
herbs and leaves or roots, to cure their ailments.
There is not an ailment they have not a remedy for;

but in other localities they are altogether devoid of succor, leaving the people to perish like cattle.

"Chastity appears to be of some repute among them. In the rearing of their offspring, they exhibit great laxity; nevertheless when the children in great numbers follow after this nation, they forbid it as not beseeming; yea, command them to return back.

"They are not, by nature, the most gentle. Were there no weapons, especially muskets, near, they would frequently kill the traders for sake of the plunder; but whole troops run before five or six muskets. At the first coming (of the whites) they were accustomed to fall prostrate on the report of the gun; but now they stand still from habit.

"Their numerals run no higher than ours; twenty being twice ten. When they desire twenty of anything, they stick the ten fingers up and point with them to the feet on which are ten toes."

(This translation of the description of Wassenaer is to be found in Jameson's Narr. of New Netherland, pp. 67-73.)

> Bright on the wigwams, painted fair
> I see each to-tem form again,
> Of Beaver, Tortoise, Wolf, and Bear,
> Of Falcon, Plover, Deer, and Crane;
> With picture-writing wondrous shown:
> All birds and beasts—all symbols whence
> The greatly wise may draw alone
> The mystery of the hidden sense.
> *(Benjamin Hathaway, The League of the Iroquois.)*

II. *The White Men.*

As the heirs of a civilization many centuries old, the white men established themselves in a new land, conquered it, and transformed it entirely. From the loose organizations of wild tribes, they made a civilized empire, steadily marching forward.

Their progress was rapid and their fame and wealth became and remains the talk of the world. But no nation ever acted towards people with such high sentiments of justice and great generosity as the United States.

Review of Interesting Events in New York.

(To designate places, names of streets of to-day are used.)

1. *Organization of the Government.* Peter Minuit, first Governor of New Netherland, 1626-1632, organized the government of the province as soon as he had obtained the title deed to Manhattan Island, 1626.

The supreme authority, executive, legislative, and judicial, had been vested in him by the West India Company, with an advisory council of five other men.

The Secretary of the council board, and also of the province, was Isaac de Razières. Jan Lampo was the "Schout-Fiscal," a sort of civil factotum, half sheriff and half attorney-general, and the special custom house officer.

2. *The Fort.* Minuit brought with him, 1626, a competent engineer, Kryn Fredrick, who built the fort, a block-house with red cedar palisades.

3. *First Warehouse and Store, 1626.* A warehouse of Manhattan stone, having a roof thatched with "reeds," was erected.

One corner of it was set apart as the village store. The people in and around New Amsterdam were generally supplied with necessary goods of all descriptions from this company's store. But it was well known that they were sold at an advance of fifty per cent on their cost, and many were the complaints.

The store was patronized to a great extent by the Indians, who came to sell their furs and drink the "white man's fire water."

4. *Horse-Mill and Religious Meetings, 1626.* A most useful building, a horse-mill, was speedily erected. It was located on what is now South William Street near Pearl, and built by the Belgian François Molemaecher.

The loft was furnished with a few rough seats and appropriated to the purposes of religious worship.

5. *First Minister, 1628.* The first minister in New Netherland, as mentioned in previous chapters, was the learned Jonas Michaelius, who administered, in French, the Lord's Supper to the Walloons. He was a warm personal friend of Governor Minuit.

6. *Comforters of the Sick, 1626.* "Comforters of the Sick" had been sent over with the Governor. These special officers, generally from the Great Consistory, and especially from the deacons, visited those overtaken suddenly by sickness and those nearing their end. Besides, every Sabbath morning, they read the Bible and lead in devotional exercises.

The Dutch called them "Krankenbezoeker" and "Ziekentrooster."

7. *Preachers acting as Physicians.* It was the custom for those who were in the pastorates of churches to assume also the practice of medicine.

8. *Patroons in 1629.* A charter termed "Freedoms and Exemptions" offered to any "member of the West India Company" who should found a colony of fifty adults in any portion of New Netherland—except Manhattan Island, which was reserved for the company—and satisfy the Indians for a tract of land of which the dimensions were specified, the title of Patroon or Chief.

He was a kind of feudal lord, owing allegiance to the West India Company, and to the States General, but independent of control within the limits of his own territory. The system was a modified relic of feudalism.

The Patroon was invested with full property rights and granted freedom of any trade—except furs, which the company reserved for themselves—with sundry limits and duties, and the privilege of hunting and fishing within his own domain. The company prohibited manufacturing, and promised protection to the colonists and defense against all enemies, a supply of negro servants, etc.

In the Patroon were centered all the rights pertaining to the position, such as the administration of justice, the appointment of civil and military officers, the settlement of clergymen and schoolmasters.

The colonists were not serfs, but tenants for a special term of years, rendering service to the patroon for a consideration.

Killian Van Rensselaer was the first patroon, 1630; his agents bought a large tract of land on the west side of the Hudson River below Albany, and in July following, other tracts on both sides of the river including the present site of Albany. Van Rensselaer formed a partnership with several of his brother directors (in the West India Company) among whom was the Flemish historian, De Laet, for the purpose of planting a colony on his land on the upper Hudson, to be known as the colony of "Rensselaer Wyck," while in this same territory an island, burg, creek and waterfall received the name of De Laet.

9. *Patroons in 1640.* A new charter of "Freedoms and Exemptions" now amended materially the obnoxious incident of 1629.

All good inhabitants of New Netherland were to select lands and form colonies to be limited to one mile along the shore of a bay or navigable river, and two miles into the country. The right-of-way by land or water was to be free to all, and disputes were to be settled by the Governor, under all circumstances.

The feudal privileges of jurisdiction, and the exclusive right of hunting, fishing, grinding corn, etc., were continued to the patroons as an estate of inheritance with descent to females as well as males. Manufactures were permitted. Another class of proprietors was soon established; Masters of Colonists they were called, and were such as should convey fine-grown persons to New Netherland, and might occupy one hundred acres of land.

Commercial privileges were very greatly extended although the company adhered to the system of onerous import duties for its own benefit. The Dutch Reformed religion was to be publicly taught and sanctioned, and ministers and schoolmasters were to be sustained.

10. *Bouwery and Plantation.* The plantations were generally only a few acres in size, rarely exceeding five, and Indian corn or tobacco were the crops raised. Farms or bouweries were much larger, and a greater variety of agricultural products was grown.

11. *Kil.* (Kill.) A stream or current of water; a small canal.

12. *Wyk.* Section of land; a territory.

13. *Burg.* A fortified castle or place; a redoubt.

14. *Dael.* A valley; new spelling "dal."

15. *First Military Force.* Wouter Van Twiller, second Governor of New Netherland, 1633-1638, arrived in Manhattan attended by one hundred and four soldiers, the first military force which landed upon our shores, and, with much wine and ceremony, he was ushered into authority.

16. *First Clergyman.* The new Governor brought with him, 1633, Dominie Bogardus, the first clergyman to reside definitively in New York.

17. *First Church, 1633.* Rev. Mr. Bogardus wanted a more appropriate place for public worship than the loft in the horse-mill. The site of this first church of Manhattan Island, as well as in New Netherland, is perhaps not to be now further ascertained than a piece of ground once called the "Oude Kerck" (Old Church), lying between Custom House Street (the portion of

Pearl Street between Whitehall and Broad Streets) and Bridge Street, and fronting on Broad Street, now known as 100 Broad Street. It was a plain wooden edifice.

18. *First Parsonage.* Near the church a parsonage was also built. It was a small Dutch cottage with a beautiful little garden, where, in the fresh summer days, pinks and tulips winked and blinked across the graveled pathways, coquetting with young vegetables. Pretty vines clambered to the very housetop, and lilacs, roses and jasmines vied with one another in gorgeous display. For many years the place was the pride of Manhattan and one of the chief attractions for strangers.

19. *First Schoolmaster, 1633.* His name was Adam Roelandsen. From some cause, perhaps because "people did not speak well of him," he could not make a living at his vocation, and so took in "washing."

There is a curious law suit recorded in the old Dutch manuscripts which shows that on the 20th of September, 1638, Adam Roelandsen demanded payment of one Gillis De Voocht for washing his linen. The latter won the suit......

20. *Cost of a House.* There is on record an agreement to build for this Roelandsen, a house on Stone Street, which was to be thirty feet long, eighteen feet wide, and eight feet high, to be tight-clapboarded, and roofed with reeden thatch, have an entry three feet wide, two doors, a pantry, a bedstead or sleeping bench (slaap-banck), a staircase, and a mantelpiece, to be ready on the first of May, 1642, for which one hundred and forty dollars was to be paid by Roel-

andsen, one-half when the timber was on the ground, and the other when the building was finished.

21. *Hotel.* A "Sleeping apartment" in the Dutch tavern of the island often accommodated several travelers at night, while during the day it was only a public room quite unencumbered in appearance.

22. *Buildings.* On a farm called "Company's Farm" extending north from Wall to Hudson Street, Governor Van Twiller—though he had a brick house within the fort—built a house, barn, brewery, boat house, etc., for his own private use.

He built also several small buildings for the tradespeople and laid out a little graveyard on the west of Broadway above Morris Street.

23. *Manhattan named New Amsterdam, 1634.* The little town or agglomeration of Manhattan now received the name of "New Amsterdam" and was invested with the prerogative of "staple right," by virtue of which all the merchandise passing up and down the river was subject to certain duties. This right gave the port the commercial monopoly of the whole province.

24. *First Police Force.* The peaceful disposition of the inhabitants was such that police regulations were almost entirely unknown in 1635. Not even a sentinel was kept on duty at night.

However, in 1643, a "Burgher Guard" was established, and in 1651 a "Rattle-Watch" was appointed. Each watchman had a rattle as a means of calling or warning—hence the name of "Rattle-Watch."

In the days of Governor Wouter Van Twiller, we find the first trace of a penal or "police system." Then, every inhabitant must not have been a model citizen for in those early days we find also a "gibet or whipping post" set up close to the water's edge.

The method of punishment was curious. The transgressors were fastened to a line by their waistband and being hoisted from the ground were left suspended, in spread-eagle fashion, for "such length of time as their offenses warranted."

Under the English, the watchmen had a bell, and so were often called "Bellmen;" the Dutch called them "Kloppermannen." They carried also a lantern and an "hour glass." At every house they cried out the time of the night and the condition of the weather: "Past two o'clock, and a dark and cloudy morning!"

They were employed only during the winter. This practice of the watch calling out the time of night was borrowed from the old towns of Europe.

25. *Dominie's Bouwery.* (Trinity Church). In 1636 a grant of sixty-two acres of land was made to Roelof Jans, beginning south of Warren Street and extending along Broadway as far as Duane Street, thence northwesterly a mile and a half to Christopher Street. This was the original conveyance of the very valuable estate since known as Trinity Church property.

Roelof Jans died soon after the grant, leaving a wife and four children. His wife, Anetje, married Dominie Everardus Bogardus (already mentioned) in the year 1638, and her farm was known as the Dominie's Bouwery.

After Bogardus' death, in 1647, this grant was confirmed by the English government to the heirs, who sold it in 1671 to Colonel Lovelace. It was afterward incorporated into the King's Farms, and in 1703 was presented by Queen Anne to Trinity Church.

26. *Captain De Vries.* Conspicuous in New Amsterdam was David Pieter De Vries. It is through the writings of this celebrated sea captain that we learn much of the irregularity existing in New Netherland at the time of Governor Wouter Van Twiller. His estate on the Hudson was called "Vriesendael."

27. *Salary of the Secretary.* Under Governor Wilhelm Kieft, 1638-1647, the Secretary of the Province of New Netherland got a salary of $250 a year; his name was Cornelis Van Tienhoven.

28. *Town Bell.* Under this Governor a curious regulation concerning the ringing of the town bell was instituted. Its chief office was to call the devout to church on the Sabbath, but Kieft ordered it rung every evening at nine o'clock, the hour for retiring! Also in the morning and evening to call persons to and from their labor; and on Thursdays to summon persons into Court.

From Dutch Manuscripts at the New York City Hall:

October 14, 1638. "For scandalizing the Governor, Hendrick Jansen is sentenced to stand at the fort entrance—at the ringing of the bell—and ask the Governor's pardon."

Under the same date. "Grietje Reiniers, for slandering the Dominie Everardus Bogardus, is condemned to appear at Fort Amsterdam—at the sounding of the bell—and declare before the Governor and Council that she knew the minister to be an honest pious man, and that she had lied falsely.''

Those evening bells!   Those evening bells!
How many a tale their music tells!
(Moore—Those Evening Bells.)

29. *Pearl Street, 1638.*   Most of the houses were in clusters, without regard to streets, and were grouped near the walls of the fort.

Pearl Street was then a simple road on the bank of the river, and undoubtedly the first street occupied for building purposes, and Kieft selected it for the best class of dwellings on account of its fine river-prospect.

30. *The Home.*   At the beginning of the settlement, the houses were one story in height with two rooms on a floor; the chimneys were of wood, and the roofs were thatched with reeds and straw.

The furniture was of the rudest kind, the stools and tables were hewn out of rough planks; wooden platters and pewter spoons took the place of more expensive objects, and naught but the indispensable chest of homespun linen and a stray piece of plate or porcelain, a treasured memento of the Fatherland, was seen to remind one of civilization.

But as the forests became cleared away, and the colony increased, the style of living experienced a material change; for some time, bricks were imported from Holland. Under Stuyvesant, enterprising citizens established a brick-yard, and on the island, stone was in abundance.

In the house, the snow white floor was sprinkled with fine sand, which was curiously stroked with a broom into fantastic curves and angles; this adornment pertained especially to the parlor, a room that was only used upon state occasions.

The most ornamental piece of furniture was usually the bed, with its heavy curtains; mattresses were unheard of, and instead was used a bed of live geese feathers. In a corner of the room stood a huge oaken, ironbound chest, filled to overflowing with household linen, spun by the feminine part of the family. At a later date, this gave place to "the chest of drawers;" in another corner stood the cupboard with its glass doors, displaying the family porcelain.

The settlers had no stoves, but enjoyed the fireplace. The great square dining table stood in the kitchen for daily use.

Small looking-glasses in narrow black frames were in general use; the flight of time long continued to be marked by sundials and hour-glasses, but about 1720, appeared the corner-clocks.

Books were rare luxuries in these times, with the exception of the libraries of the dominie and the doctor. Bibles and prayer-books contributed the sole literature of the settlement.

31. *Dutch Architecture.* What is called in New York "Dutch Architecture" or houses having in the upper portion of the construction "stepped gables" or "crow-stepped gables," sometimes called "crowsteps" is not Dutch but "Spanish architecture."

In the old cities of Belgium: Bruges, Ghent, Brussels, Antwerp, Ypres, Malines, etc., a great number of such houses can still be seen today.

32. *Windmill.* The lone windmill stood on State

Street and was, as seen from the bay, the most prominent object on the island. Near by were the bakery,
brewery and warehouse of the Company.

History does not record the date of invention of the
windmill, but it is known that it was used in Europe
as early as the twelfth century A. D.

Not only in Holland, but in Belgium and in all agricultural centers of Europe were they used.

33. *First Ferry.* I have already mentioned the
ferry in a previous chapter. It had been established
before Kieft's arrival, from the vicinity of Peck's Slip
to a point a little below the present Fulton Ferry.

Cornelis Dircksen, who had a farm in that vicinity,
came at the sound of a horn which hung against a tree,
and ferried the waiting passengers across the river
in a skiff for the charge of three stuivers in wampum
(six cents, but represented by wampum).

34. *First Liquor.* The first liquor ever made in
this country was produced from a private still on
Staten Island, erected by Kieft in 1640, and run by
Willem Hendricksen for twenty-five guilders per
month ($10.).

35. *Tapping of beer.* Governor Kieft was constantly issuing new regulations, of which there was
great need. Under date of April 11th, 1641, there was
one by which the tapping of beer during divine service, and after ten o'clock at night, was forbidden;
brawling and all kinds of offenses were to be punished
by the severest penalties.

36. *Drinking Parties.* In New Amsterdam, much
drinking was going on; nearly everyone drank wine
and stronger liquors to excess when they could be ob-

tained. For instance, a new agent arrived for Pauw's Colony at Pavonia, one Cornelis Van Vorst, and brought with him some good claret.

De Vries called there one day, and found the Governor and the minister making merry; and finally they quarreled with Van Vorst about a manslaughter which had been committed in his colony a few days before, but made it up in the end, and started for home. Van Vorst ran to give a salute to the Governor from a stone gun which stood on a pillar near his house and a spark fell upon the thatched roof, setting it on fire. There being no means of putting it out, in less than half an hour the whole building was consumed. (June, 1636). On another occasion the gunner gave a frolic, and all the dignitaries were present. The tent was erected in one of the angles of the fort, and tables and benches were placed for the guests.

When the glee was at its height, the trumpet began to blow, which caused a quarrel, and the koopmen of the stores found fault and called the trumpeter hard names. He turned around and gave them each a thrashing, and they ran for their swords, uttering terrible threats. The trumpeter hid from them that night, but the next morning, when the wine had evaporated, they feared him more than they sought him.

37. *Annual Fairs.* The Governor established two fairs to be held annually; one of cattle on the fifteenth of October and one of hogs on the first of November.

38. *Tavern.* The growth of the town, and the increasing number of travelers, brought up the subject of building a public house and Kieft decided to erect it at the company's expense. And this year, 1642, a

great clumsy stone tavern was completed; it was located on the northern corner of Pearl Street and Coenties Slip, fronting the East River.

39. *Stadt Huys.* (City Hall.) The Tavern was presented to the city in 1655 and became a Stadt Huys—State House or City Hall—containing rooms for the meetings of the Governor and his Council, etc.

Upon the roof was a cupola in which was hung a bell in the year 1656, and which was rung for the assemblage of the magistrates, and also on occasions of the publication of proclamations, which was done in front of the hall. The bell-ringer for a number of years was Jan Gillisen, familiarly called "Koeck."

The building saw many notable scenes in its day, among them the transfer of sovereignty from the Dutch to the British Government in 1664 and 1674, and the holding of the First Court of Admiralty in the province by the British Governor, Nicolls, in 1665. This ancient edifice stood until the year 1699, when it gave place to the City Hall in Wall Street, at the head of Broad Street.

40. *First Record of Sale of Lots.* The first record of the sale of city lots we find in this year 1642. There is one extant, showing that Abraham Van Steenwyck sells to Anthony Van Fees a lot on Bridge Street, thirty feet front by one hundred and ten deep, for the sum of $9.60.

41. *First Surveyor.* It was now, 1642, becoming necessary to observe regularity in drawing boundary and division lines. Andries Hudde was appointed surveyor with a salary of $80 per annum and a few additional fees.

42. *Official Interpreter.* The influx into New Amsterdam of persons who spoke only the English language (they came from New England) induced the authorities to appoint George Baxter official interpreter (1642) at an annual salary of two hundred and fifty guilders ($100.). We find Baxter as secretary and interpreter under Governor Stuyvesant.

43. *New School.* Adriaen Jansen Van Olfendam arrived from Holland in March, 1645, and started a new school in New Amsterdam. He had no competitor after Roelandsen's banishment (the first schoolmaster had to leave the country), and prospered as well as could have been expected, considering the condition of the country.

His terms of tuition were "two beavers" per annum, beavers meaning dried beaver skins. He taught in New Amsterdam until the year 1660, and among those he educated were some of the leading personages of the province[1] though the best families generally had their own private tutors direct from Europe.

44. *Latin Schoolmaster.* The "vigilant exertions" of the directors of the West India Company to provide New Amsterdam with a Latin schoolmaster resulted in the engagement of Doctor Alexander Carolus Curtius, a Professor in Lithuania, at a salary of five hundred guilders ($200.) and some perquisites. In the course of the summer of 1659 the "rector" arrived at New Amsterdam. Curtius likewise practiced as a physician.

45. *Classical School.* Assembly Journal, October

[1] Martha Lamb. Hist. of N. Y., vol. 1, p. 123.

3, 1732: Ordered, that leave be given to bring in a bill for encouraging a public school to teach Latin, Greek, Arithmetick, and Mathematicks in the City of New York; and that for the encouragement of a school-master for that purpose, the unappropriated money, to rise by the Act of licensing Hawkers and Peddlers, until the first day of December, 1737, be applied for that end; and that the said City make up the income of that fund annually, during that time, the sum of — pounds; and that in consideration thereof, the said schoolmaster shall be obliged to teach gratis, the num-ber of —— children.

46. *Early Public School Teachers.* In 1909, dur-ing the Hudson-Fulton Celebration, New York Uni-versity honored the memory of the early Dutch and Walloon schoolmasters by the unveiling of a bronze tablet applied on the University's building at 32 Waverly Place, New York.

The tablet reads: "In honor of the Seven Public School Teachers who taught under Dutch rule on Man-hattan Island: Adam Roelandsen, Jan Cornelissen, Jan Stevensen, William Vestens, Jan de la Montagne, Harmanus Van Hoboken, Evert Pietersen. 1633-1674."

47. *New York University.* Was founded in 1831. It was located at Washington Square, and a little group—glorious nucleus— of 104 students under the direction of Dr. James M. Mathews, the first chancel-lor, composed the entire University. In 1910-1911, this great institution of learning had reached the large number of 4,175 students.

Tall oaks from little acorns grow.—David Everett.

First New York University Building, 1831.
Washington Square.

In the course of that academic year, on November 9, 1911, took place the inauguration of the present learned and beloved Chancellor, Dr. Elmer Ellsworth Brown. Under his able direction and supervision the University grew still more rapidly, and to such an extent that for the year 1923-1924, the enormous figure of 17,592 students was registered.

To add to golden numbers golden numbers.—Thos. Dekker.

In the original New York University building were produced two interesting and useful inventions, by two of its most eminent professors:

48. *The Recording Electric Telegraph.* It was invented in 1835 by Professor Samuel F. B. Morse. He was also an artist of merit, and held the first Chair of Art to be established in any American College or University, at New York University's original home.

He painted the portraits of James Monroe, Chancellor Kent, Fitz Green Halleck, and Lafayette. Science began to share his attention with the Arts and finally became his dominant interest.

The statue of Morse, in Central Park, was presented to the City of New York in 1871.

49. *Photography.* In 1839, Dr. John W. Draper, Professor of Physics and Chemistry, perfected Daguerre's system of photography[1] and took the first picture of the human countenance, of his sister, Miss Catherine Dorothy Draper. He did not patent his invention but was not insensible to its commercial possibilities.

[1] Louis-Jacques Daguerre, French artist, born at Cormeilles (Seine-et-Oise) in 1789.

This same principle of photography is used today. Most pictures, therefore, are directly descended from original work done at New York University. Professor Draper, assisted by Professor Samuel F. B. Morse, opened a "photographic gallery"—the first in this country and perhaps in the world—on the top of the old University building at Washington Square, and there took portraits of the most distinguished New Yorkers of that period. Professor Draper managed the camera and developed the pictures, while Professor Morse attended to the artistic details. Together, they taught hundreds of persons to take and make daguerreotypes, and the importance of photography was soon recognized throughout the world.

Not many are aware that the two important inventions hereabove mentioned are directly connected with New York University, and among the numerous additional interesting achievements by former students of the University, I will cite:

50. *Panama Canal.* This colossal work, a marvel of engineering, was made possible by the efficient work in sanitation rendered by Surgeon-General William A. Gorgas, M. D., class of 1870.

51. *"The Monitor."* Mr. Isaac Newton, class of 1855, was in charge of the engines on the "Monitor" during the trip south from New York, and the subsequent fight with the "Merrimac" at Newport News. The importance of Mr. Newton's service in so successfully operating untried engines in a ship of revolutionary design cannot be overestimated. Wooden warships in every part of the world became obsolete as a result of this naval battle of 1862.

52. *Wisconsin Capitol.* The Wisconsin State Capitol Building was designed by Mr. George Browne Post, C. E., class of 1858. Among the many buildings designed by him, were: The New York Produce Exchange, College of the City of New York, the former Equitable Life Insurance Building, the Western Union Building in Dey Street, the Mills, Havemeyer and St. Paul Buildings, and the Liberal Arts Building at the Chicago Exposition.

53. *Mississippi River Improvements.* Much of this great work proceeded under Mr. William Starling, C. E., class of 1856, who for ten years was chief engineer of the Mississippi River Levee Commission.

54. *First "Skyscraper."* It was designed by the firm of which the late John W. Root, C. E., class of 1869, was a member. This building, known as the "Montauk Block," no longer exists. Mr. Root was part architect of the World's Columbian Exposition at Chicago.

55. *Atmospheric Nitrogen Corporation.* A subsidiary of the Allied Chemical and Dye Corporation with works at Syracuse, New York. This plant started operating September, 1921. William H. Nichols, class of 1870, chairman.

It is the most important undertaking of its kind in this country and the world, representing the latest development of a large series of undertakings in chemical engineering.

56. *The Chelsea Improvement.* On the Manhattan side of North River the $24,000,000 Chelsea Improvement was constructed by the New York City Depart-

ment of Docks and Ferries, with Charles W. Staniford, C. E., Class of 1881, serving as Chief Engineer.

57. *Hoboken Piers.* At Hoboken, N. J., the piers of the North German Lloyd, the Hamburg-American, the Holland-American, the Phoenix and the Scandinavian-American Steamship Companies were constructed by Walter Whittemore, C. E., Class of 1883.

58. *U. S. Battleships.* The United States battleships "Pennsylvania," "Nevada," "Utah," "Idaho," "Mississippi," and in fact all of the dreadnoughts constructed after and including the "Oklahoma" class, are so arranged, that when going into battle, certain selected water-tight divisions are filled with air sufficient to keep out water and retard or prevent sinking in case of penetration. The principles and methods involved were proposed and perfected by Mr. W. William Wotherspoon, C. E., class of 1898.

59. *Law.* New York University's most illustrious son of the law is Mr. Elihu Root (class of 1867).

60. *Columbia University.* The charter of King's College, the original name of Columbia, was granted by George II, and finally passed the seals on October 31, 1754, from which day the college dates its existence.

King's College played a conspicuous part in securing and confirming the independence of the United States. The Revolutionary War caused a suspension of the activities of the college, and in 1776 its building was used as a military hospital. After eight years its work was renewed by Act of the Legislature, May 1, 1784, under the name of Columbia College.

Its original site was downtown, in what became later the block bounded by College Place, Barclay,

Church and Murray Streets. In 1897, the college was reorganized as a university.

61. *Fordham University.* It was not until 1846 that the Jesuits again entered New York after a lapse of forty years. Bishop Hughes invited the French Fathers who were struggling to establish a college in Bardstown, Kentucky, to take charge of St. John's at Fordham. They accepted the offer and purchased, for what was then a very considerable sum, the old Rose Hill Mansion and subsequently the part which had been up to that time occupied by the Diocesan Seminary.

The first Rector was Father Thebaud, well known for his learned works, and with him were men like Larkin, Stack, Murphy, Stallo, Jouin and others.

The college has given many illustrious men to the Church, the bench, the bar, and to civil and military life. After many years of difficulties and trials we find it today with over five hundred pupils and with Law and Medical Departments. The grounds which were once far out in the country now form part of the city.

62. *Sarcastic Melyn.* Peter Stuyvesant was formally inaugurated governor on May 27, 1647. The whole community was present, and listened with eagerness to his well prepared speech on the occasion.

The democratic Belgian, Cornelis Melyn (already mentioned as first settler on Staten Island) who disliked Stuyvesant, afterwards wrote: "He kept the people standing with their heads uncovered for more than an hour, while he wore his "chapeau," as if he were the Czar of Muscovy."

63. *First official surveyors, 1647.* The little village of New Amsterdam, with its crooked roads winding round hilltops and ledges, its untidy houses with hog-pens and chicken coops in front, and tumble-down chimneys in the rear, had some surveyors appointed; they were: Van Dincklagen, Van der Grist, and Van Tienhoven.

The streets were straightened, great piles of accumulated rubbish were dumped into the water, and a better class of houses was erected under their supervision.

64. *Fire-Wardens.* In 1648, fire-wardens were appointed; they were to inspect the chimneys between the fort and the Fresh Water Pond.

For a foul chimney, the owner was fined three guilders. If a house was burned through carelessness in that respect, the occupant was fined twenty-five guilders. The fines were to be used to buy hooks, ladders, and buckets.

65. *Weekly markets, 1648.* The Governor established a weekly market in the open space before the Fort, the green spot which in later days became "Bowling Green." Here the farmers and butchers gathered every Monday.

66. *Notary Public, 1650.* Dirck Van Schelluyne, a Hague lawyer who was licensed to practice his profession in New Amsterdam, opened an office in one corner of a grocery store, and hung out a sign "Notary Public." His commissioned duty was "to serve process and levy executions." Later on he became the secretary of the Rensselaerswck colony.

It was in the upper part of the same grocery that Jan Cornelissen had his small school.

67. *Proclamations about cows and hogs.* In 1648, Stuyvesant had issued a proclamation that no hogs and goats should for the future be pastured between the fort and Fresh Water Pond, except within suitable inclosures and later on he issued another proclamation forbidding the running at large of cows, hogs, and goats, without a herdsman. Now, in 1650, a general law was passed to the effect that "inasmuch as the hogs spoil the roads and make them difficult of passage for wagons and carts, every man must stick rings through the noses of such animals belonging to him."

68. *Merchants and Brewers, 1650.* The merchants of those days dealt in every class of merchandise, and raised their own poultry and pork, as well as made their own butter.

Brewing seems to have been a favorite occupation, and was a source of much profit. Pieter and Jacob Couwenhoven, brothers, who came to New Amsterdam in 1633, made quite a fortune in that way, and carried on at the same time a brisk trade in flour, which was bolted in windmills.

69. *Winter of 1650.* This winter was one of great severity. It was so cold that "ink froze in the pen." There was much distress, as food was scarce and prices necessarily high.

70. *New Amsterdam gets a Municipal Government, 1653.* We have seen that in 1634 Manhattan was named "New Amsterdam" and was invested with the pre-

rogative of staple right, but there was no grant of municipal government.

Now an interesting moment arrived; a new city appeared in the annals of the world. Its birth was announced on the evening of February 2, 1653, at the feast of Candlemas[1]. A proclamation of the governor defined its exceedingly limited powers and named its first officers. There was nothing in the significant scene which inspired enthusiam. It came like a favor grudgingly granted. Its privileges were few, and even those were subsequently hampered by the most illiberal interpretations which could be devised.

Governor Stuyvesant made a speech on the occasion, in which he took care to reveal his intention of making all future municipal appointments, instead of submitting the matter to the votes of the citizens, and he gave the officers distinctly to understand from the first, that their existence did not in any way diminish his authority, but that he should often preside at their meetings, and at all times counsel them in matters of importance.

There were two burgomasters (mayors): Arent Van Hattam and Martin Cregier; the latter was the proprietor of a small tavern opposite the Bowling Green, the site of which he purchased in 1643.

There were five schepens (aldermen): Paulus Van der Grist, who owned a sloop with which he navigated the waters nearby, and opened a dry goods store, keeping groceries and knick-knacks, according to village custom; Maximilian Van Gheel; Anthony Allard, who was the consignee of a large firm in Holland, and be-

---

[1] In the Catholic and Protestant churches, the Feast of the Purification, February 2.

sides his general wholesale business, he engaged in
the retail trade for we learn by the records that he
sold a "hanger" to Jan Van Cleef "for as much
buckwheat as Anthony's fowls will eat in six months;"
Peter Van Couwenhoven, whom we have already noticed as a wealthy brewer; and William Beekman, who
was the ancestor of the well-known Beekman family,
and his name is perpetuated by two streets, William
and Beekman. He was for nine years a burgomaster
of New Amsterdam. The coat-of-arms of the Beekmans is the same as that of the Beekmans of Belgium.

In the municipality the bell-ringer was a notable
and useful indvidual. He was the court messenger,
the grave digger, the chorister, the reader, and sometimes the schoolmaster. He seems to have also been
a general waiter upon the city magistrates. He kept
the great room in which they assembled in order,
placed the chairs in their proper and precise positions, and rang the bell at the hour for coming together.

It was the business of the sheriff to convoke and
preside over this board, to prosecute offenders, and
to execute judgmentts. City officials in the Fatherland were invested with judicial and municipal powers;
but as no specific charter had been granted to our
"City Fathers," their authority was not well defined.
They heard and settled disputes between parties;
tried cases for the recovery of debt, for defamation of
character, for breaches of marriage promise, for as-
sault and theft; and even summoned parents and
guardians into their presence for withholding their
consent to the marriage of their children or wards

without sufficient cause. They sentenced and committed to prison like any other court of sessions. All their meetings were opened with a solemn and impressive form of prayer.

A pew was set apart in the church for the "City Fathers;" and on Sunday mornings these worthies left their homes early to meet in the City Hall, from which, preceded by the bell-ringer, carrying their cushions of state, they marched in solemn procession to the sanctuary in the fort. Their position was eminently respectable, but it had as yet no emoluments.

71. *First Councilor.* Nicaise de Sille (a Walloon name), an experienced lawyer, was commissioned as first councilor of the provincial government, July 24, 1653.

72. *Salaries of Officials.* Governor Stuyvesant granting the request he had received, 1654, from the city magistrates, fixed the salaries of the burgomaster and schepens at, respectively, $140 and $100 per annum.

73. *Private Library.* A noble English woman, Lady Moody, lived in Gravesend; her house contained the largest collection of books which had yet been brought into the colony.

74. *Christmas and Saint Nicholas.* At that time, in the Christian countries of Europe, Christmas was observed as a religious, domestic, and merry-making festival. It was often called the "children's festival," and the evening was devoted to the giving of presents and "Christmas trees" were everywhere in vogue.

In the Catholic church Saint Nicholas is the patron

saint of the young boys, and therefore the children's festival is celebrated on his feast day, December 6th, when the hero of the childish legend of Santa Claus is eagerly awaited, with his customary generous distribution of toys and candies.

75. *Patron Saint of New Amsterdam.* Saint Nicholas, whose image presided as the figure-head of the boat New Netherland which brought the Walloons to Manhattan Island, and for whom the first church had been named, was esteemed the patron saint of New Amsterdam. He was also the patron saint of Russia.

Several towns of Belgium and the United States bear his name.

76. *New Year's.* It was observed by the interchange of visits, as is still customary in New York. Cake, wine and punch were offered to guests. It was one of the most important social observances of the year, and was conducted with much ceremony. Gifts, in families and among intimate friends, were made. All such customs still prevail in Europe today.

77. *First Burial Ground.* It was on the west side of Broadway, near Morris Street.

78. *House of Rombouts.* Just north of that graveyard was the large stone house of Paulus Van der Grist, already cited. The orchards and gardens of the latter were highly cultivated, and extended to the very edge of the North River. Some years later this fine property was owned and occupied by the Hon. François Rombouts, a Belgian, before mentioned, who became Mayor of New York in 1679.

79. *Whitehall.* The Governor's house was getting

old and rusty. Accordingly Stuyvesant built for himself a gubernatorial mansion of hewn stone, and called it "Whitehall." It was located upon the street which was subsequently named for it.

80. *The Wedding-Place.* The settlement of Harlem was commenced through an offer by the government, 1659, to give any twenty-five families who would remove to that remote part of Manhattan Island, a court and clergyman of their own and a ferry to Long Island.

Upon the bank of the Harlem River a little tavern was built, which became quite a resort for pleasure-parties from the city. It was called the "Wedding-Place." The land travel at that time was almost exclusively on foot or on horseback; few wagons had as yet reached the country.

81. *Intolerance and Despotism.* Under Governor Stuyvesant the entente between officials was not very cordial. A leader of the opposition was Adrian Van der Donck, who, in 1649, went to Holland with a petition, asking the government to take the colony out of the hands of the Company and give it just laws. He also carried a severe arraignment of Stuyvesant, whose irritable temper and covetousness gave ample grounds of complaint.

"Religious bigotry was added to the stout old governor's love of power. He hated the Lutherans, the Independents, and the Baptists, and issued a proclamation that no public religious meetings should be held except those in accordance with the Dutch Reformed Church. The ordinance was often evaded, and there were some notable cases in which its violation was severely punished.''

''The worst was that of Robert Hodshone, a Quaker, who, for preaching at Hemstead, Long Island, was sentenced by the governor to two years of hard labor. When he refused to work he was beaten on three successive days until he fell to his feet. Then, taken before the governor, he would speak when told to hold his tongue, for which he was hung up by his hands and beaten until his back was raw. This also was repeated until the popular mind sickened of it.''

''At last the governor's sister interceded, and Hodshone was allowed to go out of the province. In spite of such severities the dissenting churches in New Netherland grew stronger.''[1]

82. *First Newspaper.* Twenty-one years elapsed from the establishment of a newspaper in Boston, before William Bradford began the ''New York Gazette'' in October, 1725. It was the fifth newspaper then in existence in the American colonies, three having already been established in Massachusetts and one in Philadelphia.

The first newspaper in Long Island was Morse's Gazetteer, published some time before 1798. In June, 1799, the ''Courier and New York and Long Island Advertiser'' was issued.

83. *First Public Library.* In July, 1729, the Rev. Dr. Millington, rector of Newington, in England, bequeathed to the ''Society for Propagating the Gospel,'' 1642 volumes of miscellaneous works, which became the foundation of the ''Society Library.''

[1] Bassett. A Short Hist. of the U. S., p. 74.

84. *First Catholic Church.* "Without consulting the ecclesiastical authorities, Hector St. Jean de Crêvecoeur [1], Jose Roiz Silva, James Stewart and Henry Duttin were incorporated by an Act of the Legislature, June 10, 1785, under the title 'The Trustees of the Roman Catholic Church in the City of New York.' "

"Crêvecoeur applied to the city authorities for permission to hold Catholic services in the Exchange, an ancient building across the foot of Broad Street, in a line with Water Street, occupied as a Courthouse, but consent was refused. Its arches were a favorite stand for itinerant preachers."

"During the summer, Father Whelan, acting on Mr. Silva's advice, bought a lease of five lots owned by the Trinity Corporation, at Barclay and Church Streets. A carpenter shop on the plot was fitted up for divine service."

"Wednesday, October 5, 1785, at the corner of Barclay and Church Streets, in the presence of a crowd of spectators, Don Diego de Gardoqui laid the cornerstone of the first Catholic church in the city of New York—St. Peter's." [2]

85. *First Directory.* The first directory of the city of New York dates from 1786. It was printed in large type; 33 small pages, 3 x 6 inches, contained the names of 933 residents. Two additional leaves in this directory have a list of the inhabitants of Brooklyn, numbering 128 names.

86. *First Bank in the State of New York.* The orig-

[1] French Consul General for New York, New Jersey and Connecticut.
[2] William H. Bennett, Catholic Footsteps in Old New York, pp. 370-373.

inal location of the "Bank of New York" was No. 67 St. George Square (afterward changed to Franklin Square) and also known as No. 156 Queen Street, afterward Pearl Street.

The building was the well-known Walton House, built by William Walton in 1752, for a private residence. In this building the "Bank of New York" commenced business on June 9, 1784. Its first president was General Alexander McDougall, and among the first directors was Alexander Hamilton.[1]

87. *First Stock Exchange.* Those who composed the nucleus of the New York Stock Exchange used to meet, 1792, at Tontine Coffee-House, corner of Wall and Water Streets; but the organization of the Exchange dates only from 1817. A meeting for "merchants" was established in 1670, on the site of what is now Exchange Place; they met every Friday morning.

88. *First Synagogue.* The first Jewish Synagogue in New York was erected about 1682, with Samuel Brown as its minister. The building was located on the south side of Beaver Street near Mill Street. The location of this Synagogue is indicated on John Miller's Map of New York, 1695.

89. *First Fire Engines.* In December, 1732, the first fire occurred at which fire engines were used. Two fire engines had recently been imported from England, and companies were formed which became the foundations of the New York Fire Department. Their efficiency was found greatly to exceed the former method

[1] Domett. Hist. of the Bank of New York.

of lines of bucket men, passing the water from hand to hand from the nearest wells or from the river.

90. *First Theatre.* An ancient deed, dated 1754, of a lot at 144 Fulton Street, mentions that is was situated "in the rear of the theatre-lot." This, therefore, must have been the site of the first theatre; it stood midway between the present Fulton and John Streets, with its entrance corresponding with No. 17 in the latter. In January, 1760, permission was given by De Lancey to build another theatre in Chapel Street, near Beekman. In the following November it was opened, the tragedy of "The Fair Penitent" being performed.

The next night was given "The Provoked Husband," which one cannot help hoping may have been a farce or a comedy, to relieve the gloom of the tragedy. The prices charged were: boxes, eight shillings; pit, five shillings; and gallery, three shillings. Popular sentiment in the future metropolis, was so much averse to this form of amusement that, in 1766, the theatre in Beekman Street was destroyed by a mob.

(The above notes were taken from many sources: Martha Lamb, James Grant Wilson, Mary Booth, David Valentine, miscellaneous works on history and chronicles.)

91. *Wampum. First Money.* The name "wampum" is closely connected with the early colonial history of New England and the Middle Atlantic States, and especially with "New Amsterdam." It was called "seawant" or "sewan."

At the advent of the whites, it was not only the money of the Indians but their jewelry. Universal in its use and unquestioned in its value, it ornamented their persons, distinguished the rich from the poor, paid ransoms, satisfied tribute, sealed contracts, atoned for injuries. In the form of a "belt," it entered largely into the ceremonial of Indian diplomacy, and it recorded the various public transactions of the tribes.

It became the most convenient medium of trade not only between the Europeans and the red men, but also between the various tribes of the Indians themselves, and later, owing to the scarcity of coin, was actually used as legal tender by the Whites.

It was made out of shells, and there were two kinds: white and dark purple; the white beads, or peag or roanoke, as it was variously called, was made from several species of conch (generally Fulgur carica or Fulgur caniculata) and the dark purple beads from the shell of the quahog or hard clam (Venus mercenaria). The former was called "wampum," signifying white, and the latter "sucki," signifying black, and though seawant was the generic name, the word wampum prevailed.

Fragments of those shells were ground down into beads, bored and strung upon the sinews of animals, or on hempen thread; the purple beads had twice the value of the white. The purple was the gold and the white the silver. Their "exchange" value was several times fixed by ordinances. In 1650 the "currency" of the province was again regulated, and "there being at present no other specie," wampum was made lawfully current, at the rate of six white or three purple beads of "commercial sewan" or of eight white or four purple of the "base strung" for one stuyver (two cents). Among the English three purple beads or six white beads were worth a penny (also two cents).

A single string of wampum of one fathom (the length of the two arms extended) is known to have reached, at time of "speculation," as high as four guilders ($1.60) in New Netherland, and five shillings ($1.25) in New England. The wampum of the Iroquois and New England Indians was inferior in quality, and rough and badly strung; the wampum of the Manhattans and Long Island was the best. By degrees, however, inferior wampum, loose and unstrung, began to take the place of the better "currency," and even, in the judgment of the Governor, to threaten "the ruin of the country."

The Dutch, in adopting the currency, applied to its manufacture the proper tools and made it at Hackensack, N. J. The coins of Europe were seldom seen in New Netherland, and wampum continued to constitute the common currency of this country long after it ceased to belong to the Dutch. On the banks of the Hudson, on the shores of the Mississippi, and even on the distant borders of the river Niger, in western Africa, the disposition or custom of using shells as a circulating medium is found to have been equally common.

The schoolmaster in Flatbush was paid his salary, in 1683, in wheat "wampum value." He was bound to provide a basin of water for the purpose of baptism, for which he received from the parents or sponsors twelve stuyvers, "in wampum," for baptism. In 1693, the ferriage for each single person from New York to Brooklyn was eight stuyvers in wampum, or a silver two-pence. For many years, the Sunday contributions in the churches were made in wampum.

After a short time the settlers learned to "counterfeit" the genuine wampum, first making it in large quantities on lathes, and later substituting glass or porcelain beads.

Wampum-making on lathes was kept up until very recent times for the western Indian trade, in Hackensack and several other New Jersey towns.

In aboriginal days, Long Island seems to have been the main seat of the wampum industry, owing to its convenient location, many shells used in the manufacture of wampum being found on its shores.

The Indian name for Long Island, "Si-wan-aki," variously translated as "Land of Shells" or "Land of Wampum," takes its origin from this source. In most shell heaps which are found along its shores from Canarsie to Montauk, the shell of the several local species of conch and of hard clam may be found.

92. *Beaver skin.* For a long time, the beaver skin also served as currency, the pelt being used instead of the coin.

In 1644, the General Chamber of Accounts recommended a series of propositions to the Company, namely that "Amsterdam weights and measures should be used throughout New Netherland," but the use of wampum and beaver-skin went on.

FORMER DUTCH COINS, WEIGHTS AND MEASURES AND THEIR EQUIVALENTS [1]

Coins

Duit (⅛ stuiver) ....$ .0025
Stuiver .... .02
Schelling (6 stuivers)....................... .12
Gulden ⎫
        ⎬ 20 stuivers .... .40
Carolus gulden ⎭
Goud gulden (1 2/5 guldens) .... .56
Daelder (1½ guldens) .... .60
Ryksdaelder (2½ guldens).................. 1.
Ducaton (3 guldens, 3 stuivers)............. 1.26
Pond Vlaamsch (6 guldens) 2.40

Linear Measures

Rhineland duim .... 1.03 inches
Rhineland voet (12 duimen) ....12.36 inches
Rhineland roede (12 voeten) ....12.36 feet
Amsterdam duim .... 1.013 inches
Amsterdam voet (11 duimen) ....11.143 inches
Amsterdam roede (13 voeten) ....12.071 feet

Uur gaands .... ⎧ 1/20 degree
                              ⎨ 3 nautical miles
Zeemyl .... ⎩ 18261 feet

                              ⎧ 1/15 degree
Geographische myl ....⎨ 4.611 statute miles
                              ⎩ 24348 feet

Square Measures

Rhineland morgen, (600 square roeden)....2.103 acres
Amsterdam morgen, (600 square roeden)..2.069 acres

---

[1] "Van Rensselaer Bowier Manuscripts" translated and edited by A. J. F. van Laer, pp. 847-849.

Liquid Measures

	Oil	Wine	Brandy	Beer	Milk
Mengel (mingel)	1.266 quarts	1.266 quarts	1.304 quarts	1.28 quarts	1.915 quarts
Stoop		2 mengelen 2.532 quarts		1 13/19 mengelen 2.15 quarts	
Steekkan	16 mengelen 5.064 gallons	16 mengelen 5.064 gallons	15 mengelen 4.89 gallons	16 mengelen 5.12 gallons	
Anker		32 mengelen 10.128 gallons			
Viertel			60 mengelen 19.56 gallons		
Aam	120 mengelen 37.98 gallons	4 ankers 128 mengelen 40.512 gallons			
Ton				128 mengelen 40.96 gallons	
Okshoofd		6 ankers 192 mengelen 60.768 gallons			
Vat	717 mengelen 226.93 gallons	4 okshoofden 728 mengelen 243.072 gallons			16 mengelen 7.66 gallons
Smalton		31.096 gallons			
Kwarteel		2 smaltonnen 62.192 gallons			

Dry Measures

	Wheat	Salt	Coal
Schepel......	0.764 bushels	1.29 bushels	....
Zak.........	3 schepels	....	....
	2.292 bushels	....	....
Mudde (mud).	4 schepels	....	....
	3. 056 bushels	....	....
Vat.........	....	4 schepels	....
	....	5.16 bushels	....
Last.........	36 zakken	....	....
	27 mudden	....	....
	82.512 bushels	....	....
Smalton.....	1/12 last	....	....
	6.876 bushels	....	....
Honderd.....	....	704.32 bushels	....
Hoed (hoet).	....	....	33.35 bushels

Ship's last = 3.71 cubic yards, 100.17 cubic feet; 2½ tons burden.

Vim (vinne) = 104 to 108 sheaves.

Weights

Amsterdam ons = 1.085 ounces (avoirdupois).

Amsterdam pond (16 onsen) = 1 pound and 1.36 ounces (avoirdupois).

"They learn to speak one language; and they raise one flag adored
  Over one people evermore, and guard it with the sword;
  In gay hours gazing on its four and forty stars above,
  And hail it with a thousand songs of glory and love.
  Old airs of many a fatherland still mingle with the cheer,

To make the love more glowing still, the glory still more
dear—
Drink up-sees out! join hands about! bear chorus all,"
chants he;
" 'Tis a good land to fall in with, men, and a pleasant land
to see!"

> —(From "Hendrick's Prophecy." The words of
> the refrain in this song are those used by Henry
> Hudson when he sailed his ship through the
> Narrows.)

III. *The Negroes.*

As labor was scarce, the charter of "Freedoms and
Exemptions" of 1629 promised to supply the colonists
with "as many blacks as the Company conveniently
could."

At first they were taken from the Dutch colonies
in the West Indies, namely Curaçoa, and as the colony
grew, it was recommended, in 1644, that as many negroes should be introduced from Brazil as the patroons, colonists, and farmers "would be willing to pay
for at a fair price." The Company had pledged itself
to a qualified support of the slave trade.

Governor Stuyvesant kept from thirty to fifty negro
slaves, besides a number of white servants, constantly
employed in the improvement of his grounds.

In 1652 the colonists were allowed to procure negroes from Africa.

The institution of slavery, as it existed in early times
in New York, was a source of constant anxiety to the
inhabitants of the city, arising from the turbulent
character of that class of the population. This arose
partly from the fact that the slave trade was then in

active operation, and New York was the mart from whence the other parts of the colony were supplied.

A slave market was established where the imported negroes were exposed for sale, and where other slaves were stood for hire. The negroes when newly arrived, were ill at ease, and differed greatly from the same class who had been born on the soil. Ignorant of the language of the country, and unused to the labor in the fields, and to the restraint under which they were held, the imported negroes were disposed to deeds of desperate outrage.

Announcement of a sale of slaves: "To be sold at Cruger's Wharf, on board the sloops Rebecca and Joseph just arrived from Arrambo in Guinea, a parcel of likely young slaves, men, women, and boys." The price of a negro averaged between one hundred and one hundred and fifty dollars.

The lot of the negro under the Dutch, was not so hopeless as his situation might lead us to expect. He was "a chattel," it is true; but he could still look forward to the hour when he too might become a freeman. In the years 1644 and 1646, several negroes and their wives, who had originally been captured from the Spaniards, had been freed from bondage, in consequence of their long and faithful services.

To enable them to provide for their support, they obtained a grant of land; but as the price of their freedom, they were bound to pay yearly twenty-two bushels and a half of corn, wheat, peas or beans, and one fat hog valued at eight dollars, failing which they were to lose their liberty and return again to their former state of servitude.

The emancipation of the parents did not, however, carry with it that of their offspring. "All their children already born, or yet to be born, remained obligated to serve the Company as slaves." The fathers were moreover obligated to serve "by water or by land" when called upon to do so. The detention of the children in slavery, after the emancipation of the parents, was highly disapproved of by the commonalty, who justly considered it a violation of the law of nature.

The West India Company, in encouraging commerce in negro slaves established an institution which unfortunately subsisted many generations after its authority had ceased.

Under the British, in 1680, a good negro was worth about thirty-five pounds ($170) in New York, but as the climate of Massachusetts was less genial to the African, he did not sell for quite so much there, when freshly imported into slavery; Boston had a great number of them. In a pamphlet entitled "Report of a French Protestant Refugee" privately printed by Mr. J. Carson Brevoort, of Brooklyn, we read: "There is much curious and novel information about Boston, in the year 1687. You may also own Negroes and Negresses; there is not a house in Boston, however small may be its means, that has not one or two. Negroes cost from twenty to forty Pistoles[1] according as they are skillful and robust."

In 1731, there was in New York a curious law requiring that no negro or Indian slave, above fourteen years, should appear in the streets south of the Fresh

[1] Old French gold coin, varying in value; about 10 francs.

Water Brook (Pearl and Chatham Streets) in the
night, after an hour succeeding sunset, without a lantern by the light of which they could be plainly seen,
or else to be in the company with a white person.

It was only in 1863 that slavery was abolished
through the initiative of the illustrious statesman
Abraham Lincoln. On March 6, 1862, he sent to Congress a message recommending "Compensated Emancipation" and on September 22 came his "Preliminary Emancipation Proclamation," soon followed, on
January 1, 1863, by his "Emancipation Proclamation,"
when the negro became a free man.

Lincoln while a member of Congress voted steadily
with the Anti-slavery Party, especially opposing the
extension of slavery to new territories. The toleration of slavery was always in Lincoln's opinion a kind
of unhappy necessity; and when the Southern States
had, by their rebellion, forfeited their claim to the protection of their peculiar institution, it was an easy
transition from this view to its withdrawal.

The successive stages by which this was effected—
the emancipation of the slaves of Confederates, and
the offer of compensation for voluntary emancipation,
followed by the constitutional amendment and uncon-
ditional emancipation without compensation—were
only the natural steps by which a change involving consequences of such vast extent is reached.

President Lincoln, on April 14, 1865, was shot in
Ford's Theatre, Washington, by John Wilkes Booth
(brother of the better known actor Edwin Booth) and
expired the following day.

Lincoln is universally looked upon as the savior of his country, and Washington himself holds no higher place in the hearts of the American people.

> "The words of mercy were upon his lips
> Forgiveness in his heart and on his pen,
> When this vile murderer brought swift eclipse
> To thoughts of peace on earth, good will to men."
> —TOM TAYLOR.

THE END

INDEX

(See the word "Names")